KT-371-455

Janet Charles

A SCHOOL IN SOUTH UIST

A SCHOOL IN
SOUTH UIST

*Reminiscences of a Hebridean
Schoolmaster, 1890-1913*

by

F. G. REA

Edited with Introduction by
JOHN LORNE CAMPBELL

Birlinn

This Edition published in 1997 by
Birlinn Limited
Canongate Venture
5 New Street
EDINBURGH EH8 8BH

First published 1964 by
Routledge and Kegan Paul Limited, London EC4

© John Lorne Campbell 1964 and 1997

No part of this publication may be reproduced, stored,
or transmitted in any form, or by any means, electronic,
mechanical, photocopying, recording or otherwise,
without the express written permission of the publisher

ISBN 1 874744 87 4

a CIP record of this book is available
from the British Library

Typeset in Monotype Baskerville

Printer and bound in Finland by WSOY

Foreword

BY KATE MACPHEE

I LOOK upon it as a privilege to help to bring more into prominence the outstanding integrity and personal charm of the author of this book, having spent the latter years of my school career under his tuition.

I was born in Garrynamonie in the parish of Daliburgh in the island of South Uist in the Outer Hebrides, within yards of Mr Rea's school, and entered it at the early age of four and a half unable to speak a word of English. But as the Infant and Primary teachers were native Gaelic speakers, we progressed slowly but well. Reaching the highest division of the school under Mr Rea's tuition seemed to me a great achievement.

At this time Mr Rea had returned to Garrynamonie school, of which he had been head teacher from 1890 to 1894, after some years' absence in England, his native country. How he must have loved the place to return once more! His wife was a charming and good woman, and must have helped a lot to make his work so successful.

In my opinion a child begins, at school age, to think more effectively as regards people and events that happen around it. I thought of Mr Rea as a most wonderful and interesting teacher; dedicated to his profession, I decided in later years, when one feels more mature to judge. Coming from an industrial town in the Midlands of England to South Uist in those days was indeed a contrast, especially when poverty was common and luxuries such as are accepted by present-day standards unknown. At Garrynamonie school he had no knowledge of his pupils' language, and conditions were primitive, but he accepted all this with sincerity and a desire to do good work. With a purpose so undaunted, he worked efficiently and successfully. He was a strict but just disciplinarian. Everyday routine lessons were full of interest, and his geography lessons carried our imagination into lands beyond our dreams. He created in us an intense love of reading—and on this subject we owed a deep sense of gratitude to a member of the Coats family of Paisley who endowed our island schools with small libraries.

Athletic events and games were not neglected. The boys were taught football and cricket and the annual 'camanachd' (shinty) match played on New Year's Day by rival teams was eagerly welcomed by young and old alike. One game we girls desperately wanted to play was cricket, so we faithfully watched the boys being taught, and then practised on our own. Mr Rea must have been so amused that he arranged a match between the boys and girls. When the great day arrived, the girls, believe it or not, won, much to the chagrin and discomforture of the boys. Not only that, but they drove us off the field in a shower of 'pluic' (clods of earth) accompanied by shouts of 'clann an d - - - - l'. However, they were severely reprimanded by Mr Rea and were taught that such behaviour was 'not cricket'!

We loved it when peat-lifting time came round, and the highest classes turned out to help. We were amply rewarded by a generous supply of sweets. As this was a case of 'many hands make light work', we set to work enjoying so much the sun and open-air freedom.

Evening classes were held during the winter months, and were well attended, Mr Rea taking chiefly the three R's and navigation, and his wife needlework and knitting. Gaelic was taught by Miss Marion McAskill of Pollachar and as a concession some of us were allowed to attend for the duration of the Gaelic lesson only. This, however, qualified us for permission to attend the country and Highland dancing session held once a week. The former was taught by a dancing teacher from Perth who used to bring her own violinist, the latter by Mr Donald (Bàn) MacDonald from Daliburgh, a renowned piper and exponent of Highland dancing. Needless to say, these were well attended.

I left Garrynamonie school in 1909 to enter Oban High School, and eventually the Teachers' Training College. But I have retained to the present day my friendship with Mr Rea's family, particularly with his eldest daughter Joyce, who was a class-mate of mine at Garrynamonie school. They, too, have always retained a deep love of South Uist, with happy memories of their childhood there. It was for them that Mr Rea wrote down these reminiscences in 1927.

In my later years as a teacher, Mr Rea's wonderful example and methods helped me very much. His adaptability to difficult conditions was, in my opinion, the keystone of his success. And no one ever heard him complain. I therefore esteem it a great privilege to add my tribute to a beloved teacher and a wonderful personality. His epitaph, were I presumptuous enough to put forward one, would surely be: 'Well done, thou good and faithful servant.'

Contents

Introduction

BY JOHN LORNE CAMPBELL

THE island of South Uist lies in the chain of the Outer Hebrides, sixty miles and more from the Scottish mainland. South Uist is about twenty-two miles long and six or seven miles broad, studded with innumerable fresh-water lochs and sea inlets. On its east coast there is a chain of hills rising to two thousand feet; its western side consists largely of low sandy ground called 'machair'. This is good grazing, but very much exposed to the frequent Atlantic storms.

In 1890 the island of South Uist, along with the islands of Benbecula and Eriskay, formed a School Board district with a total population of 5821, of whom 3430 spoke Gaelic as their only language and 2102 were bilingual in Gaelic and English. Of the remaining 289 persons whom the census of 1891 recorded as speaking English only, many must have been visitors or seamen or fishermen on vessels in local harbours. Very few persons then resident in Uist can have been entirely ignorant of Gaelic, which was then essential for anyone doing business on the island.

The social stratification then existing in South Uist, as in other parts of the Hebrides, corresponded to what can still be found in southern Italy or southern Spain or parts of Latin America. That is to say there was a wealthy absentee proprietrix, Lady Gordon Cathcart, who lived an existence remote from that of her tenants and employees; a very small middle class consisting of her representative or factor on the island and his subordinates; the clergy (three Roman Catholic priests and a Church of Scotland minister); about half a dozen big farmers holding leases from the estate; and the doctor, a few merchants, hotel-keepers, schoolmasters and government officials. Nearly all the members of this middle class were bilingual, though there was no statutory obligation on the authorities to appoint

xi

bilingual officials to Gaelic-speaking parts of the Highlands and Islands.* The third stratum or layer of local society, the vast bulk of the population, consisted of Gaelic-speaking crofters who had been tenants-at-will until the passing of the Crofters' Act in 1886, and cottars or landless labourers. The ratio of the different classes can be best appreciated from a study of the statistics of the 1891 census relating to the number of windows in the houses in South Uist and Benbecula. These figures record that in that year there were three houses in the district with no windows at all, 151 with only one window, 677 with only two windows, 286 with only three, thirty-three with four, and only twenty-two with five windows. Thirty-one houses had from six to nine windows; only ten had ten windows or more.

Seventy odd years ago South Uist was almost as inaccessible from the mainland of Scotland as the Faeroes are today. The only link was a very small steamer which then sailed from Oban in Argyllshire, stopping at other islands on the way. Such a crossing is graphically described by Mr Rea, the author of these memoirs. Few visitors braved the discomfort of crossing the stormy waters of the Minch apart from a few sportsmen and game fishermen or persons who had strong personal or business reasons for going to South Uist. I know of no English-man having gone to the island to take up prolonged residence there before Rea went to take up the position of head teacher at Garrynamonie school at the end of 1889. South Uist now has electric light, water supplies, aeroplane and bus services, a causeway to Benbecula, a seaweed factory, a tweed mill, and a rocket range: Rea went to live there at a time when most of these things had not even been thought of, and when even the appearance of a pedal bicycle was a surprise sufficient to send the island's horses and cattle careering in panic. The traditional self-sufficient life of the people, sustained by such craftsmen as the local smith and stonemason and the itinerant tailor, was still in full vigour. So was their traditional oral Gaelic literature and folksong, of which Fr Allan McDonald, in whose parish of Daliburgh Garrynamonie school is situated, was then making

* The usual practice in most parts of the British Empire has been to go to some trouble to provide officials trained in the languages of the peoples they administered. In the Highlands and Islands, however, the native population has been expected to learn English in order to deal with officials who often had no knowledge of the local language.

his fine collection. Impoverished though many of the people then were, their lives contained many elements of great interest to the folklorist and to the social historian: in many ways Uist was still a microcosm of the Highlands of the eighteenth century: even today it preserves a greater amount of Gaelic tradition than any other part of Scotland. Rea was an intelligent, sympathetic and observant man, and his description of South Uist life as it was in the 1890s is of great value and interest, much more so than are the impressions of passing visitors.

Rea's appointment to the position of head teacher at Garrynamonie school in the southern part of South Uist had a background in local politics. Under the Education Act of 1872, education became compulsory in Scotland, and became publicly financed and directed. On the local level, it was administered by elected School Boards, who had the task of supervising the schools and appointing teachers from applicants possessed of the required qualifications. Rea's appointment to the head teachership at Garrynamonie in 1889 was something of a sensational innovation; not because he was the first Englishman to be appointed to such a position in South Uist, but because he was the first Catholic to be officially appointed to a headmastership there since the Reformation.

Local tradition asserts that South Uist has been continuously Catholic since the time of St Columba. During the two generations that followed the Scottish Reformation (1560) formal Catholic observances on the island lapsed, to be revived by the heroic Irish Franciscan missionaries Fr Cornelius Ward and Fr Patrick Hegarty,* the former of whom in 1626 converted the newly appointed first Protestant minister of South Uist, Ranald MacDonald, and took him away to be trained for the priesthood at Douai—remarkably enough the first Protestant minister and the first secular Catholic priest of South Uist after the Reformation are one and the same person. Thereafter the islanders remained steadfast, even after their traditional chiefs, the Mac-Donalds of Clanranald, who had been staunch Jacobites in 1715 and 1745, had abandoned the Faith.

* The reports of the Irish Franciscans who laboured in the Hebrides between 1624 and 1647 have now been published in full by Fr Cathaldus Giblin, o.f.m., of Killiney, Co. Dublin (Latin texts and English summaries). Hitherto no Scottish historian has seen these reports. They throw a great deal of light on contemporary Highland history.

Fr Allan McDonald had been appointed parish priest of Daliburgh in July 1884.* In October of the same year he had been co-opted a member of the South Uist School Board, to which he was re-elected in the early spring of 1888. Sectarianism is happily no longer an issue in the politics of South Uist; but in the 1870s and 1880s things were very different. The grievances of the Catholic population were expressed in a letter written by Bishop Angus MacDonald, himself a scion of an old Highland landowning family, the MacDonalds of Glenaladale, to the Crofters' Commission of 1883, which is printed in the Appendix to their report, published in 1884. His letter is dated 19th May 1883:

I refer to the way in which the Catholics (*i.e.* the great bulk of the population) of South Uist and Barra have been dealt with in educational matters, in being refused Catholic teachers in schools attended almost exclusively by Catholic children. It is not my wish, and it is not necessary to discuss the question of the propriety o. combining or dissociating secular and religious instruction. As the law has been laid down by the Education Act of 1872, the decision of that, in each specific case, rests with the ratepayers, through the members they may appoint to represent their wishes. What I wish to explain is that the wishes of the ratepayers have been systematically ignored, and all educational questions settled for them by the factor,† and a very small non-Catholic minority.

Besides this special grievance, I believe that a statement of this case will tend to show the existence of a widespread evil, in the dependent and degrading position in which such tenants are apt to be placed—with no security of tenure, no guarantee against removal at will, and with the fear constantly hanging over them, that if they venture to assert their rights they may be made to suffer for it, without having the power to obtain redress. Nothing could be conceived more certain than this position to foster a low and cringing disposition, or more opposed to the formation of a manly, independent, enterprising spirit . . . .

My present official connection with this part of the West

* Fr Allan McDonald's name will be familiar to anyone who is versed in the literature of South Uist. Descriptions of him can be read in Amy Murray's *Fr Allan's Island* and in Neil Munro's *The Brave Days*; he was the original of 'Fr Ludovic' in the latter's *Children of the Tempest*. See also J. L. Campbell, *Fr Allan McDonald, Priest, Poet, and Folklorist*, revised edition, Edinburgh 1956.

† Corresponding to the English estate agent or bailiff, and a person formerly of immense power on Scottish Highland estates owned by absentee landlords.

Highlands* began in May, 1878. I was much surprised to find, amongst other things, that the whole management of educational matters was practically in the hands of a very small non-Catholic minority, who in no ways represented the feelings or wishes of the immense majority of the people. The method in which School Board members were appointed seemed to be that this minority held a meeting, and settled the whole matter for themselves. They were in the habit of leaving one or two seats to the Catholic clergy, taking care, however, to reserve to themselves the great majority of the seats, so that, with a certain show of liberality, they retained the whole administrative power in their hands. Further, they never seem to have thought it worth while to consider the wishes of the people in the selection of teachers—such a thing as a Catholic teacher in these almost entirely Catholic islands being at that time utterly unknown. On the other hand, the people earnestly desired to have teachers who would be qualified to give their children sound religious as well as secular instruction; but they were helpless to obtain this. They had the law on their side, but it was practically a dead letter. They dared not enforce it. In other Catholic districts on the mainland, Catholics had their feelings invariably respected by boards composed mainly of non-Catholic members. Here, where they could have by their votes secured a majority of seats and then looked after their own interests, they were deterred by fear from exercising that right . . . .

The fear, in fact, that if they exercised the right to elect a School Board with a Catholic majority, and appoint Catholic teachers to the schools, they would earn the instant and severe displeasure of the estate management, which would retaliate by evicting at least the supposed non-clerical ringleaders who had voted, and encouraged others to vote, against the members of the School Board supported by the estate, who in Uist consisted of the factor, the big farmers, and the Church of Scotland minister: really a kind of Protestant ascendancy oligarchy.

Bishop Angus MacDonald went on to say that in 1879 he had written to the proprietrix, Lady Gordon Cathcart, asking her for an assurance of neutrality on her part in the matter of the election of School Boards and of the appointment of Catholic teachers. He thought he had received this, but 'subsequent events have sadly undeceived me'.

* *i.e.* Benbecula, South Uist, Eriskay, and Barra—all the property of Lady Gordon Cathcart, at this time.

Whenever a new school was opened [under the 1872 Education Act, which introduced compulsory education] in South Uist, or a vacancy occurred in those which had been in operation, the requests of the Catholics for Catholic teachers was laid before the Board. The practical result was that the claim was usually ignored. If, in some cases, it was agreed to get a Catholic teacher, the simple method of leaving the negotiations to the Catholic members was not permitted, and media of advertisement were employed which practically neutralized the Board's consent.

It is hardly surprising that, when matters were administered in such a spirit, an unfavourable construction suggested itself in explanation of several unpleasant matters which occurred. For example, during the time that there was question of appointing teachers for certain Board schools in Uist, on two occasions the notice of meeting sent to the Rev. Donald Mackintosh, Benbecula, the only active Catholic member, was misdated by one day, bringing him to the appointed place just too late to take part in the proceedings. Again, an application presented by a Catholic male teacher was never produced at the meeting. Although known to have been sent, it must in some extraordinary way have miscarried, for the clerk declared that he had never received it . . . .

Bishop Angus MacDonald concluded his letter by saying that in view of the fact that the same lack of freedom and security had prevented the Uist and Barra people from voting according to their wishes in 1882, the appointment of the Royal Commission to inquire into the condition of the crofters and cottars of the Highlands and Islands presented an opportunity for obtaining redress of these grievances.

The argument may be summed up in a few words: under the 1872 Education Act, the people of South Uist and Barra had the right to vote freely in the elections of School Boards chosen to administer the local state schools, and the Boards had the right to appoint properly qualified teachers of any denomination and the duty to take into consideration the wishes of the majority of the electors. But the people of South Uist and Barra were being deprived of that right by the exercise of economic pressure which the power of instant eviction without any compensation gave to the estate authorities. And economic pressure had been one of the main means used against Catholics in Scotland under the penal laws of evil memory.

On the 6th October 1883 the Rev. Roderick MacDonald,

the Church of Scotland minister of South Uist and a member of
the local School Board, wrote a letter to the Crofters' Commission
in attempted rebuttal of Catholic grievances.* It is not a very
convincing document. In it he remarked that:

I beg leave to state boldly, and that without fear of contradiction,
that all the interest taken in the instruction of the young in the
parish of South Uist up to 1872 was taken by Protestants.

How far this is from being the case can be proved from the
following extract from the minutes (still unpublished) of the
Society in Scotland for Propagating Christian Knowledge, a
body formed in 1709 for the purpose of instituting schools in
the Highlands to extirpate the Gaelic language and the Catholic
religion. The date of the extract in question is 16th March 1727.

The Committee Reported that they had a Letter from the presbytery
of Long Island [*i.e.* the Outer Hebrides] with two representations,
one concerning the State of Southuist and Bara united into one
parish, and giving an account of the bounds thereof, and of the
Catechisable persons in every district, and shewing that they are all
papists except a very few, and pitching upon the places where Schools
may be settled, and shewing that there are two popish schools
therein.

The Committee 'recommended to Mr Alex. MacLeod and
Mr Alexander Mitchell to speak to Mr Alex. MacKenzie of
Delvine purchaser of the estate of Clan Ronald† and Doctor
Dundas & Monzie to speak to the Sollicitor to use the proper
measures to for suppressing the forsaid popish Schools'.

The Committee renewed its recommendation for the suppres-
sion of the Catholic schools in South Uist on 8th and 26th June
1727. Too often Scottish writers, and particularly writers on the
history of the Scottish Highlands, have confused 'education'
with 'Calvinist indoctrination' such as was given in the S.P.C.K.
schools in the Highlands and Islands, where the *Westminster
Confession of Faith*, the *Shorter Catechism*, *Vincents' Catechism*, the
Protestants' Resolutions, *Pool's Dialogues*, and *Guthrie's Trials*, all in
English, formed the bulk of an unattractive list of school books.

* Printed on p. 113 of the Appendix to the report.
† Clanranald's estates had been forfeited after the Jacobite rebellion of 1715.
Alexander MacKenzie of Delvine was the nominal purchaser on behalf of the
family.

Under the penal laws, there was no possibility of Catholic education developing anywhere in Scotland, and the frequent official accusations of 'ignorance' made so often against Highland Catholics rebound, in fact, against those who were ready to invoke the official ban against Catholic schools in the Highlands whenever the existence of these came to light, as in South Uist in 1727.

The Crofters' Commission issued its report in 1884. A paragraph on page 71 entitled 'The Religious Difficulty' deals with the grievances expressed by Bishop Angus MacDonald's letter.

it has been represented to us, as a grievance, on high clerical authority, that of the esteemed Roman Catholic Bishop of Argyll and the Isles, that under the present administration of the [Education] Act in South Uist and Barra, where the majority of the population are Roman Catholics, due regards has not been shown, in the selection of teachers, to the religious principles of the majority of the population. If this contention is well founded, and if the School Boards, as at present constituted, should not hereafter give due consideration to the wishes of their constituents, the remedy is in the hands of the ratepayers at any ensuing election of the Boards.

In point of fact for practical purposes the fundamental remedy lay in the excellent report made by the Commission and in the Crofters' Act of 1886, the Magna Carta of the Highlands and Islands, which conferred on the small tenants there something which the peasantry of Scandinavian countries had known for generations, security of tenure and the right to the principle of compensation for their own improvements at the termination of tenancies. Nothing was suggested in the report, or contained in the Act, to restrict absentee landlordism or limit the amount of land any one individual might own in Scotland, but for the moment a great advance had been secured.

This was the background to the first School Board election in South Uist that can be considered a really free one. It took place in the early spring of 1888, and the result was the election of four Catholic and three Protestant members, with the Rev. Roderick MacDonald previously mentioned coming at the foot of the poll of the elected members. Fr Allan McDonald himself stood third. He wrote to Bishop Angus MacDonald that though the day had been bitterly cold, only three of the 'south end' (Daliburgh parish) people stayed away from the poll, and these were hopelessly feeble. 'The manner and bearing of the people was most consoling to one who has been even only a few years here. They spoke out manfully and defiantly—a great contrast to the last election.'

Shortly afterwards the headship of the school at Garrynamonie, where the great majority of the pupils were Catholics, became vacant, and the position being advertised in the Catholic press, Mr Rea applied for it, and was selected. On the 30th December 1889 Fr Allan McDonald wrote to Bishop Angus MacDonald at Oban that 'I am to meet the Garrynamonie Schoolmaster today. According to his testimonials he is an excellent Christian and an able Teacher'. The responsibility that rested on Rea was probably heavier than he realized. The first Catholic headmaster appointed by the first School Board in South Uist with a Catholic majority was likely to be carefully scrutinized by the defeated but still influential minority, and any failings he might show would not be likely to pass unnoticed or uncriticized. In the event, his appointment was completely justified, and probably had a good deal to do with reducing sectarian tension in South Uist, though he himself may not have realized it.

Rea took up his duties as head teacher of Garrynamonie school on the 2nd January 1890. His staff then consisted of Christina McMillan, fourth-year pupil teacher, and Marion McAskill, second-year pupil teacher. Rea resigned on the 24th August 1894, presumably for the reasons of his mother's health referred to, but returned to the school as head teacher again on the 20th June 1904 and remained there until the 16th May 1913, when he relinquished duty on his appointment to a school under the Birmingham Education Authority. His memoirs, which he wrote down in 1927, were not written chronologically, and do not make it clear that he was head teacher of the school for two distinct periods, all the important incidents of his Uist career being described as if they had taken place during the first of the two spells that he spent there. That is presumably why there is no reference to the funeral of Fr Allan McDonald, a big occasion on Eriskay, which took place in October 1905, and which Rea attended.

In his memoirs (which were brought to my attention by Miss Kate MacPhee, who was first a pupil and then a pupil teacher under Mr Rea at Garrynamonie school during his second period there, and are now published with the consent of his family) Rea remarked in his preface that he had avoided mentioning names of persons and places as far as possible. He often refers to them by rather clumsy circumlocutions. This reticence being now quite unnecessary, I have restored the real names of the persons and places mentioned whenever possible.

The school log book, which the present head master of Garrynamonie school, Mr MacKay, has kindly allowed me to consult, gives much interesting information on Rea's difficulties. In the 1890s the south end of South Uist (of which an interesting account can be read in Margaret Fay Shaw's *Folksongs and Folklore of South Uist*) was one of the poorest districts in the Outer Hebrides. Roads were often no more than rough tracks across the mountain moorland or over the storm-swept machair, and there were no public conveyances to bring the children to school. Epidemics were frequent; there was no medical inspection of the school before 1915. Children were frequently needed to help at home with planting potatoes and herding cattle in the spring, and for helping with the harvest in the autumn. Rea's very first entry in the school log book on 2nd January 1890 reads: 'Very poor attendance today, in consequence of wet stormy weather.' Some other characteristic entries may be quoted:

20th January 1890: No school today. Children kept away by frost and snow. A visit from the Compulsory Officer, who reports much sickness among the poorer children.

4th April 1890: Attendance of elder children not so good as hitherto —parents taking them to assist in field-work.

30th May 1890: The attendance fell much lower this week owing to the commencement of the herding-season.

20th January 1891: Today there was no school held, owing to cold stormy weather.

23rd January 1891: No school was held on Wednesday or Thursday, owing to exceptionally severe weather.

30th January 1891: There is much sickness among the people, consequently the attendance was very low.

The poverty of the people, their low standard of living, the inadequate medical service, and the constant exposure of the children to wind and weather on their way walking to and from school, resulted in devastating effects on attendance. Thus the school was closed from 14th February to 28th April 1898 for scarlet fever; from 22nd November 1898 to 23rd January 1899 for measles; from 23rd January to 15th April 1901 for whooping-cough (after which it was recorded that many children were weak); from 17th February to 4th April 1904 for a smallpox outbreak; from 6th May to 20th June 1904 for mumps; from 20th February to 19th March 1907 for influenza; from 16th November 1910 to 9th January 1911 for whooping-cough; and from 23rd February to 18th March 1912 for scarlet fever. On 24th April 1893 Rea recorded that 'many children in the district, not yet on books of the School, are unable to attend owing to ill-health and distance'. On 8th December 1893, there was 'exceptionally severe and boisterous weather, the attendance suffering in consequence—many parents of scholars were obliged to accompany their children to and from school, the wind being actually dangerous'. The school building too had its deficiencies; even as late as May 1939 H.M. Inspector reported that 'many things—sunless rooms, disrepair, draughts, smoke, grime, ancient furniture—make this perhaps the most depressing school building in the County'—and it had been improved since Rea came first to Uist!

Rea's memoirs show how he strove to meet these difficulties. They, and the recollection of his former pupils, show him to have been a sincere, conscientious, hard-working man, an excellent teacher interested not only in the intellectual progress but also in the spiritual and physical well-being of his pupils. Some men in his position have tended to isolate themselves, but Rea had a keen power of observation, an interest in the unfamiliar scenes and happenings around him, and the ability to record them with a vividness that overrides his sometimes old-fashioned and slightly pedantic style. In view of this, it is really rather surprising that his writings do not seem to reveal any intellectual curiosity on his part about the Gaelic language which was universally spoken around him, or about its literature, on which Fr Allan McDonald could have given him plenty of information. The Catholic victory in the School Board election had made the appointment of Catholic teachers to the South Uist and Barra schools a possibility, but unfortunately the institutions in

Britain in which Catholic teachers were then trained did not include Gaelic in their curricula. The result was that while no doubt individually excellent appointments were made, such as Rea's, collectively the Uist and Barra schools at this time came to be headed by an assortment of teachers from Edinburgh, Aberdeen, Glasgow and England, all of whom were ignorant of Gaelic, and very few of whom were ever able to unbend sufficiently to take an interest in it. A system of education whereby the head teacher was entirely ignorant of the only language with which his pupils entered school, and was dependent upon pupil teachers and monitors to act as his interpreters, cannot possibly be considered satisfactory. Young children came, often a considerable distance on foot, often stupefied by hunger and cold, to be instructed through the medium of a foreign language, and when they were examined or inspected, this was done according to standards devised entirely for monoglot English-speaking children on the mainland. In fact, under the 1872 Education Act no attempt was made to devise an intelligent system of bilingual instruction for Hebridean children whatever. It is not surprising that one inspection report after another refers to the indistinct utterance of the Garrynamonie school pupils when reading or speaking English. Gaelic itself was then hardly thought worthy of inclusion in the school curriculum. Things are very different today, as the Inverness-shire Education Authority tries conscientiously to fill teaching positions in Gaelic-speaking areas with Gaelic-speaking teachers, and is (belatedly) experimenting with Gaelic-medium instruction in some of the Uist schools. It was not until the 1918 Education Act that adequate provision was made for the teaching of Gaelic as a special subject.*

Apart from this reservation, Rea was admirably suited for the position he was chosen to fill, and his vivid and unprejudiced account of contemporary life on South Uist is an important contribution to the social history of the Hebrides and should be read with interest by many people, particularly those who are already acquainted with the islands of South Uist and Barra and with their literature.

In conclusion, I must express thanks to the late Rt Rev.

---

* For the history of bilingualism in Highland education, see J. L. Campbell, *Gaelic in Scottish Education and Life*, 1950 edition.

Kenneth Grant, Bishop of Argyll and the Isles, for permission to quote from Fr Allan McDonald's letters to Bishop Angus MacDonald; to P. J. W. Kilpatrick, for permission to use photographs taken by Walter Blaikie in Uist and Eriskay in 1898 and 1899; to Margaret Fay Shaw, for photographs of South Uist reproduced here; and to Mr MacKay, the present headmaster of Garrynamonie school, Miss Kate MacPhee, formerly teacher there, Mr McGinn, headmaster of Daliburgh school, Mr Donald MacDonald, headmaster of Eriskay school, Mr H. D. MacIntyre the present factor of South Uist, Mr Neil MacLennan, postmaster at Lochboisdale, and Mr John Mac-Innes, Clerk to the South Uist District Council, for information and encouragement in preparing Frederick Rea's memoirs for publication.

J. L. C.

Isle of Canna
12th September 1963

Addendum

IT WAS the author's comments in the introduction that he had 'restored the real names of the persons and places mentioned wherever possible' that has prompted the following notes to be added to this edition, which might interest today's readers, particularly those who know the island as many of the readers will.

Page 11: last line: The Garrynamonie school was built in 1876 to a standard design for Board schools in the Highlands (the result of the 1872 Education Act) by the prolific Highland architect Alexander Ross. It is currently disused and under threat of demolition.

Page 13: last paragraph: Boisdale House, South Loch Boisdale (not to be confused with the old house of the Boisdale Estate at Kilbride, demolished early twentieth century).

Page 24: line 17: (a) The (RC) Church, Our Lady Star of the Sea, 1888 by G Woulfe Brenan and (b) The Church of Scotland, 1892–3 by Hardy & Wight (now derelict). The school – Standard Alexander Ross design, 1879 (disused and at risk).

Page 47: line 21: The school – also by Alexander Ross, 1876 – today stands disused and falling into dereliction. The schoolhouse has been refurbished and is occupied.

Page 58: line 26: Kilbride House, formerly known as Boisdale House as it was the house for the Boisdale Estate at the south end of the Island (not to be confused with the house referred to on page 13). A lofty Georgian Laird's house, it was built in the 1760s by Colin Macdonald of Boisdale and demolished in the early twentieth century. The great garden walls still stand.

Page 60: line 5: The Macdonalds of Boisdale were not chieftains, but a cadet branch of the Clanranalds. The Clanranald family were proprietors of South Uist, Benbecula, Eigg, Canna, Arisaig and Moidart until the early nineteenth century.

Page 62: line 19: The stones were also used for an extension to the Lochboisdale Hotel.

Page 82: line 9: This large farmhouse is the old Boisdale House at Kilbride, now demolished (see page 58).

Page 145: line 33: The referee was Captain T A Mackenzie (yr of Ord) who was at the time adjutant of the 2nd (Militia) Battalion, The Queen's Own Cameron Highlanders.

Page 150: line 15: The Camerons were never at Dargai, but Rea was probably muddling it with Tel-el-Kebir, where Captain T A Mackenzie did fight in 1882.

Page 191: line 1: Dr Alasdair Maclean has confirmed that this was Alasdair Macdonald, son of the Rev Roderick Macdonald, Minister at Howmore, who worked the farm of Grogarry, which was later adopted as the estate home farm. The house described here and in the following pages is the old manse at Grogarry.

Page 197: footnote: Alasdair Macdonald, son of the Rev Roderick Macdonald, minister at Howmore.

Page 202: line 5: The old school at Kyles Flodda, closed around the middle of the twentieth century.

Page 204: line 34: Howmore Post Office, the building still stands but was later reconstructed as a barn.
Line 37: The Howmore School (Alexander Ross 1870) still stands but is disused.

Page 208: footnote: It was here that the Napier Commission heard the Benbecula crofters' grievances.

Chapter One

IN 1889 I was a young certificated assistant of twenty-one, teaching in a large school in a midland city of England, at a salary of seventy pounds a year. Having to share in the support of a widowed semi-invalid mother, I applied for any teaching post which seemed to promise an increased income.

Well I remember receiving at school, one December morning, a telegram asking me to send references at once; it was addressed from Lochboisdale and was signed by A. McDonald, 'Chairman'. I had no recollection of having applied for a post outside England, but came to the conclusion that among my applications for various posts I had inadvertently included one at a Scottish school.

Inspection of a map showed me that Lochboisdale was a seaport on South Uist, an island of the Hebrides. But, being young and venturesome, I decided that this should not deter me, providing the post promised improvement in my financial position. I sent 'references' with a request for particulars, and soon learnt that the vacant post was the headmastership of a school of some hundred and forty boys and girls.

On looking back to that time, I now feel no surprise that my relations and friends regarded the whole affair as a huge joke. It is not easy to realize in these days of the aeroplane, motoring, and of the many facilities for comfortable travel, how people of forty years back [from 1927] looked upon such a venture as I contemplated—less surprise would be created nowadays if a person proposed to take a school post in Spain or Greece. I looked upon the matter as an adventure, and though only a few days were left for preparation, I accepted the post.

The morning of my departure approached; having to leave by an early train I had to bid my farewells the previous night.

Even then it was not realized that I was in earnest, for I well remember my elder brother exclaiming: 'What! Going to Scotland really? Why on earth do you want to go to Scotland?' To which I replied: 'To gain experience.'

It was a cold, dark December morning when I set out alone on the first stage of what I considered a great adventure. My recollections of the long train journey north are now somewhat dim, but having lived all my life till then in a Midland city, I was deeply interested in the different types of people who joined or left the train at the various stopping places; and the new experiences as we proceeded further and further north delighted me, especially the changing scenery. But a long railway journey in winter was no light undertaking in those days, for the carriages were not heated; tin footwarmers filled with hot water were supplied to a few passengers, but these soon cooled, so were of little use.

My first recollection of Scotland is of the train stopping at a smallish station, soon after leaving Carlisle. Among the few people on the station platform I especially noticed some whom I took to be Elders of the Kirk: tall, severe-countenanced men, sombrely clad, pacing slowly up and down the platform. They might have stepped straight from one of Scott's novels. The dull leaden-skied winter afternoon, with a piercing cold wind blowing across the bare landscape seemed completely in keeping with them. I remember how, with a heart sinking in foreboding, I murmured to myself: '*Now* I am in Scotland!'

Vague impressions linger still of travelling on in the darkness till we reached a badly lighted, bare-looking station* where I was to change for the last stage of my railway journey. Soon a short train of two or three comparatively empty carriages drew in and I was shown into an empty, dim, dismal, bare-looking compartment by a muffled-up guard.

I had now been some twelve to fourteen hours on my journey, so that memories of what followed are somewhat dim; but the chief are those of feeling desperately cold, tired and hungry; of being often wakened from dozing by frequent violent jerks, then of the sudden stopping of the train, followed by voices of men calling to each other. At last, at one of the stops I ventured to open the window, though this let in the bitter night air, and I

* Probably Stirling.

2

saw men with lanterns walking beside the track, talking in loud voices. As the guard, lantern in hand, passed the window, I asked what was the matter, and was informed that at certain parts of the route rocks from the mountain slopes often rolled across the track, necessitating extreme caution and stops to remove obstacles. So, grimly closing the window and trusting to Providence, I curled myself up on the uncushioned seat to obtain all the warmth I possibly could. I often compare the discomfort and danger of that tedious railway journey with the comfort, safety and speed with which it may now be accomplished.

Eventually, I was awakened from a fitful sleep by the sudden opening of the carriage door, and a man with a lantern announcing that we had reached the railway terminus.* I got out on to the platform of an open station, semi-lighted, around which seemed nothing but blackness.

On my asking for the boat that was to convey me to my destined island, the lanterned man led me, stumbling in the darkness, between trucks, across railway lines, to the quayside, pointed out a steeply sloping gangway, and left me to get on board as best I could. Before me was a steeply inclined gangway which seemed to go miles down into obscurity. Valise in hand and holding on tightly to a rail of the gangway, I carefully descended till I found myself on what, by the light of a single oil lamp, appeared to be the deck of a boat. Stumbling about in the darkness and cold, I at last came to a flight of stairs lighted by another oil lamp. Having descended these I found myself in what I concluded to be the cabin with a table in the middle, and a kind of divan running round three walls. It was now about five o'clock in the morning, and, as no one appeared, I put down my baggage and, utterly weary, fell asleep in a corner of the divan.

What awakened me I cannot say with certainty. Perhaps it was the uneasy motion of the cabin, or the clatter of knives, forks and crockery at the table, accompanied by men's voices talking in a guttural tongue, which I fancied was Gaelic. Half-awake, I gradually realized where I was, and from a blended aroma of coffee and bacon surmised that breakfast was proceeding. Seated on benches on either side of the table were several

* Oban.

3

men, three of whom were in thick, dark blue clothes, relieved with gold lace, whom I took to be the officers. Two were short and thickset, with very blue eyes and weather-beaten countenances, the third looked slim and tall. I afterwards learnt that the former were captain and mate, the latter the purser. A steward was attending to the gastronomic requirements of these and one other, whom I took to be a fellow-passenger. Feeling hungry myself I took a seat at the table, being greeted by a gruff 'Good morning!'

I had previously determined to economize for I did not know when to expect any salary at my new school, and I would have to meet essential expenses out of the little store left from my last receipt of salary. From what I could see, the others had breakfasted on fish, preceded by porridge, then ham and eggs, followed by a chop or steak, then buttered roll and marmalade. Though I was hungry and felt that I could vie with any of them as a trencherman, I took only rolls and butter, with a cup of coffee.

Alas, for the plans of men! After consuming my modest breakfast, I asked the steward the charge. He told me that breakfast charge was half a crown, irrespective of what was consumed. I paid him without further question, with a mental reservation that I would more than make up this surcharge at the first opportunity—as I subsequently did.

The rolling motion of the stair as I ascended to the deck was a novelty, for my previous experience of boats had been confined to the row-boats and skiffs on pools of city public parks. Reaching the deck, I was surprised at the smallness of the vessel and wondered how she could venture to cross the seas. Everything around me was of interest: the wet deck; the mate clad in oilskins on the bridge with the man at the wheel; the few deck hands stowing luggage or coiling ropes; the smoke from the one funnel swirled away by the winds; the cries of the sea-gulls as they circled around the tops of the two short masts—all these were a delight to me, a landsman; and, as I faced the stiff breeze, inhaling breaths of the good clean air, I felt invigorated by a buoyancy new to my experience. Though I am now looking back some forty years, this memory is as vivid as ever, and I still recall the thrill of it.

The vessel was steaming along a channel,* from two to five

* The Sound of Mull.

miles in width, flanked by low shores receding in the distance to high mountains, the bare landscape rendered more sombre by forests of dark fir.

As we approached the mouth of the channel, a little later in the morning, the waves of the sea increased in height and length, while the motions of our little ship became more violent; so I was frequently forced to hold on tight to whatever bar or stanchion offered to save myself from being thrown headlong against the bulwarks or going over the side, but I know that I enjoyed it as being new to any of my previous experiences.

The shore on our right ended in a high promontory where stood a lonely lighthouse. Interested, I asked one of the sailors what it was. He shouted in my ear what sounded like 'Ahhrrd-nahlchmrrchn'. I considered this, and then came to the conclusion that it was Ardnamurchan Point, the most westerly point of the mainland of Scotland.

When we came abreast of this important lighthouse, our course was altered towards the south, and in an hour or two we were passing between two low, sandy, wind-swept islands.* Soon I noticed one of the few passengers wildly gesticulating, stamping, and shouting, seemingly in anger. Eventually I ascertained that he intended to buy cattle and sheep on these two islands. But, as neither island had a pier, it was the custom to land passengers and goods from the steamer by means of large boats putting out to her from the shore while she lay to. But this day the sea was too rough for boats to come out, or for the vessel to attempt to lie to among the heaving seas. As the steamer passed there once a week only, I am sure no one could wonder at the cattle dealer's violently expressed chagrin: for this was the third successive week that he had made the round of the Isles in the hope of purchasing and procuring his animals, his hope being defeated each time by high seas. I trust that the poor man attained his object eventually!

This incident gave me furiously to think: I thought how little city people could realize the contrast between their easy means of reaching their destination and this poor man's.

After passing between these two islands we now met the full seas: three thousand miles of water straight ahead of us! How puny our little vessel seemed as she rolled and tossed in the long

* Coll and Tiree.

5

waves! I watched the latter as they rose ahead of us: up, up, some higher than the mastheads, till I thought we should be buried in a mountain of water. But, strange to say, we shipped comparatively little, and I can but think this was due to the fine seamanship of the captain and his mate. Sometimes I looked at their faces, and their steady, calm looks made me feel ashamed of any fears that might assail me.

Early in the afternoon the course became more northerly, and by and by the waves became less huge, but a misty rain came on, mingling with the spray. I knew that we must be nearing the scene of my new labours and peered ahead for any sign of land. After what seemed hours of watching, I discerned that we were steaming between two high hills partially obscured by mist; also that our ship was steady on her keel; dimly seen land seemed to close in around us; the steamer's engines changed from their steady throb to a gentle purr, and soon we ran alongside a wooden pier, which was supported on strong piles. At last I had reached Lochboisdale whence had been despatched the telegram so short a time before, but which had wrought such a change in my life.

While our gallant little boat was being warped safely to the pier head, I gazed curiously about me. Beyond the pier, the ground rose in a low hill, topped by what I took to be an hotel. Behind this, the ground seemed to rise abruptly to bare rocky heights only partially visible in the swathes of mist wrapped in a warm rain that swept across the landscape.

A few men were grouped on the little pier, among whom stood a tall figure clad in clerical black. As I reached the end of the gangway on to the pier, this figure left the group and advanced towards me with extended hand. 'You are the new schoolmaster, I believe,' he said in a deep, strong voice, and with a stronger grasp of the hand. He was a well-proportioned figure, over six feet in height with strongly marked weather-beaten features, about thirty years of age, and his grey eyes under bushy sandy-coloured eyebrows bent upon me kindly but penetrating looks.

Seizing my bag with a short 'Come along' to me, and a wave of the hand to the group he had left, he started off through driving misty rain along a rough stony road. Having caught him up, I told him that as it was nearly dark I had previously thought of staying at the hotel for the night. He dismissed my suggestion in a few words as he walked on, saying that I should stay that night at his house and as it was only three miles away there was no need for a conveyance of any kind. Though tired and hungry, I fell in beside him, and we headed into the damp breeze, which struck me as peculiarly warm for December, and we trudged on. I felt that I was now really in the isles of the Highlands of Scotland. Somehow I sensed that my companion was trying me out. So I there and then determined to show that Englishmen are not easily daunted. Taking my bag from his hand, I put as good a face on matters as I could, talking and asking questions as we went along.

I learnt that my companion was the Rev. Allan McDonald, generally called 'Father Allan'; that he was chairman of the School Board under whose jurisdiction were eight or nine schools, serving a population of five thousand; that the position of my school was some six miles from the pier. It seemed to me that I had to make all the conversation, my companion contenting himself with saying as little as possible.

I shall not forget the shock I had, after a mile or so searching the road right and left for dwelling houses and only seeing in the fast failing light, a few what looked to be large isolated heaps of stones or earth, lying well back some hundred yards or so from the road we were traversing. I burst out: 'But where are the houses?' Pointing to one of the black-looking heaps I had noticed, my conductor replied: 'Those are the houses!'

At last lights began to show ahead dimly, and we were soon passing through a stone gateway, along a shingly path which took us to a door beside which was a lighted window. Father Allan opened the door and we entered a small passage lighted by a small paraffin lamp. Here we hung up our wet coats and head covering, and went into a small, poorly but comfortably furnished sitting-room, where a fine fire was burning. This fire was a novelty to me, as it was of peat, which I had never seen before. I now know whence came that strange elusive aromatic scent which I noted upon first landing from the steamer—the smell of burning peat.

After we had warmed ourselves at the fire a frugal meal was laid on the table by an oldish woman with a weather-beaten but kindly face. My host became more conversational, under the

7

influence of food and warmth. Almost the first thing he said during the meal, as he looked across the table, was: 'I am glad!' On my asking of what he was glad, he exclaimed: 'Your English is so clear, and anyone can easily understand every word you say.' I did not know quite how to take this; but when he went on to explain that most of the Englishmen he had met were visitors who came to the hotel for the salmon and trout fishing, I had a shrewd idea of what he meant; for often the exaggerated accent and drawl affected by some of my countrymen when visiting abroad is appalling. Subsequently the correctness of my conclusion was verified when I, with an Edinburgh school-master, sat in the hotel coffee room listening to the conversation of the anglers as they prepared their tackle for the day's fishing. Every now and then my companion nudged me and said: 'There, can you understand what he said? I can't!' Of course, having heard this sort of thing before, I was able to retail exactly what was said by eliminating the affectation.

A little later, Father Allan remarked that I must be tired and that all matters concerning my work must be left till the morrow. As I had been some forty hours without proper sleep I was not loth to retire. Lighted candle in my hand, my host led the way up the uncarpeted stairs, and showed me into a barely furnished room, and with a blessing went out, leaving the lighted candle behind him.

I was soon in a small, clean bed, and, though it was of Spartan hardness, sleep overtook me almost immediately, while I was still wondering what the future was holding in store for me.

Chapter Two

BREAKFAST next morning consisted of oatmeal porridge and milk, salted herring, newly made scones, oatcake, butter and weak tea. The porridge in soup plates was served first, each plate being accompanied with a large basin of cold milk. This, being new in my experience of taking porridge, caused me considerable diffidence; but Father Allan, tactfully ignoring my hesitancy, commenced his portion, while I followed suit, imitating him as well as I could. We had our basins of milk before us, the plate of porridge on the right; a little of the hot porridge was taken in a large spoon which was then dipped into the cold milk, and porridge and milk then placed in the mouth. I am afraid that I was rather clumsy at first, letting the porridge slip from the spoon into the basin of milk, and having to fish about for it, or taking too large a portion of hot porridge to be cooled quickly and consequently burning my mouth; but I attained greater dexterity before finishing.

Over our meal we discussed my future work. It appeared that my school was the southernmost of those on the island, between three and four miles from the church at Daliburgh to which was attached the priest's house where we then were. On expressing my wish of finding apartments as soon as possible, I was told that I should be expected to take up my quarters at the schoolhouse attached to the school, when I took up duty. All my objections, among which was that I was not ready to set up housekeeping, and that I first wanted to feel my way, were airily waved aside.

On rising from the table, my host proposed that we should go and look over the schoolhouse; with which we set out. The misty rain of yesterday had given place to a clear sunny day, with a steady breeze from the sea. I noticed that the church and

9

house were built of big blocks of stone set in cement, enclosed by a field or paddock fenced by walls of large stones or pieces of rock. As we stood a little way from the house door I found we were on rising ground down which ran a shingly road some hundred yards long, and about eight feet wide, ending at a wide gate.

Allowing my gaze to wander beyond these to the horizon on either side, I took in the view. To the east stretched a road, evidently the road we had traversed the evening before from Lochboisdale; but all along that horizon running from north to south were hills and mountains standing out grandly in the clear air. To the south gently undulating land, upon which I caught a glimpse of a road, ended in a hill some miles from where we stood. The air was so clear that a building standing on this hill was quite distinct to my gaze. Raising an arm Father Allan pointed to this prominent building, saying: 'That is your school.' To the west as we passed through the paddock there were only low sandhills or dunes, and I seemed to know instinctively that there lay the sea.

Closing the gate as we left the paddock, we turned east along a stony road, parts of which were formed of the solid rock. On either hand, back from the road, were small one-storeyed houses which in the murk of the evening before I had mistaken for heaps of earth or stone.

They were built of rough stone and thatched with straw and heather, and had small windows deeply set in the walls; some had chimneys, and some only a hole in the roof to let out the peat smoke, but each stood in its own plot of ground. Outside these houses we saw an occasional rough-bearded man, who would raise his cap as we passed by. I noticed curious shy children peeping from behind neatly piled stacks of peat, but they always bobbed back out of sight if we appeared to look their way. We paused on a plank bridge where our road crossed a chasm through which a broiling stream of clear water rushed sparkling in the sunlight. I now began to take in the bareness of the landscape; hitherto I had been so interested in new surroundings that this bareness had not previously struck me. Of course, the season would account for the bare dark look of the ground and shrivelled, coarse grass. But the landscape lacked something besides hedges, whose place was taken by stone walls.

Suddenly it flashed upon me—no trees! Look where I would there was no sign of a single tree anywhere. My heart sank for it was like suddenly losing dear friends. My guide told me that the storms prevented trees from becoming firmly rooted. As we walked along, I felt while gazing at the rocky hills and mountains that Nature knew best and that their wild stern grandeur would be spoilt by trees.

After going some distance along our easterly road, we turned south on to a road less stony which stretched north and south, and which, I learnt, extended from the extreme north of the island to the south end, a distance of twenty miles. Rising ground now hid my school from view, but from its summit I gained a better view. The hill on which the building stood now seemed higher and the building itself larger. I suppose it was but natural for me to be anxiously curious about my new home! A gently falling valley lay before us through which our road undulated on and on until it passed from view over the hill of the school. Below us, on our right, lay a large loch dancing in the sunlight and, seemingly floating near its centre, an island clothed in bushes of heather; and further on I had glimpses of other lochs. On my left rose the majestic hills, which I determined to climb before long.

We had passed few houses since gaining this main road; but as we descended a house appeared round a bend on our left, while on the other side of the road facing the house was a group of three men, clad in coarse blue cloth trousers and blue jerseys, hauling on a rope. We stopped, wondering what they were doing, and then saw the head and shoulders of a cow appearing out of the ground with the rope attached to its horns. It appeared that she had wandered across the road into a bog on the other side. With much hauling and pulling, in which Father Allan and I lent our aid, the poor beast was soon free, but with hindquarters clothed in mud. If aid had not been forthcoming the bog would have swallowed the terrified creature. The men were profuse with their thanks, of course in Gaelic, and we went on our way. At last we breasted the hill on which stood my school, looking rather imposing on its elevation.

From the main road another short one led to a wide iron gate set in a stone wall, surrounding a fair-sized piece of land in which stood the block of buildings, all built of stone. On the right was evidently the gable end of the school, with large high windows, while the part facing the gate appeared to be the school house. The latter was a compact-looking place; the double door, sitting-room window, with two dormer windows above, rather took my fancy. Entering the house by a fair-sized vestibule, fitted with a rail for hats and coats, we passed through a glass-panelled door into the house proper. From a small hall a staircase ran up on the right with a pantry underneath. Two doors were on the left, that of the front sitting-room facing the stairs, the other opening into a fairly large kitchen, from which another door opened into a small scullery. I was particularly struck by the thickness of the walls which was shown by the window embrasures of nearly three feet depth. I soon learnt the reason for this! After viewing the upper floor of the house, consisting of three bedrooms and a small room fitted with a skylight instead of a window, we passed through the scullery to the back of the house.

What a view! To the south the main road wound down to the sea less than two miles away, its dancing blue stretching to a number of smaller islands, and beyond to larger ones rising into mountains. My eyes ranged round from these to the west, and there lay the Atlantic, its mighty swell surging in towards us from as far as the eyes could reach. The awe I felt at this beautiful scene is with me even now as I write. It was not exactly a garden in which we stood, for its thin turf gave place to bare rock in many places, and Father Allan told me that this school had its foundation sunk in solid rock, as it was the highest of them all, and the most exposed to the elements. Here and there, dotted about, could be seen the thatched stone cottages of crofters who eked out a living from their crofts, or small farms, aided by their earnings in the fishing season.

Retiring to the schoolhouse we discussed my setting up house there. I was rather dismayed to learn that salaries were paid half-yearly, the next pay-day being some four months ahead. Of articles of furniture of any kind the house was entirely devoid with the exception of a pine table and two hard chairs, and, as I had only a few pounds remaining from my little store, I was somewhat in a quandary. Father Allan said that I could easily manage for I could get what I needed from a merchant whom we would see next day.

As it was now Thursday* it was decided that I should take up duty on the following Monday, going to the house during the Sunday afternoon. A sister-in-law of the local postman would come in and cook my meals. We went over the school which consisted of a large room with as accommodation long desks with seats for about a hundred children, and a galleried† classroom for forty or fifty more. The entrances were on the east through a small cloak room or porch for the boys, and another on the west side for the girls. There was a separate playground for each. The schoolrooms had large open fireplaces; but not having seen any fuel except a stack of peat by the house, I enquired about school fires. It appeared that each child was expected to bring to school each morning a piece of peat which should last through the day as the winter days were short. An allowance for cleaning utensils was made, but the head teachers had to make their own arrangements about the actual cleaning. I do not think that I showed the surprise I felt at this, as I had determined to see it through.

Leaving the school and house, we started on our way back to the priest's house, where I was to stay in the meantime. I had noticed that the school and house had not been locked up and remarked upon this. Another surprise!—no one bothered to lock their doors, robbery being unknown on the island.

Very hungry and tired I was glad when dinner was served— vegetable soup served from a large tureen, followed by roast fowl which must have been far beyond the laying age for it resisted all the efforts of my host to dismember it, and only after much sharpening of the knife and many attempts was he able to obtain a few morsels from its tough carcass: indeed, the bird had to be taken from the table almost intact. I supposed that the good frugal housekeeper would not think of sacrificing a fowl not past the laying age. I began to realize the economical and the stern frugality with which my host had to live. We partook of more soup instead, followed by milk pudding.

Next day we walked over a hill called Carishaval to the store of the local merchant situated about two miles from the school. It lay in a well-sheltered nook beside an arm of the sea. A large roomy comfortable-looking stone house with slated roof was

---

* 31st December 1889.
† The gallery was later removed.

13

attached to a sort of general store. In front of the house was the first attempt at a garden I had seen since landing; and, wonder of wonders—trees! These were only smallish willow trees, about ten feet high: but still, trees! I thought that they had a softening effect on their surroundings. The proprietor, Mr Donald Ferguson, a black-bearded youngish man, was introduced, in English, as a member of the School Board, and one of the managers of my future school. He was quite affable, and spoke to me in good English; then he and Father Allan conversed in Gaelic for a considerable time. At last I found that they had settled for me what I was to purchase; the goods would be sent to the schoolhouse the next day. When I asked for the bill I was told not to worry about that: it would follow in due course. The simple, casual way in which things were done rather amused me.

Sunday arrived and after a cup of tea and some oat-cake we watched the people coming to church. As Father Allan had to say the eleven o'clock Mass, of course he was fasting. From before ten o'clock I could see figures, single or in groups, approaching in a leisurely manner from all directions, as far as the eye could reach; some were seen on the road, some crossing boggy ground, but all walking, although I had previously seen many on shaggy ponies, riding bareback. As they arrived in the vicinity of the church the men stopped, resting in groups against walls, or on rocks, evidently engaged in conversation. The women, mostly wrapped in plaid shawls, with a smaller one over their heads and tied tightly at the back of the neck, entered at the paddock gate, steadily advanced up the road and entered the church without pause.

Eleven o'clock arrived and passed, Father Allan went occasionally to the window, and then returned to his chair, saying that he could see more coming in the distance. It was nearer twelve o'clock than eleven before he gave the order for the bell —one salvaged from a wrecked ship—to be rung. Explaining the delay he said: 'Some of them have to come a long way, and not many have clocks, so I do not ring the bell till all have gathered.' Afterwards I learnt that some came from an island called Eriskay by boat to the other side of the hills, and walked six to eight miles to hear Mass.

The interior of the church looked very bare—small pictures

of the Stations of the Cross being the only ornaments—but it was full, men on one side and women on the other. The people worshipped with great decorum and devotion. The language of the Mass, being in Latin, was the same as in the city I had left. I realized the value of this to one away from his native land. The concluding prayers were said in Gaelic, which sounded very strange to me.

Looking through the window just before sitting down to our late breakfast, I could see the congregation dispersing in all directions as they had come—I believe some of them could not reach home before well into the night. This manifestation of faith impressed me strongly.

Soon after our meal, a little man with a forest of whiskers came for my baggage. As he lived a little south of my school I was to accompany him; so leaving Father Allan standing on his step, assuring me that he would be at the school during the week, we set off, I summoning all my courage to meet the future. The walk to the school seemed longer than before: my companion could not speak a word of English and when I addressed him only grinned and answered volubly in Gaelic. On no account would he allow me to carry any of my luggage, behaving as if it were a privilege to carry it for me; nor would he accept anything in the way of gratuity on arrival at the schoolhouse, but dumped the things at the door, grinned at me again, and started off down the road—Poor Hamish! I often think of him. A more willing, cheerful and helpful soul I never met. Indeed, it was through these very qualities that he later met his death— he saw a runaway horse with a woman in a light cart, and in trying to stop it had his chest crushed in by the shaft and died shortly after. Many must have missed him.

I smiled to myself when I saw the preparations that had been made for my setting up house, and I wondered what the folks at home would have thought had they seen them. A peat fire was burning in the front sitting-room, a tin paraffin lamp was alight on the table. All I could find of the furniture supplied by the merchant was a cushioned chair convertible into a camp bed, beneath the cushions of which were a couple of blankets. As I went into the kitchen I heard a slight noise followed by the stealthy closing of the back door. A fire burnt in the grate there, a large black iron kettle was standing on one hob, a small brown teapot on the other. A paraffin lamp with tin reflector hung on the wall lighting up the table on which was a coarse tablecloth, a cup, saucer, spoon, plate and a knife—all of a very common and coarse kind. To eat, there were oatcakes, warm scones, and salt butter; a little milk in a small corked medicine bottle and some wet sugar completed the table equipment. All was dark and still outside; so I sat down and made as good a meal as I could. While unpacking my baggage in the sitting-room a little later, I heard stealthy movements in the kitchen. Assuming that the person who had prepared my meal and had disappeared so surreptitiously had returned to clear away, I did not venture from the sitting-room for some time, wishing to defer to any possible shyness she might feel.

Some hour or so later I entered the kitchen. Standing over a large iron pot from which steam arose, a tilted plate of oatmeal in one hand, the other occupied in stirring the contents of the pot with a long spoon, was a youngish gipsy-like woman. As she glanced up, then turned away and bent her head over the pot, I noticed her aquiline-featured and weather-beaten countenance, her large dark eyes and her blue black hair caught up in a knot behind her head. She was wearing a clean light-coloured blouse, a short skirt, and was in bare feet. I politely said: 'Good evening', she turned her head, smiled, showing very white teeth, and said something in Gaelic, and resumed her stirring of what I judged to be porridge. Returning to the other room I occupied myself till I thought she had gone, then I went to look for supper. On the table was a soup plate of porridge, the sugar, and the remains of the milk in the bottle. Whoever the departed woman was I came to the conclusion that she knew how to make porridge—I had often had porridge before and have, many times since, but I have never tasted porridge to compare with what this woman could make. Having thoroughly enjoyed my supper and made up my camp bed, I put out the lights and was soon asleep.

I had previously gathered that, during the interim between the leaving of my predecessor and my taking up duty, the school had been conducted by a temporary schoolmistress, assisted by two pupil (student) teachers, one in her first year of apprenticeship, and one in her second year; that school commenced at ten o'clock in the winter, and at four o'clock in the summer. So, rising fairly early the next morning I went, after a frugal breakfast of tea, egg, scone and butter, to the school.

Seated at one of the school desks with books before them were two young women, one fair and one dark, whom I took to be the student teachers. With a polite 'Good morning' I advanced and asked to see what studies they were doing. To my surprise they made no response, but looked at each other and burst out laughing. After several attempts to get them to say something, I opened a history book for each and gave them a chapter to study.

I got on better when the temporary mistress arrived, a little before ten o'clock, for she spoke passable English quite readily. I learnt from her that I was the first teacher at the school who spoke solely English; and that hitherto all instruction had been given in Gaelic. To an extent this explained my getting no response from the student teachers—they had probably heard little English, and my strange accent and the fact that I was their first man teacher might account for this.

The temporary mistress told me that she was to stay and help for a time; so I directed her to continue as usual.

The scene of the children of all ages entering at the doors, each with a piece of peat which was deposited on the floor near the fire, was quite novel. Though it was winter time none of the children wore shoes or stockings and all the boys with the exception of a few of the biggest wore kilts of home-spun cloth. Most of them, boys and girls alike, looked hardy and weather-beaten. Many curious but shy glances were cast on me as the children proceeded to their places, and an occasional smile from me evoked no answering smile from any one of them.

While the lessons, given in Gaelic, proceeded, I read the log book, and recorded therein the fact that I had that day taken up duty. I then followed as far as possible the instruction that was being given, went round overlooking those who were inscribing in books or on slates, and making mental notes for future guidance. There was no break in the session from ten o'clock in the morning till dismissal at three o'clock in the afternoon. Before the school children dispersed I addressed a few words to them which they met with solid silence. It was getting dark, so retiring to the house, feeling none too cheerful after the first day's experience of my new school, I set to work planning how

17

best to cope with matters. While I was so engaged there was a tap upon the sitting-room door; it was opened, and a voice said: 'Teee.' I went to the kitchen, but my housekeeper had disappeared as before, so I had my meal of boiled salted ling and potatoes, the latter with their skins on.

The rest of the evening I spent in the preparation of school work; and after a supper which was a duplicate of that of the night before, I went to sleep while thinking of my plans for the future.*

Matters in school were a little better next day. I gained a 'Yess' or a 'Naw' from my student teachers, now and then, in answer to my questions—probably they had thought over their conduct of the previous morning. But they astonished me by the way in which they had memorized the chapter of history I had given them to study; page after page they reeled off, absolutely word perfect; and this faculty they evinced throughout the whole course of their subsequent study. This, of course, was very valuable, but apt to prove embarrassing when I wanted them to reason things out for themselves as in mathematics, or from causes to effects.

I myself took charge of the top class throughout that day but could get no English from them except when they were actually reading English from the books. The next day or so it was the same, and it was fully a month before I began to get any response in English. I knew that mutually we had difficulties. Theirs lay in shyness of trying to express themselves in (to them) a foreign language; that they had never had a man teacher before; and that his pronunciation of fairly familiar words was different from any they had ever heard before; so that it was not easy for them to grasp the exact meaning of what I said. Above all, I believe that they had an acute fear of ridicule from each other. My difficulties are fairly obvious, I think. However, by

* Rea's first entry in the school log book reads: 'No school yesterday, New Year's Day. Very poor attendance today, in consequence of wet stormy weather. On this date, January 2nd 1890, I commenced my duties as Head Teacher of this School.

    Staff: Fred. Geo. Rea, Head Teacher.
            Christine McMillan, Frth. Yr. P.T.
            Marion McAskell, Sec. Frth. Yr. P.T.'

His predecessor was Mary MacDonald, a native of Perthshire, who was assisted by her sister, Isabella MacDonald, and the two pupil teachers mentioned above, at the time of her retirement in 1889.

a combination of patience, perseverance and sympathetic consideration for them, before many weeks were over I had overcome much of these difficulties and established a modicum of mutual confidence.

During the week Father Allan visited the school,* and, after examining the registers and making an entry, he left me at the door with an invitation to dine with him on the following Sunday. I looked forward to this most of the week as I had no one to converse with and out of school I was utterly alone. I remember a loud knock at the door late one night and hoping it was someone I could talk to. On my opening the door a voice said: 'Post' and a bundle of letters was thrust into my hand. I tried to keep the postman for a minute with some remarks about the weather; but with a short 'Oh, aye!' he turned on his heel and went away: so I had to be content with the written words of my correspondents.

Sunday came and I enjoyed the respite from my loneliness. It passed all too soon though, but I brought back with me several historical novels lent to me by my host. How glad I was of these during the evenings of the ensuing week! Up to this the weather had been wonderfully fine, clear, and warm for January. That Sunday night I was awakened suddenly by a tremendous gust striking the house, and I felt my bed heave and the whole building seemed to rock. Blast after blast struck as if with a giant hand. These soon gave place to an appallingly loud booming, rising higher and higher in pitch into terrifying shrieks that seemed those of ten thousand angry Furies trying to rip the house from the face of the earth. All through that night of storm I sat, starting up now and again as the wind struck with extra violence. I remember thinking how well those builders had worked so as to enable the house to withstand the storm. Well did I now understand the three-feet-thick stone walls!

By school time the next morning it was blowing a strong, steady gale. When I ventured out of my door to go to the school, it was as though I was being pushed by a board to the wall and pressed hard against it. By dint of holding on to the stones and pulling myself sideways, the wind pressing me tightly against

* The visit took place on 9th January 1890, at 11.25 a.m. One hundred and one pupils were present, of whom ninety-nine had been marked in the register, and two were unpunctual.

19

the wall all the time, I managed to reach the opening into the playground where I was at once torn from my hold and whirled away right past the school door. Fortunately this brought me under the lee of the school gable and by careful manœuvring I gradually reached the shelter of the school door.

No school session was held that day as only a few children who lived near by were present. How the teachers reached the school I could not imagine, but arrive there they did. Now and then during the morning there was a slight lessening in the loud booming of the gale. During one of these lulls I went to the school door and saw some big bearded men clad in oilskins and sou'westers peeping out from the lee side of the school wall. These men, I could only think, must have brought the children to school, and, probably, were waiting to take them home: but they were too shy to come to the door, for they would betray their ignorance of any knowledge of English. During these lulls the children left the school, I holding the hands of the smaller, one on either side of me, and took them to the waiting men. I was alarmed as I took the first two children for, when we reached the opening through which I had passed in trying to get into school that morning, they were lifted right up in the air while I, hanging on grimly to their hands as they were blown out straight before me, only just managed to get them safely across to a sheltered part. Eventually we got them all safely away from school, and the two student women teachers disappeared after the last child was placed in the care of his protector. I do not remember exactly how I got back into my house, but I have a lingering impression of crawling on all fours, occasionally having to turn round from the wind to recover breath. Fortunately I have been athletic and physically strong all my life so I now can look back to this experience with a certain amount of the pleasure I then felt in battling with the elements—later on I had bets with friends, challenging them to get round the gable end of my house when a steady south-west gale was blowing; and I won every time.*

* Rea recorded 'very stormy weather' in the school log book on 7th and 13th January, and 'continuous stormy weather' on the 17th (1891).

Chapter Three

THE gale lasted three days during which time school procedure was very similar to that of the previous Monday. While I was reading in the evening of the third day, for I was now more accustomed to the sound of the storm, I was rather startled by a sudden silence—the storm had ceased! I remember thinking that it was as though some Greater Power had said: 'That is enough!' and instant obedience had followed.

The temporary schoolmistress, a tall brawny masculine type of woman with high cheek bones, told me that she was due to leave the school the following week. On the Friday morning of that week she said that she was crossing to Barra to stay with a schoolmistress friend there, and if I cared to visit the school-master who conducted a large school on the same island she was sure that he would be delighted to meet a colleague. At the south end of our main road, which passed my school, stood an inn, Pollachar, and it had been arranged that a boat from there should take her across the sound to a bay where her friend's school was situated. At the thought of a talk with a fellow school-master I jumped at her suggestion of visiting him. Shortly after school closed we set off for the inn some two miles from the schoolhouse.

The inn was a low rambling stone erection, half inn and half farmhouse, standing within a few yards of the shore, upon which were two or three boats drawn well up clear of the sea. As a boat had to be launched and there was no sign of a crew, my companion led the way into the inn. As we were passing down the long hallway a door opened to our left and from it came a young woman wiping her flour-smeared hands on a clean apron. Judge of my surprise when I recognized her to be Marion Mc-Askill, one of my student teachers! Confusedly she explained that she was busy making scones for tea and showed us to a little room in which were two people whom my companion introduced to me as the father and the mother of my student teacher. I cannot attempt to describe them—the gentle, kind, refined face of the latter, and the rugged bewhiskered weather-beaten countenance of the former, whose broad strong figure seemed to express in every movement an innate courtesy of welcome, will always be imprinted on my mind. There was a natural dignity about them that deeply impressed me as they cordially welcomed me in very good English; my companion they evidently knew well.

While our host went to see about the boat his wife regaled us with wine and biscuits. Intimation came almost immediately that the boat was ready and with a hasty good-bye we climbed across some rocks into a smallish boat. With a wave of the hand from our late host as our crew of two men hauled up the sail, and a fluttering of handkerchiefs from the boat, we shot out from the small bay.

The evening was closing down as our little vessel scudded along across the choppy sea of Barra Sound and shore lights began to twinkle in the distance. The wind was rising and I noticed that one of the men began reefing the sail while the other man steered, watching the sail all the time. The sea was becoming rough, night was coming on, and the wind getting stronger every moment. Reef after reef was taken in the sail as the wind increased and I heard the two who formed the crew shouting at each other in Gaelic. Soon lights appeared ahead and there was the sound of heavy breakers beating on the shore. Suddenly the man at the helm seized my hand, put it on the helm, yelled something in Gaelic, and the two men sprang to the sail and pulled it down till only a fragment of it caught the wind. All I could see was churning white water boiling on either side of the boat while we were racing along between in a channel of black water.

I cannot say what I felt at the time, but I know that my energies were concentrated on keeping the boat equally distant from the water churning on either side of us, for this obviously denoted rocks. The men at the sail were peering ahead, occasionally looking at me, but all I could do was to keep the helm as I thought right and to trust to Providence. At last one of the men took the helm from me and ran us up on to a sandy sheltered beach. Through it all my schoolmistress companion had sat imperturbably in the boat as though she were quite accustomed to such experiences. After we had landed she told me we were some six miles from her friend's house, and we should have to walk there. We left the men making their boat secure, and started off into the darkness, my companion leading the way.

I stumbled along over sandhills, grass, heather and rocks after my guide, who never appeared to hesitate in her sense of direction, and eventually we arrived at the door of Northbay schoolhouse about midnight. The inmates had to be roused from their sleep; and shortly two young ladies* came downstairs clad somewhat *en deshabille*, and proved to be the schoolmistress and her sister. There was some embarrassment, for I was not expected, and it was too late for me to find my way, as I intended, to the schoolmaster's house at Castlebay six miles off.

After much discussion in which I gathered that accommodation was very limited, I elected to sleep on the hearth rug for the rest of the night. I also undertook to leave the house before six in the morning providing they now told me the route to the other school: for I began to sense that they feared scandal might be caused by my having slept there. So milk and biscuits were left on the table and they retired.

I slept only fitfully and was up before daylight. Having consumed the milk and biscuits I gathered my belongings and quickly crept outside as dawn was breaking over a lovely little bay facing the school. I have often thought of that scene since as one of the most beautiful I can remember. The school and house were built in an armchair-like sheltered fold of the hills so close that by reaching from the windows you could almost touch the grass and delicate little ferns that covered the slopes. The spot was so sheltered all round and the air seemed so clear, gentle, and mild that I thought: 'One could grow anything here!' From the buildings the ground, covered with soft grass like that of a lawn, sloped gently down to perfectly white sand that almost circled the tiny bay whose water was as clear as crystal. As I took in the whole view I almost gasped with delight.

Recalling the necessity for haste I started off along the road directed the previous night. It slowly wound up a hillside, over

* Jessie Thomson and her sister Annie. They were from Forres.

23

the shoulder of a mountain, down into a valley. I met no one till I had crossed this valley and was ascending a hill. I had passed by several cottages similar to those on my own island without seeing man, woman or child. Coming over the crest of the hill towards me were two men carrying something on their shoulders. As they came near I judged them to be fishermen as they were carrying a large-mesh net between them and were dressed in coarse blue jerseys. I stopped and ascertained that I was only a mile or so from the schoolmaster's house. They spoke in fair English—I judged them to be fishermen returning from the night's fishing with nets to mend.

When I reached the crest of the hill I looked down to a large bay on which quite a number of boats lay at anchor; most of them were large, bearing two masts. Around the shores of the bay stone buildings were congregated, also long wooden sheds—I was looking down on a little town, Castlebay. I soon located two churches and a school, the latter similar to mine but larger: Noting with satisfaction that smoke was issuing from the school-house chimney, I descended to the sea front and proceeded to the schoolhouse.

I need not be diffuse on our meeting and how my new friend seemed as delighted to shake the hand of another man teacher as was I. He was a voluble, youngish man from London, though I should not have thought so from his flowing black beard and rather unkempt hair, but he was the soul of hospitality, as was his wife; she was suffering from toothache and I remember wondering if the nearest dentist were on the mainland. Retailing our experiences, our mutual, also our individual, difficulties fully occupied the time we spent together. In fact I remember his sitting at the foot of my bed that night telling me of a school-mistress who had come from London to take a school on Barra Head, one of the neighbouring islands.

This schoolmistress was teaching in London and, seeing this vacant post advertised, applied for it and was appointed. After a long railway journey she arrived at Oban. Here she asked for a cab to take her to her school. Of course it was explained to her that she would have to go by steamer. She landed at Castlebay. Here she again asked for a cab to take her to her school. Again she was told that she would have to go by boat. There was a lighthouse on the island where her school was

24

situated, only approachable by boat in calm weather. The people were few and mostly connected with the lighthouse. Intercourse with Barra Head could only be maintained during fine weather in the summer months owing to the enormous swell from the ocean which made it impossible to land at other times. The last boat of the season went, as a rule, towards the end of August; all communication was then cut off from the island till May of the following year. It happened to be this last boat of the season that took the schoolmistress to the island. Early in May of the following year, when the first boat of the season went to the island, the schoolmistress returned in her, went straight on board the steamer that was about to leave and nothing more was ever heard of her.

Time for my departure from my new friend's house came all too soon and with many promises of frequent correspondence and with mutual regard we parted, both of us stimulated by our congenial intercourse and the exchange of thought and ideas.

Chapter Four

BY degrees more confidence was established between the schoolchildren and myself. The teaching of games new to them was a great help in establishing a good spirit in the school.

I remember making the first kite the children had ever seen. The bigger boys watched me with keen interest: and choosing a suitable day we had the first flight. As the kite ascended into the air their loud exclamations and their capering in delight fully rewarded me for my trouble. Some of the women from nearby houses came out at the noise of the boys' shouts; but, seeing the kite, dashed inside again and slammed their doors. I think they imagined I was a kind of wizard who was hauling a bird from the sky. Under my supervision some of the more reliable boys, in turn, were allowed to fly it. The pull of the string amazed them, and when I flew it into some low clouds out of sight and sent messengers of paper travelling up the kite's string, their delight was unbounded.

That evening I allowed the postman's son, a boy of twelve who lived near by, to fly it himself in front of my house. A fresh north wind was blowing, so he soon had let out all the string. There he stood in sheer happiness and I had not the heart to interrupt him though it was now nearly dark. When it was quite dark he began to haul in. Suddenly, with a shout of consternation, and crying out 'It's away!' he dropped the string and vanished into the darkness. I knew from the position of the kite when last seen flying that it would with its broken string drop into, or somewhere near, a large loch lying to the south of us. How long he was gone I cannot say, but he returned with it having found it on the far side of the loch. How he succeeded in finding it in the pitchy darkness was a mystery to me: he must have had the eyes of a hawk!

The attendance officer, Donald MacCormick, visited the school at intervals for reports of the attendance. He was a type of man I had never met before. A fairly educated man who spoke, read and wrote Gaelic and English quite fluently, he had a thoroughly independent outlook on men and matters, and his logical critical view on life in general tinged with a little philosophy quite interested me. He was a native of the island, between forty and fifty years of age, of medium height and build, hair turning grey, and had clean-cut good features in which were set a pair of keen grey eyes. I judged that he had travelled a lot in his earlier days but he had evidently settled down, for he then had a fair farm and quite a number of cows and horses.

If he came to the school in the afternoon I generally invited him to the house when lessons were over, for I enjoyed conversing with him. His knowledge of the then current politics and prominent men, and his keen judgment of them: his power of discussing the merits and demerits of standard authors and their works really astounded me; for *here* was, perhaps, the last place I should have looked for such a character.

One evening while talking of books and facts, I asked him, suddenly, if he believed in 'second sight'—I had read of such in Scott's and other works. He paused for a minute, then leant across the table and said: 'I was *made* to believe in it!' Knowing him for the hard-headed matter-of-fact man he was, I said sceptically: 'Go on! You don't.' For a moment he looked offended, then in a serious voice said: 'I was made to believe in it when I was a youth, and I will tell you how.'

He told me how youths were left to look after the cattle during summer and took them to water at the lochs at intervals. One day he was with another youth and they were driving the cows to the loch for water. Just as they neared the loch shore his companion called out: 'Who are those people?' He said: 'What people?' and his companion, pointing to the other end of the loch replied: 'Look, man! There are a lot of them!'

My informant said he had heard it rumoured that this youth had second sight, but he himself ridiculed the idea, so he said: 'Rubbish! You can't pull my leg!' The other replied: 'I'll make you see them,' and rushing behind placed his two open hands one on each side of his eyes like the blinkers of a horse's bridle.

Quite calm and serious, the attendance officer told me that

immediately the extended hands were placed beside his eyes he saw a procession of men slowly crossing rough ground towards the other end of the loch from where the two youths were standing. He told the other to keep his hands there 'For,' he said to me, 'I was curious to see what would happen and I knew that I should see nothing if he took his hands away.' As the procession neared the loch he could see that the men were in black and seemed to be carrying something. At last they reached the lochside where they stopped and gathered round in a large group, but he could not see what they were doing. Then there seemed to be a loud crack at his feet and the whole group of black figures vanished.

He turned to me and said: 'You asked me if I believe in second sight and I could only tell you this one and only experience of mine.' He went on to say that years after in reading old Gaelic annals of clan warfare he found that the Macleods from Skye had landed near there on a raid, and that a desperate fight ended in great slaughter, the slain being buried by the monks near the loch. *

Apart from sudden winter storms the climate was remarkably even and mild; some days were perfect, more like those of summer than of winter. I remember my taking advantage of one such day, a Saturday, to put into execution my previously mentioned desire to climb the range that ran down the whole of the eastern side of the island. Away to the north rose two dominating peaks of some two thousand feet; but opposite my house the range would be a little under a thousand feet, running along like a wall shutting out the eastern shore from my view. Off I started across the road and up the rising ground beyond, down which tiny rivulets ran. Now and then when standing on a level

* Rea recorded in the log book on 5th June 1891 that 'the newly appointed Compulsory Officer visited school today and was instructed to visit and warn parents who persist in keeping their children to assist out-door work. Attendance low throughout week'.

Subsequently Donald MacCormick wrote the notice of his visit in the log book with his own hand on 1st March 1892, and again on 8th March 1892, signing the entry himself on the latter occasion.

Donald MacCormick was a remarkable man: he had taught himself to read and write Gaelic, and had made a collection of Gaelic proverbs, which was copied by Fr Allan McDonald into one of his notebooks. Later he made a collection of the words of thirty-seven waulking songs in 1893; this MS was preserved amongst Father Allan's papers, as well as one or two letters in Gaelic written by MacCormick, and an elegy in Gaelic on Fr George Rigg, who died in 1897.

green bit I would notice the whole piece of ground quaking and it was only great wariness and lightness of foot, together with the aid of my stick, that took me to firmer ground. When I judged myself to be nearly half-way up I turned to rest and to look at my house and school below. I was amazed to see how tiny they looked. Beyond them the ground sloped down to a long stretch of sand extending all along the western shore of the island. Beyond this again lay the ocean so calm, yet mighty and awesome. Stifling my emotions I resumed my climb and at last reached the top. The range gradually sloped down into a valley bounded on all sides by hills broken by deep glens. I wanted to see the sea on this side of the island; some subconscious influence urged me on, and I descended into the valley. Here I began to feel lonely. Since passing the crofters' cottages near the school I had not seen man, woman nor child, only a few sheep on the other side of the hills, and here was only an eerie silence. Determinedly pushing on I went due east, mile after mile, past still lochs, and on and on till an isolated hill barred my way. But I soon reached the top of this and climbed to its pinnacle. I was amply rewarded for my pains. The sea was at my feet and from the elevation on which I sat I saw the islands of the Inner Hebrides, the mountains of Skye and Rum, and the lower-lying Eigg, and Canna. I suddenly became aware that the sea-gulls from the sea were flying around me with loud discordant cries; then some swooped close past me shrieking in my ears, others seemed to fly straight at my face so that I struck at them with my stick; they were very large and became so menacing that I scrambled down into the valley and commenced my return.

Eventually, I reached home without mishap with the exception of one incident which might have proved serious. While ascending the east side of the hills which faced my house a rock which I had gained gave way and I rolled down the hillside into a bush of heather which startled two huge snowy owls, the only sign of life I had seen since crossing the hills in the morning, with the sole exception of the sea-gulls. I reached home just before dark. Afterwards I learnt that I had been to the most easterly point of the island and that probably none of the inhabitants had ever been there.

A few nights later I was disturbed in my sleep by a knocking sound somewhere in the vicinity of my house. There was a muffled deadly monotony about it that seemed queer in the quietude of night. The next evening I understood. A knock at the front door had taken me to it when something wrapped in brown paper was thrust into my hand by the postman with a 'Please do that'. On returning to my sitting-room and opening the paper I found a piece of black-painted tin, also a scrap of paper with the name of a male person followed by the letters 'R.I.P.' It was a coffin plate! I am afraid that my attempt at a suitable superscription was of little merit, but it was done with a feeling of sympathy for the bereaved. Anyway, I was asked to go to the funeral next day.

A number of men were gathered about the house when I arrived, and one of them whom I recognized as my attendance officer began to marshall them in twos to form a procession, I taking a place among them: then he led the way from the house to the road, the men following two by two. As we proceeded slowly along the road the leader left his place at the head of the procession and stood on a hillock beside the way, and reviewed us as an officer might his men on the march; then he proceeded to the head again and I noticed the three leading couples divide, fall out and stand three on each side of the passing line. This procedure having occurred several times it became my turn to fall out and I stood with the others facing the procession, three of us on either side. Wondering what we should have to do I glanced towards the rear of the procession as it came nearer, and I understood. On a small platform nailed upon three poles which projected about two feet on either side and borne by six men was the coffin, while immediately behind walked a woman and a youth, these mourners forming the end of the procession —she was the only woman there. The coffin having arrived opposite us we six quickly relieved the other six bearers who moved to their position immediately in front of the coffin, all done with the slightest of delays. So we proceeded to the grave, the leader regulating the pace and the bearer reliefs with quiet efficiency. By and by the head of the procession turned off the main road along a lesser but rougher road leading to the west. I felt very nervous of stumbling here while acting as a bearer, and we had to exercise great care, for the coffin was only kept in position on the little platform by pieces of wood skilfully nailed around it as wedges. The road gave place to sandhills formed by winds from the ocean. On a ridge of these was an enclosure with a wall of boulders, and smaller stones surrounding it. Entering through a gap to the enclosure we were in the graveyard, as the low mounds with here and there a wooden cross denoted. The platform with its burden was laid on the ground near a spot where two men commenced to dig while the rest gathered round taking turns at the spades till a grave of sufficient depth was made in the sandy soil. While the digging was proceeding the priest, Father Allan, arrived. As we all stood around I noted the demeanour of the men—all were silent beyond a whispered word of direction now and then, their weather-beaten faces showing no other emotion than that of a quiet serious attention.

The grave dug, the platform was lifted beside it, the wedges knocked off, the ropes were slung round the two ends of the coffin which was then lowered to its last resting place. The priest assumed a stole, stepped to the side of the grave and recited the beautiful service for the burial of the dead, ending with sprinkling on the coffin lid the holy water from a small bottle which he had brought with him. Each and all of us in turn stepped forward to look down upon the coffin and then retired to a little distance from the grave. A momentous pause and silence next intervened as the youth mourner stepped forward when a spade was placed in his hands. Alone, he advanced to the pile of excavated earth, filled his spade, turned to the grave, and gently sprinkled the earth upon the coffin—that of his father. Willing hands then took the spade from him and the grave was rapidly filled. All stayed till sods were cut, laid on the grave and beaten down firmly, while finally pieces of rock were placed on these to keep them in place. With scarcely a word, all then dispersed to their respective avocations.

On fine evenings I was fond of climbing the hills and of exploring the shoulders and hollows with which they abounded. On one of these evenings I had wandered farther than I had intended and it began to get dark as I started for home; in descending the hillside I had to exercise extreme care in rounding boulders or the large knolls. Darkness closed in as I was nearing a larger cluster of these when I heard a weird sound rising and falling with a certain queer rhythm on the night air. As I advanced, the sound became a little louder. Cautiously moving round a boulder I found my face level with a small lighted window. I had found the source of the strange sound. The window through which I looked must have been high up in the room wall, for I gazed down on to a long table round which were seated a number of women crooning a strange kind of song. Descending to the level and going round to the door, I knocked in order to ask my way. The song ceased, the door was opened by a man who exclaimed in Gaelic 'The Schoolmaster!' and in English welcomed me in. I was shown to a seat by the fireside where two or three men were seated on a bench and who politely rose till I was seated. I explained my difficulty about getting home, but was told to rest a while and someone with a lantern would see me home. Having thanked them I was now at liberty to look around me. A large lamp suspended from a beam above the table cast a good light below. Seated on benches round the table were fourteen or fifteen women with sleeves rolled up to the shoulder, hands on table all grasping what looked like a long coarse blanket. At the head of the table sat one who appeared to be the leader for she sprinkled the portion of cloth before her with some liquid taken from a tub at her side, passed a large bar of soap across it two or three times, then the next woman on her left drew it towards her. This was repeated, the cloth being passed from hand to hand all round till the whole had been sprinkled and soaped. Now the leader commenced a weird slow chanting song in Gaelic raising her portion of the cloth in both hands, and then pounding it on the table in rhythm with her song, all the other women following suit and joining in the chorus. Gradually the rhythm of the song and of the pounding on the table increased in pace and volume as the cloth was passed along till the arms were soon moving with bewildering speed, yet in perfect time. Sweat was pouring from brow, face and neck of these women when the pace began to slacken. They slowed down till the movement almost ceased, when another woman commenced another song and they proceeded as before. I could but admire the fine physique of the women and the skill with which they worked. They must have been specially selected by the woman of the house.*

While this had been going on I had noticed that at intervals

* Some of the waulking songs sung in South Uist can be found in *Folksongs and Folklore of South Uist* by Margaret Fay Shaw.

a few men had entered, singly or in pairs. Suddenly the singing and the dub-a-dub-dub ceased. The cloth and tub were removed from sight and the table moved, leaving the centre of the room clear. I was told that a dance was now to take place; but, as it was late, I asked if it would be convenient for me to leave. The man who had opened the door on my arrival found a man who was leaving, and who lived near the school. All stood as I shook hands with the men and bowed to the women, and left with this new experience behind me. My companion with the lantern could speak no English, but he safely guided me home, leaving me at my gate.

Chapter Five

ONE fine Saturday morning soon after my first experience of cloth shrinking at the hillside house, Father Allan called at the schoolhouse. He informed me that he was on his way to celebrate Mass on the neighbouring island of Eriskay on the following day, and if I cared to accompany him I might do so. Accepting the invitation with youthful alacrity and putting a few things together, I started off with him down the road to the south. Of course he had walked from his house as he always did while I knew him—whatever the distance or the state of the weather; on sick-call visits or other missions, he always walked, disdaining any aid but that of his own legs. We turned off to our left across some braes after going some distance along the main road. Passing the end of a stony-shored loch of clear water and a cottage near by, where a man doffed his cap to us, we started to climb the south shoulder of the hill range. During this climb I learnt by experience that it was a great saving of breath and of exertion to climb in a somewhat zigzag fashion, taking advantage of parts of sheep paths and so lessening the steepness. On arriving at the summit we without pause began to descend towards the sea.

Below us to the south lay a beautiful wild glen studded with boulders and carpeted with heather, soft grass, and many varieties of fern, among which I recognized the royal fern. The beauty of this sheltered place was enhanced by the fine bright day and the gentle soft air. Descending to near the sea my companion stopped on a large elevated rock, the flat top of which was scorched. 'This is the priest's point,' he said, 'and we must light a fire.' I looked for the wherewithal for lighting it, but he was already picking dry grass and ferns and I did likewise. Gathering these together in one heap we descended to the shore to search for driftwood and soon gathered a fair quantity from crevices of the rocks—large and small pieces washed up by the waves but now bleached perfectly dry; a ribbon-like whitish seaweed dry as tinder was also carefully gathered, and the whole of our spoil carried to the site for our fire. I watched Father Allan start the fire: first he made a heap of the specially selected dry seaweed, then placed some smaller pieces of wood on this, applied a lighted match and the whole began to burn. On this fire we next put the heather and ferns together with some of the larger pieces of wood and then returned to the shore to gather heaps of half-dried coarser dark brown seaweed which we carried to where the fire burned. When this darker seaweed was placed upon the fire a dense smoke was given off.

My companion seemed quite satisfied now, and he led the way to a comfortable nook well up on the hillside, sat down, filled and lighted his pipe saying: 'This is the Highlander's glory—with back to the wind and face to the sun!' I joined him and then gazed about me wondering what was to happen next. Down below us beyond the rocky shore lay a stretch of sea and beyond this again a number of islands; Eriskay, the one immediately opposite to us, looking larger than the rest, was our destination I learned. Father Allan gazed intently at this island for a time, then left our perch to put more damp seaweed on the fire which gave off a denser smoke; then he returned to me to ask if I could see any thick smoke across on the other island. This performance had been repeated several times, when, gazing across again, he sat down with an exclamation of satisfaction. Looking steadily across the sound, which was some two to three miles wide, I could see a column of smoke rising from a high point on the opposite shore. Our signal was answered!

My companion said that the answering smoke signified that his signal had been seen and a boat would come for him: they knew it was the priest, for no one else ever lighted a fire on this particular point. As the tide was low and there were sandbanks in the sound it would be some time before a boat could cross to our shore; so we lay back contentedly with our pipes and talked while our fire burned itself out. One of the first things my companion said was: 'Well, do you want to be back in your city?' I did not answer at once but thought for a moment or two. My mind travelled back to the scenes I knew so well: the city's streets, its shops, its rows and rows of houses, its factories and their smoke-stacks, its crowds hurrying to work, others idling and gazing into shop windows; I could tell almost exactly what was taking place there at that particular moment—the same drab round, year after year. Then I looked at the scene before me: the blue sea and the sky in which birds were soaring, wheeling and diving swiftly into the water after fish, the towering hills and mountains which never looked the same two days together. My companion must have been watching me and following the thoughts perhaps reflected in my face, for he sighed and said: 'Ah! God made the country and the deil made the toon!'

He then spoke of Eriskay, the island to which we were soon to cross. Its population of some three hundred souls used to live in comparative comfort and contentment in the glens and the valleys of South Uist, the families supporting themselves by the cultivation of small farms and by fishing. An owner of our island had sold or let extensive tracts of the best land to large-scale farmers, and the displaced crofters, becoming homeless, were allowed to go to the then uninhabited island lying before us. We suddenly paused in our converse for we saw a boat putting out from the opposite island, its red-brown sail shining in the sunlight. We watched it crossing towards us and noticed the sail being lowered then hauled up again as its crew tacked; to avoid sandbanks, my companion said. He seemed to know when she was on her last tack, for gathering his belongings he started off at an angle for the shore, I followed and we were soon clambering over rocks. I in my inexperience, of course, frequently sliding and skidding on the slippery seaweed covering them. Following Father Allan across these as best I could, for every now and then he disappeared from my sight, I abruptly came face to face with a grey-bearded weatherbeaten old man whose face had suddenly appeared above the slippery rock I was attempting to negotiate. He steadied me with his outstretched hand and I climbed over to see a small boat below lying in a small inlet between the rocks while a young lad was standing on a ledge of rock holding her gunwale to shore. At the helm sat Father Allan. I slipped, rather than got, into the boat; the old man loosed the painter from a rock, then came aboard and the lad, giving the boat a push, jumped nimbly aboard. Clear of the rocks I, a landsman, watched them with interest as they hoisted the sail: I was particularly struck with the nimbleness and surefootedness of the boy. I judged him to be about ten years of age but he seemed thoroughly at home in the boat, running along the gunwale to tighten or loosen a halyard as she leaned over to the breezes. Father Allan was at the helm and seemed quite at home while I sat near him enjoying myself and thinking: 'I would rather be here than walking a city pavement!' There was a sudden Gaelic exclamation, down came the sail, and the boat slowed to a standstill. To my surprise, overboard went the old man and the boy, and they were standing in the water beside the boat and pushing— we were on a sandbank. I looked round at Father Allan—he had taken off his boots and socks and was rolling up the legs of his trousers as far as he could. Telling me to remain where I was he was overboard in a minute pushing the boat with his shoulders like the others. With a gentle 'sweesh!' she slid into deep water as they all three clambered aboard. Sail was set and the old man took the helm. He knew every rock, shoal, current and sandbank; it was said that he could steer his boat blind-folded through any part of that ten-mile sound—and I believe it. I had a shrewd idea afterwards that I had seen a slight twinkle in his eye when the incident happened and that he secretly chuckled to himself. He is dead now, but I have heard that his son (the ten-year-old boy aforementioned) succeeded him as ferryman on attaining manhood, and is as skilful, daring, reliable and shrewd as was the old man, his father.

Without further mishap we came under the shadow of cliffs of sheer rock then round a bend into a good-sized bay desig-nated the 'Haun' or 'Haven'. Here, resting at anchor, were a number of large two-masted fishing boats while smaller ones similar to ours were drawn up on the shingle on the west side of the bay whose eastern shore was a pile of rocks. The sail was lowered; we soon ran alongside one of these rocks; the boy leapt ashore and steadied the boat while we landed. Looking around me I saw that the shore of the bay rose in more or less rocky ascent on all sides, a little shingle or sand showing here and there. A youth descended to us and touched his forehead as he took our impediments from us and we climbed after him up the slope. At the top stood a long low corrugated iron building

37

which I judged to be the store as I saw a number of boxes and tea chests outside it, while new oilskins, seaboots and other paraphernalia hung at the door. Spread out on the rocks near the building lay huge fish (cod and ling) which had been split open and were drying in the sun.

Turning to the right we skirted the top of the shore to the west and there we found much sand as well as rock. This part of the coast appeared to culminate on the north in a hill of rock facing the island we had left so shortly before. In a sandy hollow before us lay the school and schoolhouse which, being similar in design to mine, I recognized as such at once. From here the ground sloped in waves of sand down to the western seashore. Arrived at the school I was introduced to the schoolmistress. She was a youngish widow with a charming little daughter of seven or eight years of age. Her husband had been a sea captain, had caught fever in the East Indies and had died leaving her with a small pension. Being fond of the sea (though brought up in Edinburgh) she accepted this post here and with the aid of her pension lived in comparative comfort, if not in luxury. As accommodation was limited it was arranged that I should sleep that night on a camp-bed in the sitting-room. After a hearty, and almost luxurious, meal followed by a smoke and a talk, Father Allan and I went out for a walk.

We made first for the rocky hill to the north. A glorious view stretched around us when we reached the top. At our feet lay the sound we had crossed, the hills and mountains of our island receding in wonderful graduation of light and shade far into the distance and its white sands gently lapped by the sea. Away to the south-west, past several smaller islands, was Barra, the island I had previously visited to make the acquaintance of my new schoolmaster friend; beyond this again lay the limitless expanse of the Atlantic Ocean. The island on which we stood seemed to be constituted principally of bare rock with soil interspersed here and there; the chief feature was a barren-looking mountain, sombre and grim, looking sternly down upon the land below. The only redeeming feature of this grimness was the silvery white sand on the western shore whereon, I was told, Prince Charlie had set foot while on his way to raise the Highland clans in the 'Forty-five'.

My companion suggested that we should climb along the

cliff, and started off down a sheep path, I following. The path abruptly ended and my companion disappeared; I discovered him spreadeagled on the face of the rocky cliff to my right, while the sea boiled some hundred feet below. Youth is notably foolhardy; I thought: 'Where he can go, I can!' Holding on to a crevice in the rock face with my hands, and groping for one to put my feet, I started to follow! Only dour doggedness carried me on. When I ventured to look below I felt dizzy: but sanity returned and I thought of Shakespeare's 'Cowards die many times before their deaths', and clung on, seeking hand- and foot-holds. Now and then my companion called out: 'Want to go back?' My answer was a laconic 'Go on!'—I felt that I would follow, no matter what the cost. I cannot attempt to analyse my motives. That climb was a nightmare to a young man who had spent all his life hitherto in a city. However, I remember my blended feelings of relief and triumph when I had completed the circuit of the face of the cliff and stood beside my companion on a path leading to more level ground. This we crossed and found a seat by some rocks near the gently sloping sandy western shore.

While we were smoking and resting I saw a large silvery fish shoot from the blue sea close at hand, it turned in the air then fell back again into the water with a loud splash. On my asking what the fish was my companion told me that it was a salmon trying to get rid of parasites from its skin—these powerful fish dart through the water, spring out and splash back, the friction and shock ridding them of some of these troublesome guests.

Then my companion began to talk of climbing; and I thought he now regarded me with a more kindly eye while he spoke of his experiences with other climbers who were Highlanders and whom he seemed to regard with a slight contempt, for he had tried them and found them wanting in courage or stamina— he himself was born at the foot of Ben Nevis, and I thought his rugged features and tall powerful figure typified his birthplace. He told me of the men of wild lonely St Kilda, an island of lofty precipitous cliffs far out in the North Atlantic. He said that they were the finest cragsmen in the world. None of them was entitled to be called 'a man' unless he had undergone the cragsman's test, and till he had passed that test no St Kildan maiden would look at him as a prospective husband. The test

39

took place at the edge of a special cliff of rock rising sheer from the boiling surge of the sea some hundreds of feet into the air. The candidate for manhood's estate had to advance barefoot to the edge of this cliff, stand upright with his toes protruding over it, and then bend forward to touch his toes. I said: 'But if he falls over, what then?' The reply was: 'Oh! they would say that he was not worthy to be called a man, and was no loss.'

Next morning Father Allan asked me to serve Mass, so I accompanied him, carrying some of the vestments and necessary vessels. We soon reached the church,* a long low stone house with thatched roof. The wooden partitions used to subdivide such cottages had been removed and the result was a fairly large floor space of beaten earth. At the far end from the open door was a long wooden table, scrubbed spotlessly clean, set cross-wise. We advanced to this, the altar, bearing the appurtenances we had brought with us. The stand on which to place the missal was a roughly shaped piece of rock, while the other accessories were almost as primitive. Father Allan took a small portable altar-stone from a case he had brought with him and placed it in the centre of the altar. He then began to vest, assisted by me. The people began to troop in, every man in fisherman's garb of blue cloth and blue jersey, the women in plaid shawls with small black shawls on their heads. They crowded in together, filling the floor and overflowing to the ground outside, the men on one side, the women on the other. There was the utmost quiet and devotion during the Mass, after which the people trooped out. While the priest was removing his vestments a number of men came in bearing planks which they rested on rocks ranged round the walls The congregation then returned and sat round on these while some stood during the time the priest delivered a sermon in Gaelic. After he had given a blessing they all dispersed, and we returned to the schoolhouse in company with its mistress. Father Allan must have needed the meal of which we then partook, for he had of course been fasting since the night before.

We now set out for a ramble round to 'Prince Charlie's Landing Place'. On our way we passed along the western base of the bare-looking mountain, Beinn Sgrithinn, a mass of rock. My

* Not the church now in use on Eriskay, which was built in 1902.

companion told me that the eastern side of it was composed of lodestone which deranged ships' compasses and had caused many wrecks, but mariners who knew of it gave the dangerous coast a wide berth. Far up on the side of the mountain I could see small dark heaps. I asked Father Allan what they were and he told me they were stacks of peat. The soil of the island consisted of sand, but well up the mountainside in some of the crevices were banks of peat. The people had to cut their fuel there and then stack it in heaps to dry. There were no horses or ponies on the island so the women went up and carried down supplies on their backs in creels, or baskets, slung from their shoulders. The men were all fishermen to a man, for the barren soil was useless for farming. The population was entirely Catholic with the sole exception of the storekeeper, Ewen MacLennan.

My companion rather startled me by adding that it was his ambition to come some day and spend his life among these poor people.*

Soon we came to a loch, the only one on the island; it contained no fish of any kind, its still brown waters and its shores of grey rock suggested complete absence of life. We came to the shore on the south-west, a beautiful sandy beach interspersed with rocks sloping down into deep blue water. As we arrived here I saw large dark bodies slipping from the rocks and disappearing in the sea—seals! The landing place of the Stuart Prince having been pointed out to me and also the flower plant *Convolvulus maritima*, he himself was said to have planted, we commenced our return to the schoolhouse.

The youth was waiting to take our belongings to the boat for he said that the tide was just right for our return. We took leave of our hospitable hostess and descended to our boat lying by the landing rock in the 'Haun'.† The sail was soon hoisted and we headed out into the sound. As we rounded the rocky cliff towering above us whose face we had scaled the day before, I viewed it with a new interest. Instead of making across the sound towards the Priest's Point near which we had embarked on the previous day, the boat was steered by our old boatman due west along the middle of the sound. On our right lay the long

* As soon occurred. Father Allan was removed by his bishop from Daliburgh to Eriskay in January 1894, after an illness, and lived there until his death in 1905.
† From the Norse word *havn*, meaning 'harbour'

broken line of heather and grass-clad hills and mountains; to our left the rocky island we had just left gave place to some other low grassy islets with stretches of blue water separating them. The perfect day, with a fair south-east breeze, a calm sea, and the sun casting a radiance over all awakened in me feelings unknown to me before. Quietly taking in the delights of the scene I heard Father Allan say: 'Look at the rascals. They seem to know that we have no guns!' Swimming, rolling over, diving and basking in the sun were seals: two or three were swimming alongside, and as I leant over the side of the boat they looked up into my face and their brown doglike eyes seemed almost human. Something probably alarmed them, for like a flash they all disappeared.

I now gave my attention to the shores of South Uist with a view to rambles in the future. The rocky character of the more eastern part changed to green with a long white sandy shore. A straggling line of white stone-slated buildings appeared; one a large house rising from the summit of a small hill next took my attention. Cattle were grazing on the hillside and braes and my thought travelled to England—a farm! The swell of the sea soon began to assume larger dimensions, but passing a long sandy spit of land the helmsman turned the boat sharp to the right, the sail was lowered, and we ran up on to a shingly beach. Disembarking, we climbed to higher ground and I found we were outside the inn where lived my student teacher.

Our welcome was as warm as the one I had received on the occasion of my former visit. We stayed for but a few minutes, saw our boat start on its return to the island, while Father Allan and I, belongings in hand, started north for home along our island's main road. Some distance along the road we paused to rest at a large white gate on the right which guarded the entrance to a side road with fields on either side of it. I ascertained that this road led to the farm I had seen from the boat. Looking north I saw at the top of the rising my house and school silhouetted against the sky. Gathering our baggage we proceeded and were met by smiling Hamish, who took it from us, shouldered it and led the way up the hilly road. Soon we reached the end of the road leading to my house. Here I wanted to know what was the cost of our outing for I wanted to contribute my share. 'Nothing,' was the reply. 'But how much did the boatman charge?' said I. 'Charge! He is only too proud to convey me or my friends. Don't you ever offer them money. They would be insulted!' Pondering somewhat deeply over this I left Father Allan and Hamish as they started off, and entered my house occupied with many thoughts.

Chapter Six

ONE evening after tea I thought that I would pay Father Allan a visit, and off I set stick in hand. I always took a stick with me to drive off any cattle that might meet me on the road —I had learnt from experience that these shaggy beasts would often charge if excited, but would sheer off at once if a stick were waved at them.

It was dusk when I started and before I had gone half-way to my destination, night had come down. I think it was the blackest night I had ever experienced and I could only tell that I was on the road by tapping with my stick and cautiously feeling with it for the deep ditches which lay on either side of this main road. To judge how far I had proceeded on my way was difficult, for the only guide I had was the rise and fall of the road. At last after a very long rise I judged that I had reached the summit of the hill near which Father Allan and I had helped to haul the cow from the bog.

Pausing here I rested amid total blackness and silence. I distinctly remember holding my hand before my face and thinking. 'This is literally a darkness where you cannot see your hand before your face.' Quite suddenly lights began to move about on either side and across the road in front of me. I called out: 'Who is there?' Receiving no answer I advanced and struck at them with my stick, but each time it met with no obstacle. Rather puzzled and thinking that perhaps someone was playing tricks I started off again down the other side of the hill; but soon heavy rain, driven by a gusty wind, came on. This quickly rose into a storm, while battered and bewildered by the wind and rain, I struggled on. All I remember of what then happened is a vague recollection of having turned, as I thought, on to the road which led to Father Allan's house; of suddenly finding

44

myself struggling among reeds in water and mud; of plunging hither and thither in an endeavour to reach firm ground and only finding greater depth on either side; of being beaten by the elements so that I lost all sense of direction. Dimly I remember how, utterly confused and exhausted, I was about to give up all hope and was resigning myself to my fate when I saw a light near at hand. How I managed to reach that light I cannot say, but can only surmise that only by swimming and desperate struggling I reached the house where the light shone. Impressions of my battering on the door, of my being taken within and of some strong-smelling liquid being poured down my throat while I was being warmed at a peat fire linger still, but very faintly.

Somewhat recovered I found that I was in one of the small stone thatch-covered cottages which I, on landing, had taken to be heaps of stones or earth. Very warm and comparatively comfortable it was. The good man and his wife could not do enough in order to express their sympathy; learning that I was anxious to reach Father Allan's, the man took a large smouldering peat from the fire and opening the door led the way. The smouldering peat burst into flame in the wind, scattering sparks in all directions; this was an excellent torch and lighted up the road so that we soon reached Father Allan's house, quite near.

The priest was in the church conducting the wedding ceremony of a local couple, so I meanwhile dried myself as best I could at his sitting-room fire. Soon I heard the sound of bagpipes being tuned up somewhere at hand and Father Allan came to me and said that I must come and congratulate the newly wedded pair. Paying no heed to my attire, for I was now fairly dry, I followed him into the kitchen. There I found a party of four, evidently the bride and bridegroom with the bridesmaid and the best man. The two women wore subdued-coloured dresses and looked very demure, while the men were bright and smiling—all wore sprigs of artificial orange blossom. A young piper with his instrument, the priest's housekeeper, Father Allan and I completed the company. One of the two men of the bridal party held a wine-glass minus its stem in one hand, and a bottle of whisky in the other. With considerable solemnity, as though he were performing an important

45

ceremony, he filled the glass from the bottle and handed it to the priest, who put it to his lips, then handed it back. The three women each took a sip; a pretence of refilling from the bottle was made each time as the glass was handed back. A big tall black-bearded man, who was the bridegroom, took the brimming glass and nearly emptied it at one mouthful; when refilled it was handed to me. I had never drunk neat whisky before so took only a modest sip, and I was glad that I did for it tasted very strong and fiery. The piper and the best man, the latter being the last to drink, both emptied a brimming glassful at a gulp. All this was done with such seriousness and decorum, and in such grave silence, that I was secretly amused.

I had often heard the pipes being played before, but always at a distance. They had then sounded melancholy, yet with a certain wildness strangely in keeping with the mountains, hills, lochs and the restless beat of waves on the shores of the island. I had often stood in my garden on a beautiful evening listening to the rise and fall of the sound of the pipes and I had thought how incongruous would be the playing of a brass band in such surroundings. I found a happiness in listening—strange and barbarous as the bagpipes may sound to the unattuned ear of the average Englishman.

But the swirl of the air set up in this little kitchen seemed to grip me up and whirl me around with its rousing rhythm; and as the ripples of the notes rose and fell they made my toes ache to dance. The bridegroom took the bridesmaid to one side of the kitchen while I willy-nilly stood aside and watched the scene. To my consternation the bride took the orange-blossom from her hair, advanced to me and fixed it in my coat while all the others clapped and laughingly told me that I could not refuse the dance. How I acquitted myself in this, my first Highland reel, I would not venture to say; but having always been light of foot with a keen sense of correct timing, I was saved from making a hash of it—I know I enjoyed it. Another reel was danced, then there came the sound of many voices outside. At this the bridal party prepared to leave. With handshakes and the good wishes of us in the kitchen they departed, headed by the piper playing a march and escorted on their way with a group of people carrying lighted torches. At intervals one or another of these stepped aside and fired a gun over the heads

46

of the rest in salutation of the happy couple. We watched the torchlighted procession as it wound along the road. The sound of the pipes and of the gunshots gradually faded in the distance so Father Allan and I retired to his sitting-room and it was arranged that I should stay there the night.

He was much concerned on learning of my adventurous journey to his house that evening, and he advised me never to commence one again unless there was a reasonable chance of my completing it before dark; storms rose very suddenly and often stopped quite as suddenly, but it was unwise to be so exposed after dark. The dancing lights I had seen on the road he explained as the phenomenon of the will-o'-the-wisp. We talked of many things that night before retiring. Among others he told me that a young schoolmaster from Aberdeen was coming to take charge of Daliburgh school which was being temporarily conducted by an old parochial schoolmaster to whom he would introduce me on the morrow. With pleasant thoughts of soon having a young colleague fairly near me, I went to bed.

Soon after breakfast next morning we started off to visit Daliburgh school. We had nearly reached Father Allan's gate when he heard the galloping of a horse. Along the road came at full gallop a large white horse with a young woman seated sideways on its back. Just as we reached the gate it stopped and she slid easily to the ground almost before it came to a standstill. I noted she had ridden without saddle or bridle. After a rapid conversation in Gaelic, she put her foot on a bar of the gate, sprang lightly to the back of the horse which immediately started off at full gallop on receiving a slap from its rider. It transpired that she had come with some important message from the priest of Bornish, the next parish eight miles away. On my speaking of her remarkable riding my companion exclaimed: 'Oh, that's nothing,' as if it were not worthy of comment.

Reaching the near-by Daliburgh school with the teacher's house attached, I found it similar in build to mine but with a loch running along outside the wall farthest from the road. Gates from the road opened directly into the teacher's garden and the school playground. Another gate led out of this garden into a sort of paddock in which stood a low stone-built house with small corn-stacks standing near it. Father Allan did not take me to the school building but through this latter gate to the other house, explaining meanwhile that the old parochial schoolmaster had had this built for himself. It was now the local post and telegraph office, the schoolmaster acting as postmaster and registrar for the district.

Through the open door, a small counter faced us and on the right was an opened door disclosing an old man with snowy hair and a long white beard seated at a table writing. He raised his venerable-looking head and gazed at us through large steel-rimmed spectacles. Slowly rising from the table he calmly advanced towards us. He said something in Gaelic to my companion, then coolly taking a pinch of snuff he looked me up and down and said: 'Well, well! So this is the young schoolmaster from England! Come away in to the fire.' Father Allan, saying that he would leave us together, departed leaving me with my venerable colleague.

One of the first things he said was: 'And what were they doing in England when you left?' Rather confusedly, I fear, I gave some account of the chief happenings of the time when I left, while he listened, quietly watching me with a pair of very shrewd steel-grey eyes. When I had finished he sniffed contemptuously and said: 'Ach! Let them play at it!' Then he went on to tell me how he had studied as a young man and passed his examination in Edinburgh. He had come to the island and opened the parish school. School was only held in the winter months: during the summer all were engaged on the land. He was disgusted with the idea of children going to school during the fine-weather season saying that they should be out in the open air gaining health and strength. He said that as the years rolled on and newfangled ideas and regulations came into being so he acquired a farm and built himself a house. He never went from the island for a holiday. Some years before he had been persuaded to go to Edinburgh with the Free Church minister for the vacation. But he walked the hotel bedroom floor most of the night: the loud noises of the traffic and the various clatterings startled him and made him so nervous that he told his companion that he would be happier among his own cabbages; so he left by the first train and came straight back to the island; he had never been from the island since.

I noticed how a current of broad philosophy ran through his

talk. If he were alive now, I could fancy hearing him say: 'Ach! With your motor cars, your cinemas, aeroplanes, speed boats and your rush! What has it brought the world to?'

With a promise to pay him another visit in the near future I took leave of him and returned to my home on the hill.

Chapter Seven

THE spring was now well advanced and having now received my salary I arranged to send for my invalid mother in the hope that the pure sea air would restore her to better health. I duly heard that she would soon be coming under the charge of my elder sister, a governess, taking her holiday from France.

Meanwhile the young Aberdeen schoolmaster arrived and took up duty at the school at Daliburgh hitherto conducted by the old parochial schoolmaster.

On the Saturday following I went to make myself known to him and found him staying temporarily at the post-office with the old, now retired, schoolmaster. I found them sitting in the room I had been in before, one on each side of the peat fire. My new colleague was a young man a year or so older than myself apparently; of medium height, dark haired, with good features and wearing a black moustache. His manner was phlegmatic and I felt rather chilled by this; when sitting, all three together, his sole contribution to our conversation consisted of an occasional 'Hmn! Hmn!' He sat smoking a briar pipe which he removed from his mouth when he gave forth this expression. At the time I thought that this manner might be due to the impressions of his new environment, but I afterwards found that this was his habitual manner unless stirred by some suddenly mentioned subject that awakened his interest and enthusiasm—in time, I grew very fond of him and often echoed Father Allan's expressed 'I like C - - - !'

The old retired schoolmaster told us of the *Dunara Castle*, the large cargo steamer from Glasgow that called at our port of Lochboisdale at irregular intervals all through the year. She called for goods and passengers at most of the ports of the

Hebrides and was the only means of communication with the lonely St Kilda which she included in her calls during three months of the summer only; for the rest of the year its population of seventy souls were cut off from the rest of the world. She had that week put into our port with a missionary from St Kilda on board, but he was quite insane. At the boat's last St Kilda visit, some nine months before, he, a young ecclesiastical student, had landed there as missionary, schoolmaster, registrar and postmaster. As he could not speak Gaelic, imagination only can give any idea of what that young man had been through.

Our host did not smoke, and I smoked cigarettes, which I had learnt to make, as ready-made cigarettes were then unknown on the island. I made them from sailor's plug tobacco which I cut with a razor and then shredded and dried. The old schoolmaster watched me making one from my pouch then said: 'Will you make me a paper pipe?' He joined us in our smoke but soon began to cough and choke so threw the cigarette in the fire. Not to be outdone he, by and by, took a tea caddy from the mantelshelf and asked me to make one from tea as it would not be so strong. I complied and we all three sat and smoked, our host proudly puffing away with his bearded chin raised to prevent the dry tea falling out. Before I left he brought into the room some tea leaves moist from the tea pot and asked me to show him how to make a cigarette. Drying these at the fire we managed fairly well. Afterwards I often saw him puffing away at one of his tea-leaf 'paper pipes'. While I was there a policeman called to have a signed entry made on his sheet recording the fact that he had visited this place on his rounds. After he had gone I gathered that he was the only policeman for South Uist and two other islands containing altogether a population of seven thousand, but that his post was a sinecure as the people were most peaceful. He travelled on foot for most of his thirty-mile round, calling upon people of various kinds and authority for a report and a signature verifying the fact that he had visited them in person.

A letter awaited me at home acquainting me of the probable date of the arrival of my mother and sister at Lochboisdale. I proceeded with my preparations, augmenting to some extent the meagre supply of household furniture and equipment. I visited Pollachar inn, where lived my student teacher, to see if

I could arrange for a vehicle to bring my people from the pier some eight miles away. It was arranged that a two-wheeled dog-cart with seating room for two people in front and two behind should be available. A live hen was purchased for sixpence (!) and kept in a shed till the eve of the day of my people's arrival, then it was to be killed, plucked and made ready for cooking.

At last came a telegram announcing that I was to expect them by the next afternoon's boat. My feelings may be well imagined when it is realized that I had been cut off from my kinsfolk for months and now expected to have my mother and sister with me within the next twenty-four hours. Needless to say, I was early down at the inn for the vehicle to convey them from the pier. With some impatience I watched the deliberate way in which they harnessed the horse to the trap; the farmer superintending the operation himself, tightening or loosening a strap or buckle here and there. When all was ready the latter told me to climb in. On my reaching the seat he thrust the reins into my hand, and it dawned on me that I was expected to drive to the pier alone. My protests that I had never driven a vehicle before and could not drive, were unheeded. The inn-keeper said no one could be spared to drive, and I should be all right with Jack, the horse; he gave the latter a slap and off we started up the road at a good trot. 'I am up against it again,' thought I; so putting my mind to the business I managed to get along better than I expected—I am afraid this was due more to Jack's intelligence than to any skill I acquired on the road. As we reached the top of the hill and passed my house I tried to assume the manner of an experienced driver but soon had many qualms when descending hills for fear the horse might trip on the rough road and I be flung headlong from the vehicle. However, at such places I kept his head up and we soon covered the five miles to my young colleague's school, where a three-mile road turned sharp to the right, terminating at Lochbois-dale pier. Just before reaching my colleague's school at Dali-burgh we had passed a part of the road which ran between two lochs, with a low parapet about two feet high and built of stones guarding each side of the road. The approach to either end of this bit of road was very steep, and I felt some trepidation when negotiating this particular portion—the two lochs, in reality, were halves of one large loch through which this part of the main road had been built. In rough weather, with certain winds, it was dangerous to attempt to pass here, as large waves were dashed across the road from one side of it to the other.

As I drove along the pier road I noticed quite a number of lochs on either hand lying well back on the moorland that footed the hills. On we went till the road rose at the hill that overlooked Lochboisdale and the pier. Here was the old parochial school, now empty but for an old couple who stayed there and in whose care I was to leave the horse and trap till I was ready to return. Descending the hill on the side nearer the pier I found a few stone buildings, the post-office, the bank, a baker's shop, and a general store, while standing apart on higher ground was the hotel. I advanced to the pier whereon were stacked scores of new herring barrels ready for the herring fishing which had just started. Several of the fishermen standing about recognized me and touched their caps when I went to inquire for news of the steamer. I ascertained that she was late and would not be in for an hour or so. This made me slightly anxious for I did not anticipate with relish a drive home in the dark; but I occupied my time by making some purchases and packing them safely in the trap.

I will not dwell on the arrival of the steamer, with my mother and sister on board, on our greetings, nor on the difficulty of getting the luggage and ourselves safely stowed in the trap, which I had fetched nearer the pier. All was done with as little delay as possible: the lamps on the vehicle were lighted, as it was getting dark. Before we had traversed the three-mile road from the pier darkness had settled down. Realizing my responsibility put me into anything but a happy frame of mind. My two companions of the journey told me afterwards they had assumed from my manner that I had learned all about driving during the time I had been on the island. This was exactly what I wished to convey, so that they should not share any anxiety. The darkness was now so intense that it was difficult for me to recognize when we had reached the main road, where we had to turn sharp left in order to reach my school three miles off. The candle lamps of the trap gave so feeble a light that they were of little or no assistance. When the innkeeper had said to me: 'You will be all right with Jack' he had spoken the truth, for I am sure Jack turned on the main road of his own accord. The danger of the passage between the two lochs now loomed before me for the wind had risen and it was a dense black night. Soon I could hear the rush of waves and guessed we were nearing the danger. Checking the slow trot of the horse to a walk I let the reins lie quite loose and trusted to the animal's instinct. I am sure Providence was with us that night. The roar of the water of the lochs increased and the next minute I felt the trap going down the steep decline. Jack seemed to feel his way at every step for the whole way across to the other side while the waves enveloped us in spray: he went on as cautiously as the highest intelligence might have directed.

I shall never forget my feeling of thankfulness when the motion of the trap told me that we were ascending the acclivity at the other end of this road through the loch. As we reached the top a 'Thank God!' burst from me. My sister asked me what I said, but I took up the reins and called to Jack who now went on at a sure trot. When I pulled up at the short road leading to my house a man from the inn was waiting with a lantern to take the pony and trap back to the inn.

There was a happy trio assembled that night at the teacher's house on the hill.

At one of the thatched houses situated on the brae opposite my house lived an old man and his wife together with a son and a daughter. The son would be about twenty-five years of age but his hair was perfectly white. I had often wondered about this, and subsequently I learned the cause of it. Like many other of the youths this young man was very fond of 'tickling' for trout. The 'tickler' generally went out at night to a loch or stream and selected a likely spot. Then, rolling his sleeves right up to the shoulder, he lay or knelt on the bank and gently lowered his hands and arms into the water under the bank. With extreme patience he waited until he felt a fish which he then very carefully and gently began to tickle. When the fish seemed to have become accustomed to the movement the 'tickler' at the right moment lifted it from the water and threw it backwards to the grass behind him—one tap on the back of the fish's head and it was dead.

The young man, Sandy, was an expert 'tickler', and one night he went down to the loch near my house on the south side of which the postman's son had recovered the kite after exclaiming:

'It's away!' After securing several fish at one part of the loch he was seeking a fresh place in the darkness when he felt the ground give way beneath his feet—he was in a bog! Quickly he was sucked down, his struggles and efforts availing nothing against the bog's relentless grip. Fortunately the bog was not deep so that when it reached his shoulders his feet rested on a firm sandy bottom. There he remained all night till he was found next morning—his hair had turned white.

His sister, Catriona, was about seventeen or eighteen years of age. I had often seen her about their croft driving the cow to pasture or turning the stirk out from the rickyard. She was a sturdy girl—I remember seeing her one day chasing the stirk and getting angry with it because it would not go the way she wanted. Suddenly she made a dart at it, seized it bodily in her arms and lifting it in the air threw it over the rickyard wall. When I came from school on the morning following the arrival of my mother and sister I found them at my gate talking to this girl. There was some quality in my dear mother that always engendered respect, confidence and friendship in people, and she and Catriona had become friends already. Catriona apparently could speak English very well; but, I suppose, had been too shy to betray this fact before. She from now on became invaluable to us. Were she going to make purchases at Donald Ferguson's store some few miles away or were her brother going to the pier six miles off, she never failed to come first and see if we wanted anything. She thought nothing of carrying on her back across the hills from the store a boll (140 pounds) of flour or meal, besides other purchases.

If Sandy went to the pier during the fishing season he usually brought us back a bucket of herring freshly caught that morning. Herring! I had never tasted herring of such flavour as these from the Atlantic; rich in oil, they needed no lard or fat for frying; their flavour, compared with those I had tasted in England, was like comparing that of real sardines with sprats!

I was told afterwards that all the barrels of herring were shipped to the Baltic ports. As the fish were landed from the local boats, an auctioneer sold them to the merchant who made the highest bid per cran. The fish were then gutted, cleaned, sorted and thrown into barrels by a number of women and girls engaged for the purpose by the merchants. The barrels

55

were then closed and stacked ready for shipment on the cargo boats that made special trips during the season. I asked why we could not get herring like these in England. 'They won't pay the price,' was the reply. The Russians, I was told, would pay £9 to £12 a barrel for these herring so rich in oil and flavour—a good price even could be got for a cup of the pickle that remained in the barrel! At the time of which I am writing, the shoals of herring chased by whales from the Atlantic came first to these Outer Isles where the natural feeding grounds produced their first-class condition. Passing from these feeding grounds the shoals of fish circled round the north of Scotland, past Aberdeen, down the east coast on to Grimsby and Yarmouth, losing considerably in condition and flavour on the way.

When I left afternoon school on this day of my mother making the acquaintance of Catriona, I found the former missing from the house. On inquiry I heard that she had gone across to see the latter's parents. Following her I came to their house door where I was met by a silver-haired smiling old man who blinked at me while saying: 'I am verra much obleejed!' Entering the peat-smoke-filled cottage I found my mother bending over a large wooden contrivance of wood and strings at which an old-white-haired woman was seated while Catriona explained to my mother the process of weaving—it was a hand-loom for weaving cloth. They were a dear gentle old couple, poor but quite happy and contented, as appeared from the kind inquiries of my mother interpreted by Catriona, whose parents ventured no further English than what was said at my entrance. I believe that they both read much Gaelic literature though.

My elusive housekeeper had become more elusive than ever now that my mother and sister were with me. Beyond preparing the morning fire and putting into the cupboard milk and some newly made-scones—she always had made these daily at the house of her brother-in-law, the postman—she kept away from my house. I thought that not speaking English, she was shy of meeting them or considered that my people would now cater for me.

The peat fire in the kitchen had never been extinguished since I had first arrived at the house and my sister was most interested in the setting of it for the night. A piece of glowing peat was taken from the centre of the fire and pushed deep into the ash under the grate; two large dampish pieces of peat were then pressed down on this and the fire was set for the night. In the morning the whole would be redly smouldering, and it was only the work of a moment to put the glowing pieces into the grate with the tongs, then a few dry peat pieces on this, then with a puff there was a fire ready for cooking breakfast.

My purchases at Lochboisdale pier had ensured that we should fare comparatively well on this the first day after the arrival of my people. Added to this there was a knock at the front door before morning school, and one of my pupils stood there. She was from the farm of Kilbride which I had seen from the boat when returning from Eriskay, and stood there bearing a basket. This contained a lump of farm butter wrapped in a clean white linen cloth, and also a large bottle of milk. On learning that these came from the farm I intimated that I would call and thank them shortly.

Chapter Eight

WITH the intention of trying to arrange for a regular supply
of butter and milk from Kilbride farm, I left my house on
the following, a Saturday, morning to pay them a visit. It was
a glorious May day, and as I proceeded south down the hilly
road I occasionally paused to listen to larks carolling in the sky.
I had heard larks singing in my own country, England, but
never had I heard so many in the air at a time—the clear sky
seemed full of them bursting into song as if they would rend
their little throats in ecstasy. Exhilarated and filled with the joy
of spring, I soon reached the white gate by which Father Allan
and I had rested on our way home from the island, and which
guarded the private road to the farm.

Passing through the gateway and cheerfully fastening the
gate after me, I walked along a rough road bordered on either
side with well-cultivated fields, the hills rising at some distance
on my left, while curlews swept with shrill cries over the sandy
ground on my right, beyond which I knew lay the sea. Some
distance along the road I gained a view of the shore of the sound
lying away some hundred yards or more to the south. Straight
in front of me to the east I could see the road skirting a large
group of weather-beaten buildings. Reaching these I began to
explore while keeping a sharp eye for any of the inhabitants of
the farm and for watch-dogs. Quite a number of the buildings
were stables, cow-houses, and barns; but standing apart from
these and crowning a large mound stood a large old stone house
of many gables and chimneys. A long flight of wide stone steps
led up to its main entrance which looked so imposing that I did
not venture here but wandered round to the other part till I
found what apparently would be the kitchens and domestic
offices. Here I heard voices talking in Gaelic which ceased on
my making some noise to attract attention.

From a door here there issued a typical buxom farmer's wife clad in clean print dress and wiping her hands on a white apron. On my explaining the reason for my visit she said: 'Yes, yes! Of course! Come away in,' and led the way round to the flight of steps and the main entrance. The spacious long hall with its wide flight of stairs leading to the upper regions, the trophies of the chase adorning it (stag's heads, stuffed seals, eagles, heron and many other things) quite astonished me. Opening one of several doors on our left my conductress ushered me into a kind of anteroom and with a 'Sit you there,' disappeared, closing the door behind her.

Wonderingly I looked around me. The house must be some hundreds of years old I thought—the stone steps at the entrance, the large flags of the hall all so worn in the middle, seemed to record the passage of many generations of men; the blackened oak beams of the ceilings and the whole interior, even the room in which I sat, seemed to betoken age. While I was sitting here the door opened suddenly and a maid appeared bearing some pieces of peat. As she without word or look lightly stepped to the fireplace, my breath almost stopped—she was physically the most perfect type of womanhood I had ever seen. Tall, the sleeveless open-necked blouse, short skirt, bare feet and legs revealed a perfectly moulded form whose natural grace and ease of movement, reminding one of the deer, denoted perfect health and well-balanced strength. As she knelt to light the fire, her hair, fastened in a careless knot in the nape of her neck, glinted, for it was of that rare shade of brown that has a trick of changing into gold in subtle lights, and I almost gasped at her in wonderment. The fire lighted, she disappeared from the room as lithely and as silently as she had entered it. I never saw her again: but I always think that a beautiful woman with a beautiful soul is one of the most perfect things in God's creation.

Bearing a tray with decanters and sandwiches my hostess now re-entered. While I ate and drank we soon settled that the children from the farm should bring butter and milk to my house regularly, for which an account would be rendered for settlement.

From the room in which we had been sitting I was taken to another larger room, indeed it was a room whose size surprised

59

me—my hostess called it the dining-room, I think, but it was large enough for serving a banquet. I modestly remarked to her on the size and apparent antiquity of the place when she told me that in the old days the house was the island residence of a line of chieftains of the clan Macdonald, the MacDonalds of Bornish,* and here they often held high revel or had meetings with their leaders. It was here 'Bonnie Prince Charlie' conferred with the then clan chieftain when the Prince first landed in the islands to commence the raising of the clans for the 'Forty-five'. She showed me in the wall beside the huge fireplace the secret panel which gave access to a passage to the kitchens, by which means a fugitive could slip from the room out through the kitchens to a boat on the shore close by or to the adjacent hills whose countless rocks provided many secure hiding-places. She regretted that her husband was not in but said I should probably find him somewhere about outside. Taking my leave I left the house to look for him.

Near the house was a large enclosure surrounded by a high wall made from pieces of rock cemented together which stood some ten to twelve feet in height. From the house to the south the ground sloped down to a small sandy bay, on the east of which rose a low hill covered with grass and broken rocks. Approaching this hill I came to a stop upon hearing close at hand the growl of a dog. There rose from behind a rock the figure of a little grey man—grey clothed and grey bearded. He evidently knew me and expected me to speak for he advanced with extended hand and welcomed me to his farm. As he showed me round, especially his garden within the high wall that had been built to protect the plants from the high winds, and he pointed out the chief features of his domain, I could tell that he was a man of education and of considerable refinement. The main road through his farm, to which the large white gate had first given me entrance, continued on between the garden and the low hill. Continuing on this road which now rose a little we reached its summit and his land now swept right on due east alongside the sound, out past the Priest's Point as far as I could see. This stretch of land would be nearly two miles wide, the

* *Recte* the MacDonalds of Boisdale. Alexander MacDonald of Boisdale did his best to persuade Prince Charlie to return to France in 1745, having no confidence in the success of the rising.

north side bounded by the high hills which afforded his farm shelter from cold winds.

Gazing around me I referred to Prince Charlie having stayed here. My companion averred this to be a fact, alleging that the Prince returned from the mainland to hide here when later he was being hunted by the soldiery. He told me how he hid among the lonely hills for weeks while the islanders secretly provided him with food; how they mendaciously put his hunters on a false scent; that though £45,000* reward had been placed upon his head, any islander would have execrated himself at a thought of betraying him. But my companion said that he had heard of one exception. This was that of an ingenuous lad who had been on the hills and had actually seen the Prince in a cave. On reaching the valley the lad met a search party of soldiers and told them that he had seen a man hiding in a cave over the top of the hill. They jeered at him and said they had been sent off on a wild goose chase too often before. This was the only case on record where a particle of information as to the whereabouts of the Prince had been given by anyone on the island.

To our left lay a beautiful lake, its edges covered with fern and heather, its still deep waters glowing in the sunshine. The road ended here, giving place to an enormous bank of shingle composed of large stones—it reached out before us for nearly a quarter of a mile and would be at least fifty feet in width. My companion told me that the loch on our left had been a part of the sea, but in one night's gale these thousands of tons of stones had been cast up and had completely isolated the loch.

The negotiating of a passage across the large stones of this bank was most trying and the thought of it makes the soles of my feet ache even now. We reached the other end of the shingle, pausing in relief on the grass and heather to which it had given place. As we stood, a large fish sprang clean into the air from the loch beside us. 'An eight-pound sea-trout,' remarked my companion quietly. 'Do you fish?' I confessed that I did not. 'A pity!' he said. 'I have some good sport in these lochs.' Crossing the heather we came quite suddenly upon another larger loch from which rose several coveys of wild duck, their harsh cries and whirring wings somewhat startling me. Standing on a knoll I stood and took in the scene, and looking seaward watched

* Actually £30,000.

61

birds of all sizes floating in the air above the waves. Every now and then I noticed a large white bird with black-tipped wings drop from a height like a stone into the sea and disappear. Noting my interest, the farmer remarked: 'Solan geese! They never miss!' He told me that they hovered in the air till their keen eyes detected a likely fish, when they dived after their prey. I watched closely for a while and noticed that each dive was succeeded shortly after by a bird emerging from the water with a fish in its beak.

My companion now pointed with his stick to some browsing cattle scattered on the hillside, and remarked that he was going after them. He pointed out a short way to my home across the hills, so with a few words and a shake of the hand we parted, he to go after his cattle which his dog was already rounding up, I to climb the hills before me and reach home, which I did without further incident of note.

Gone today is the grand old house of the chieftain Islesman, its historic stones scattered hither and thither or used to build crofters' cottages—if these stones had tongues what tales of intrigue, romance, and barbarous deeds might they not tell!

Chapter Nine

ABOUT this time I had noticed that the stack of peat in my garden was diminishing, so I tried to ascertain the procedure for replenishing my supply. I learned that the people cut peat once a year in the early summer and this supply had to last the whole twelve months. Seven men of neighbouring houses in one day cut sufficient fuel to last a house for the whole year. They did this for each of seven days, by which time all their houses had a year's supply of fuel cut. Every crofter had his own special peat bank on the hillside from which to cut fuel and no one ever attempted to infringe on another's. Most of these peat banks were situated well up the hillside and the peat, when ready for stacking, had to be carried in creels down to the roadside, whence it was carted and then built into a large peat stack near the crofter's house. The piece of land appertaining to the schoolhouse, I found, lay near the main road opposite the school, much obviating the labour of carrying of peat to my house.

I consulted with Sandy of the white hair, and with his sister, Catriona, about my supply of fuel for the year. The former told me that we should need a crew of fourteen men and he undertook to obtain them—he said that he could do so easily as they would consider it an honour to be asked to cut peat for the schoolmaster. His sister and mine then went into the matter of the supply of refreshment to the men. The whole affair was such a novelty to my sister and myself that I think we were really enjoying ourselves. Eventually it was decided to fix the following Saturday for the event. We were warned not to speak of paying the men—they would feel insulted and not a man would come. So we arranged to give them breakfast preceded by a dram of whisky and followed by the gift of an ounce of sailor's twist tobacco, dinner preceded by another dram, and finally, after the day's work was finished, tea preceded and followed by the important dram of whisky. Catriona undertook to procure the supplies of food and to make the scones and she and my sister were to do the cooking and catering; Sandy was to get a pound of tobacco from a shop at the pier and I to order a gallon of whisky from the inn at Pollachar.

To fulfil my part in the preparations I set out for the inn soon after tea the next evening. When I was nearing the white gate leading to the farm I became aware of a cloud of dust on the road somewhat before me. As I approached it I could see that the dust was being raised by some animal careering along the road. On it came at a tremendous pace and as it came near I jumped into the ditch to avoid it. Almost like a flash it went by, but I could see that it was a black young cow or bullock and that something was trailing behind it and was swaying from side to side of the road, raising the dust as it brushed the ground. The thought in my mind was: 'It has come from the farm belonging to the inn. Something has got entangled with it and it has dashed off mad with fright.' To me the object dragged behind looked like the apron-cloth from the dogcart or a piece of sail.

For a moment I watched the animal careering towards the hill on which my house stood, then I hastened on to the inn. Entering at the open door I explained to those within what I had seen. Without a word the men sprang to their feet and rushed out of the house. I remained some little time and, having arranged about the gallon of whisky being delivered at my house ready for the peat-cutting, I proceeded to the open inn door. Here I found men grouped round a much bedraggled man and a black bullock with three or four of the men holding ropes tied securely to the beast's horns and snout.

From the innkeeper I learnt that he was to buy this animal from one of the crofters who had led it down to the inn that evening for the purpose of selling. They had inspected it and a bargain was made. The innkeeper went indoors to fetch the money, leaving the man outside holding the rope attached to the beast's horns. Something frightening the animal, it had jumped and knocked the man over who clung on to the rope. It had dashed off up the road dragging the man behind it. So, what I had taken to be a piece of cloth dragging on the road when the creature had rushed by me previously was a real live sentient man. The party of men who ran from the inn had overtaken them both near the top of the hill near my house with the man still clinging on to the rope attached to his charge. As I returned home I reflected with mixed feelings on the tenacity, endurance—and the grip—of the man who had been dragged with such violence for nearly two miles. I believe that he resumed his work as usual the next day, taking the experience as 'All in the day's march'.

When I arrived home that evening I found that we had a visitor, the officer of excise, a Mr T - - - . My mother and sister had been entertaining him in my absence till I returned. He was last stationed in a Lancashire town so that we had much of mutual interest to discuss. He had been longer on the island than I had, and had many incidents of interest to relate to us. I was rather struck with the contrast of our respective positions: he was suspicious of there being secret whisky stills and the people regarded him in no lovable light, so that his whole attitude towards them appeared antagonistic. My position was just the opposite one: I was for the securing of mutual help and trust. Approaching local questions from different points of view proved most interesting and we all spent a very pleasant evening together. One of the many incidents of which he told us and which amused us more than others now occurs to my mind. At Howmore, some ten miles north of my school, he told us, he one evening met a cart. The driver was seated on the dashboard and a man on horseback was riding behind the cart, the contents of which were covered by a piece of sailcloth. Feeling suspicious the exciseman stopped them instead of passing by and asked to see what they had in the cart. Receiving an evasive answer he drew the cloth covering aside and discovered a number of filled whisky kegs on the bottom of the cart. It was now getting dark, so, pleased with his capture, he climbed on to the other side of the dashboard and told them to drive to the house of the nearest justice of peace some two or three miles further on. When they arrived at the house the magistrate was summoned to the cart and the charge was made against the two men. To the exciseman's dismay, when the cloth was removed the cart was found to be empty. Our visitor remarked with some amount of chagrin that he could not be certain as to how the kegs had been removed but he had a shrewd idea that the man riding horseback behind the cart must have done it. Probably, unnoticed in the darkness he had quietly taken a keg at a time from the cart, slowed up and dropped it into the ditch beside the road, then regained his position at the cart-tail, and repeated the process till he had emptied the cart of kegs. At daylight the road was searched but our friend never saw the kegs again. During our conversation cards happened to be mentioned, so as our guest showed a keenness for the game of whist we four sat down to the table and played a most enjoyable rubber. The exciseman was a very good player and subsequently he never failed to drop in for a game of whist whenever his duties brought him to our vicinity.

Saturday morning came with the sound of men's voices, the clattering of feet, and the ring of metal on stones near the house. My party of peat-cutters had assembled, fourteen of them all told, with Sandy at their head. I led the way into school where a long table improvised from school benches had been set for breakfast. They followed me, leaving their tools outside. My sister and Catriona were busy preparing fried ham and eggs, and strong tea in large pots and jugs. Piles of scones, butter, cheese and jam were already on the table at which the men seated themselves. A hot plate of ham and eggs with a cup of tea was placed before each and to my surprise they all sat solemnly still gazing in front of them without saying a word. I was wondering if they were waiting for me to say 'grace' when Catriona whispered in my ear: 'The whisky!' This was produced and white-haired Sandy passed round the table handing each a brimming wine-glass of whisky, the contents of which were tossed off without a blink or word and with the utmost solemnity. All sat silent till the last man had drained the glass, then first looking round at each other they began to eat heartily of all before them. Before long they were talking to each other in Gaelic and seemed more natural—the effect of the food and perhaps the whisky, thought I. When they had breakfasted to repletion—and I noticed each man said a grace of thanksgiving, signing himself with a cross as he did so—an ounce of tobacco was given to each from which they shaved and rolled a pipeful, then they sat comfortably smoking and talking in low tones. At a word spoken in Gaelic by Sandy, they all rose and, putting on their caps at the school door, took up their tools and started for the peat banks.

I was curious to see this process of peat-cutting, so followed. We arrived on a raised piece of grass-covered ground which was intersected here and there with ditches. Four or five of the men threw off their coats and with spades removed the turf along the top of the bank bordering a ditch, while others with shovels removed the surface soil that lay beneath the turf. A smooth damp-looking close-fibred brown substance was then revealed. The white-haired leader told me that this first process was known as 'skinning the binks' and the ground was now ready for cutting the peat. Two men now came forward to the front edge of the raised peat bank and one of them jumped into the ditch below. The other man carried in his hand a most strange implement called 'the iron'. The upper part was just like that of the ordinary spade, but the lower part, made of heavy steel about fifteen inches long and three inches wide, had a ten-inch keen-looking knife-blade some eight or nine inches from its end. This man advanced to the front of the bank and placed the base of 'the iron' on the peat so that the knife-blade was directly to his front with its point exactly on the front edge of the bank. He then pressed a foot on a protuberance on the shank of his implement just above the blade and the iron part sank into the damp peat to its own depth. With a jerk of the handle a clean-cut piece of peat fell from the bank into the hands of the man waiting in the ditch below who immediately threw it with a sliding motion of the hands on to the bank of the other side of the ditch. Stepping back the length of the knife-blade the man on the bank cut another piece, and so on for the whole length of the peat bank, one man cutting and jerking, the other catching and throwing with such regularity that the movements appeared to be automatic.

I watched very closely for I was very interested in the process. By this time the whole crew were at work in twos on the other peat banks. From one pair of workers to another I wandered and began to feel a desire to try my hand at 'the iron'. Sandy gave me first trial and a sad bungle I made of it, I fear; 'the iron' was heavy and clumsy, the knife-blade would not bite just where I intended and I was in mortal fear that I might stab the man below when I jerked the handle. However, I persevered, trying with one couple and then another and though my efforts caused some laughter at first this gave place to encouraging smiles as I acquired a little more skill. The work was arduous and I marvelled at the steady skilful labour of these men, which continued throughout the morning.

Dinner was taken in the school but was not quite the solemn affair as was breakfast: there was conversation in Gaelic and now and then an English word or two was spoken by some of the more venturesome; but the drams were taken with the usual solemnity of ritual. After dinner and a smoke they all returned to the banks and laboured till evening. I confess that I did not do much peat-cutting that afternoon. About six o'clock word came for me at the house that I was wanted at the peat banks. I found the crew standing resting on their spades and their cutting implements. Sandy said they wanted me to inspect the peat they had cut and to know if I were satisfied. The ground was strewn with cut peat in all directions; they had cut three 'iron' depths of peat from each bank, about a hundred cart-loads I was told. Of course, I thanked them and led the way to the school for tea. I am sure they well deserved the hearty meal which they ate and the extra dram and the twist tobacco which I gave them with a shake of the hand on parting.

After the clearing away and the washing-up of crocks, glasses, and the knives, forks and spoons, my sister, mother and I experienced a mutual feeling of thankfulness that all was over for the day; and as we stood together in the garden that peaceful early summer evening, drinking in the soft air and the calm beauty reigning around us over land, hill, sea and sky, I am sure we thanked God in our hearts for all that had been vouchsafed us.

Chapter Ten

THE summer evenings I found to be delightfully long and I often sat out in the garden reading till nearly midnight. Of course, as I was then some four hundred miles nearer the North Pole than when in my native city, I might have expected a considerable difference in the duration of twilight, but the extent of the difference I now realized. Distinctly I remember being with my mother and sister and watching the gorgeous sunset in the north-west over the sea—crimson, purple, orange and deep blue; then, as we turned to the north-east, dawn was already breaking behind the mountain peaks; as the glorious colours of the sunset faded those of the sunrise strengthened, and we marvelled at the wonders of nature opened to us as never before.

On one such evening after tea I set out to visit my colleague at his school three miles away to the north. Swinging along the road, enjoying the fresh sea air and feeling that indeed life was good, I had travelled about half-way to my destination when, reaching the top of the hill which the road crossed, I heard a voice say: 'A verra fine evening!' It was Donald MacCormick, my attendance officer. He was sitting on the brae beside the road, a dog lying at his side. I stopped and asked him what he was doing there, to which he replied that his flock of sheep was just over the hill-top and that he was going to gather them and take them to fresh pasture. He spoke a word in Gaelic to the dog and it was off like an arrow up the hill-side, disappearing over the top. I remained to watch. Shortly after, scores of sheep appeared on the sky-line at the top of the hill; more joined them and they began to descend towards us; then the dog appeared and stood still, silhouetted on a rock against the sky. Donald gave a short whistle and the dog left his perch and followed the flock, steadily driving them towards us. Some of the more timid broke away, some to the north, some to the south. The dog stood still and Donald again whistled shortly, when the dog darted away to the north, rounded up the truants and gently ushered them back to the main flock. Again standing still he waited for orders. Another from Donald and he began to shepherd the flock towards the south. At another signal he was off after those sheep that had broken away south. Rounding these up he quietly turned them towards the flock. At a long loud whistle he lay flat and watched at a distance from them while the sheep gradually settled down on the new pasture. I have since witnessed sheep-dog trials in England and Wales and have marvelled at the displays of dog intelligence and man's training of it; for quiet unostentatious training I would give Donald the palm. During our little chat that followed I was amused somewhat at my companion's views with regard to training animals. 'When I get a new horse or a new dog,' he said, 'I always give it a good thrashing straight away, for you must prove to them that you are master. Maybe,' said he with a twinkle in his eye, 'women should be treated the same.' Donald was a bachelor, I believe! He was an interesting character but though I always much enjoyed exchanging views with him I did not linger any longer but proceeded on my way.

Reaching my colleague's gate I saw him in his garden near the wall that overlooked the loch by his house. He held a light fishing-rod in his hand. With a bright hail he beckoned me. Closing the gate behind me I advanced to his side. There was no sign of his usual phlegmatic manner now. 'Look at that!' said he with delight in his voice. At his feet lay a large fish nearly a couple of feet in length. I had never seen a trout out of water before; but, as I looked at its beautiful form, its spots and lovely colouring, I could only say: 'What a beauty!' My friend was all excitement now as he told me of how, after tea, he had taken his rod, climbed the wall and worked his way along the rocks below the wall, casting his flies, when he saw a fish rise far out. Lengthening his line he had been able to cast near the rising fish, when he felt a touch, so struck and hooked the fish. He had just landed it when I appeared. I accompanied him across to the post-office to have it weighed; it was just under six pounds.

He invited me to the schoolhouse, where he had set up house-keeping, with a cousin to attend to household matters. I found his house similar to mine and just as meagrely furnished; but its situation and outlook bore no comparison: whereas mine stood on a hill commanding views of mountain and sea, his was on low flat land and the view from the front was that of the main road with neighbouring buildings consisting of crofters' cottages, the Free Church with minister's house attached, and a few fairly well built slate-roofed roomy houses of dressed stone.

What a change had come over my usually phlegmatic friend! He was evidently an enthusiastic angler. Over a supper of broiled trout which was delicious eating, he waxed most eloquent. From boyhood he had fished the streams of eastern Scotland, commencing with a hazel stick, string, hook and worm, later acquiring skill with jointed rod, flies and landing-net. Now and again in recounting some fishing exploit he would burst out with: 'Aye mon, but it was fine!' I, no fisherman, was secretly amused at his intense enthusiasm over such a subject—indeed, I remember, in my ignorance, feeling a little contempt, and growing somewhat weary of the topic. However, before leaving, I promised to go out with him on the following Saturday morning for I rather yearned for the companionship of a man of contemporary age and avocation. It was now rather late but it was quite light all the way home. My friend accompanied me as far as the hill where I had parted from Donald MacCormick with his sheep; but though we talked on many subjects as we walked along, my companion showed no special enthusiasm for any but that of fishing. One of the subjects we discussed was that of shaving, and half in joke and half in earnest we both undertook not to shave but to grow beards. With a friendly challenge as to who could grow the longer beard, I and my friend parted with a promise from me to be at his house early on the Saturday morning.

Feeling rather unkempt, as I had not shaved, in accordance with our compact, I duly arrived at my friend's house about nine o'clock on Saturday morning as promised and found him in bed smoking a briar pipe. 'What's the hurry?' said he. Of course I told him that I was in his hands and I felt less unkempt as I noticed the black stubble on his chin while mine, being fair, did not show so much. In quite a leisurely manner he rose and dressed while we joked about, and caressed, our respective beards. Descending to the sitting-room, where his breakfast was laid, I smoked and drank tea while he took his meal. The leisurely way in which he took his breakfast, and the deliberateness with which he afterwards fetched his fishing-rod and tackle, carefully testing each joint of the rod and each cast of flies, soaking the latter in a saucer of cold water as he proceeded, rather exasperated me. Perhaps he noticed my impatience, for he made the remark: 'The fisherman catches his fish before he starts!' On my asking for enlightenment he told me that the experienced angler chooses his day; he knows beforehand whether it is a fishing day: 'When the wind is in the north the fish jump forth (over the flies); when the wind is in the south it blows the fly into the fish's mouth (and is blown out); when the wind is in the east the fish take the least (cold and dry—fish shy); when the wind is in the west the fish take the best.' When the wind is as the last, and cloudy skies prevail with the sun just peeping through them, one is sure of plenty of sport, he told me. Again, he had lost many a good fish through a cracked rod joint, a frayed piece of gut, or a badly tied fly. I now began to be ashamed of my impatience and asked him how the day promised. Without answering he went outside and returned in a few minutes remarking: 'Only fair.' Considerably later we set off along the main road towards the north and leaving the township behind us proceeded a mile or so before turning off to the west across a moorland. Quite suddenly we came upon a large loch whose rocky shores gave many bays of deep dark waters.

I had never before been interested in the subject of fishing, for all I had previously seen of it consisted of men sitting beside the canal or a pond holding substantial rods in their hands and watching a float, with an occasional jerking of the heavy line from the water and a dangling bait; sometimes I had seen a small fish attached to the hook swung on shore and the removing of this hook seemed such a dirty messy process that I had always felt not a little disgusted. I had not fished myself since the stick, string and bent-pin period of early boyhood.

Nevertheless, I was rather interested in watching my friend set about his business of fishing, and closely observed his actions. His rod was in three separate joints which he proceeded to fit together: he first carefully pushed the very thin top joint into the socket of its fellow, then pushed this into the socket of the bottom joint, all the time talking of the relative merits of the different builds of rods and their most suitable lengths and weights for the various kinds of fishing. Now he swished the jointed rod about. I thought this was to test its security, and I could not help but admire its slender tapering length and suppleness. Taking a reel of line from his pocket, he fitted the reel in the slot on the butt of the rod and threaded the line through the rings of the respective joints. He next took from a pocket-book a coiled cast of flies and, uncoiling it, put the loop of it in his mouth while he smoothed out the gut cast with a piece of rubber taken from his waistcoat pocket.

Telling me to remain where I was with the landing-net, he advanced along the top of a rock jutting out into the loch. Reaching the point of this he whirled his rod round his head so that the tail of his three-fly cast described figures of eight in the air, then at a sharp forward jerk of his wrist the line stretched out straight in front and the cast of flies fell gently on to the surface of the water—I admired the skill with which he made this cast and thought that it must have been the result of long practice. With slight jerks of his wrist he made the flies dance along on the ripples of the water. Watching his flies I noticed a swirl of the water, my friend gave a sharp turn of his wrist and his reel gave a whirring sound as the line rushed out. I noticed that he had raised the point of the rod which was now bent like a bow and I knew that he had hooked a fish. Evidently the creature was dashing towards the middle of the loch, and the loud whirring of the reel spoke of the length of line being run out, while I was fearing that there would not be enough. My friend was keeping some pressure on him as I could see by the bowed top joint; then the angler began to reel in and I noted the rod was less bowed. Again there was a rapid whirring of the reel—the fish had rushed off in another direction. Suddenly it leapt into the air and fell with a loud splash back into the water, my friend relieving the pressure on him by lowering the point of the rod—the line went slack, the fish was rushing in towards us. My friend was reeling in as fast as he could, stepping backwards till he could again feel the fish on the line when he stopped. He called to me to bring the landing-net. Advancing to the edge of the rock, the net in my hand, I waited; yard after yard was reeled in, when the hair-like gut of the cast appeared and I knew that the fish was at hand. But with a whirl of the tail he was off, dashing hither and thither, while I stood by expecting the fine gut of the cast to break at any moment. Three times my friend skilfully manœuvred the fish near us but each time he made off—I did not know which to admire more, the endurance and fighting qualities of the fish or the cool patience and skill of the fisherman, for the least excess of pressure on the line would have snapped the fine tackle like cotton thread. At last, as my friend drew him gently near the rock, the fish lay on his side exhausted and when my friend called: 'Now!' I slipped the net into the water under its head and with two hands lifted him well ashore. He jumped and sprang about full of vigour; but my friend gave him his quietus with a tap at the back of the head and the fish stirred no more—he was a beauty, judged to be of between four and five pounds.

I began to feel rather an ignoramus, for up till this I had regarded anglers with a certain amount of contempt: but this experience showed me a sport where all the chances are against the angler and where it was only by the exercise of patience, skill and coolness that he could hope to land his fish—the small hook had caught this fish in the upper lip, and had there been too much pressure the hook would have torn through the skin at once. My friend caught several more trout, I assisting with the landing-net. After hooking one of these he handed me the rod and told me to 'play' the fish. I shall never forget this, my first experience of such work—my hopes and fears, the constant vigilance required so as not to put too much or too little strain on the line—and, when I gradually coaxed him shoreward near enough for my friend to net him, I was a proud man indeed. For his size I believe the trout is the most powerful and the gamest of all fish.

Needless to say, I was now a complete convert to fishing. That evening over a meal at my friend's house, I was as enthusiastic on the sport as was he; and long and serious were our deliberations over the kind of rod I should procure, the casts and the merits of their different makes, the best killing flies, and so on. We settled on a ten-foot six-inch three-jointed greenheart rod with snake rings, and a spare lance-wood top, four drawn-gut casts of flies (I remember the names of some: Zulu, Greenwell's Glory, Teal-and-Green, March Brown), a fly-hook, check-reel with line, creel and landing-net. Before we parted I had written an order for these from a firm then advertising in the *Fishing Gazette*, whom my friend specially recommended, and I started for home with joyous speculations on many fishing expeditions in the future.

Chapter Eleven

THE weather had been remarkably dry for some time and Catriona, the Useful, told us that 'the peats should be lifted' now; she suggested that school-children volunteers should do it in the interval between morning and afternoon school sessions. As I was curious to know the process of 'lifting the peats' I accompanied her to my peat banks. When we reached the ground I saw that the damp slabs of peat cut not long before were perfectly dry and crinkled on the upper side which had been exposed to the air. Stooping, Catriona picked up two slabs of peat, leant them against each other on end, dry side inwards, when I saw that the under sides that had lain next the ground were quite wet; against the corners of these two slabs she leant four others dry side inwards, and finally another slab, wet side up, on the top, which steadied the whole small stack of seven peats. So I now saw the meaning of the term 'lifting the peats' which I had heard in school recently as a reason for children's absence from school: 'Please sir, I was lifting the peats.' Catriona told me that if the dry weather continued the peat would be ready for 'carrying home' in two or three weeks after the 'lifting'.

Some days later, after procuring a seven-pound jar of sweets, of which, I had learned, all the people (from the youngest to the oldest) were very fond, I asked for boy volunteers for 'peat-lifting', making no mention of any reward. I was surprised at the eagerness shown, and afterwards learned that they looked upon it as a privilege to be allowed 'to lift the schoolmaster's peats'. Choosing two crews, each consisting of twelve boys, and appointing two of them as captains, I led them to the peat banks and saw them start making the little peat stacks, the two crews working at a distance from each other. Seeing that they thoroughly understood the process I left them at it. At intervals I returned to see how they were getting on and complimented them on their progress. A little before school assembly I visited them, looked around, expressed approval, distributed sweets, and dismissed them from the ground—three such days completed the 'peat-lifting'.

That evening, while in the garden, I noticed that the long line of the western shore was spaced out with columns of smoke rising high into the clear air. When I made inquiries I heard that these were the fires of the kelp burners. During the gales of the winter much seaweed from the Atlantic is thrown up on the western shores, and among it the long thick 'tangle' or roots as thick as, or thicker than, a man's wrist. The men hasten to the shore with long forks and drag this wrack from the waves high up on to the shore out of reach of the sea; here it is piled up and left in heaps until spring. As soon as dry weather comes it is burnt in a kiln or kind of pit, the resultant ash being left to cool and solidify. This is the kelp from which iodine, soda and other products are obtained at the chemical works in Glasgow. I think I remember my informant saying that twenty shillings a ton was paid to a crofter obtaining this kelp, and that a man and two boys could make ten to twenty and even thirty, tons in a few weeks if fine weather prevailed. I remember thinking to myself at the time: 'Poverty as found in towns is unknown here; no man here need starve, for he can get fish from the sea, potatoes for the sowing, fuel from the hillside, and water from springs or fresh-water lochs, and money for clothes from kelp burning.'

My water supply came from a galvanized-iron tank outside my kitchen door; this tank was the receptacle for the rain water draining from the roof of house and school. It was about seven feet long, four feet wide, and the same in depth, holding between four and five hundred gallons of water. At frequent intervals, when rain was imminent, I donned my bathing dress, climbed into the tank which was mounted on strong trestles, and removing the plug inside near the bottom, scrubbed and sluiced it out thoroughly. When the rain came shortly afterwards, the resultant water supply was delightfully clear and fresh as the air was remarkably pure. Owing to the dry weather the tank supply of water was rather low, so I inquired about the situation of the nearest spring to the school. As usual it was Catriona who pointed out the purest and the best for our purposes; but she warned us not to drink water from any of the lochs and in support of this advice told us a story. In all seriousness (I am sure she believed it) she told us the following.

One summer a young woman friend of hers was taken ill with internal pains. Her people tried different remedies but the pains continued, so a man was sent for the doctor who lived some twenty miles away. After examining and questioning her he prescribed medicine and treatment and left saying he would see her again shortly. On his next visit she was little better and he seemed to be puzzled, but prescribed other medicine and treatment. The patient became no better, and got thinner and thinner. The doctor frankly became puzzled with the case, and questioned them more minutely. After considerable reflection he left them with strict instructions not to give her any food nor drink of any kind for three days and nights. Though her people were hard put to it to resist the appeals of the patient, especially for water, they held out and would not allow her anything in the way of food or liquid, in accordance with the doctor's instructions. On the third day the medical man arrived, and after ascertaining that his behests had been faithfully followed, he asked for a pudding-dish full of water with a little oatmeal floating in it. Taking off his coat and rolling up his shirt-sleeves he took the large dish of water and meal and advanced to the bedside of the patient. Resting the dish by the bed he told the girl to open her mouth as wide as she could. He knelt beside the bed and looked well into her mouth and throat. Raising the dish he brought it to the girl's mouth, then slowly withdrew it. He repeated this action several times while gazing into her mouth. Suddenly the onlookers were amazed and horrified to see a narrow-looking head appear at the mouth of the girl. The doctor repeated the action of putting the dish of water to the girl's mouth and when the head issued as though to drink of drawing it back. At last the head protruded a little further from the girl's mouth than before, and with a lightning-like snatch the doctor grasped the creature and drew from the girl's throat—an eel! From the lack of results from his earlier diagnosis and treatment, and from later answers to his questions, he suspected that in drinking water from the loch she had swallowed a tiny eel which had remained living in the stomach of the girl since.

That was Catriona's story and she was rather indignant at our expressing scepticism as to its being true. However, my mother soothed her feelings and told her how much we had enjoyed the story. Long ago as this was, I must confess that I have been careful ever since about water for drinking purposes. *

The shortage of water for doing the household washing at the schoolhouse was causing us difficulty. As usual, Catriona came to the rescue; she obtained a very large iron pot and an armful of peat which she took down to the loch-side which lay a quarter of a mile to the south; she next came for soap and the clothes, which she took away with her. My sister and I went down to her later on and found that she had set up on the shore of a little bay some stones at intervals, forming a circle, lighted a fire of peat in this circle, filled the pot with loch water, put in clothes, and by the time we arrived the pot was boiling merrily. Quite near was a shallow tub of water. Removing some clothes from the boiling pot, she laid them on a sloping piece of rock, rubbed them well with the bar of soap, then, putting them in a shallow tub, lifted up her short skirt, stepped into the tub barefooted and barelegged, and stamped and danced on the clothes with great vigour. She poured off the water from the tub, renewed it, stepped in again and repeated the process till she was satisfied that she had stamped out all the dirt. She now waded out into the little bay and thoroughly rinsed each article in the loch water. To dry them she laid them on the rocks in the sunshine, placing stones on the corners to prevent them blowing away. By midday when we visited the loch again quite a number of women were at work round the loch-side, engaged in doing their family washing in a similar way to Catriona's method. It was quite a novel sight to my sister and myself; the fires burning, the pots boiling and

* Miss Peggy MacRae, whose name will be familiar to readers of *Folksongs and Folklore of South Uist*, has recorded an almost identical story of the cure of a boy of the same trouble in her mother's time. The cure was attributed to the Rev. Fr James MacGregor who was parish priest of Iochdar from 1827 to 1867. He is said to have had some medical training before he was ordained, and stories of his medical skill are still current in Uist.

It was firmly believed that hairs left in standing water would eventually turn into eels which were very dangerous if drunk. In fact, there is a long thin water worm which does look very much like an animated hair.

steaming, the bare-legged women stamping in the tubs while laughing, singing, or calling to each other.

After school the next day the three of us at the schoolhouse took our tea to the western shore less than a mile from our house. We took the rough road that I had previously traversed in funeral processions. This road ended in a broad sandy plain extending some seven or eight hundred yards to the western sea-shore, and north and south as far as the eye could reach. Large fields of oats, barley, and rye waved in the gentle summer breeze. Where no crops were shown myriads of small wild flowers carpeted the plain, in blues, yellows and reds— my mother and sister were charmed with the beauty of this part of the island which is called 'the machair'. Crossing this, we climbed up the landward side of a line of sand-hills piled up from the shore by westerly gales; descending the seaward side of a sandhill we found the tide out and a long stretch of gently sloping hard dry white sand a hundred yards wide stretching away in the distance north and south. On the slope of a sand-hill we took our meal, while the rolling green waves of the ocean broke softly on the shore, a gentle sea breeze fanned us, and the whole scene gave us a feeling of calm and contentment.

Of course, after the meal my sister and I went down to the sea and paddled, enjoying the soft swish of the cooling waves over our feet and legs. Edging along and picking up some of the beautiful shells and starfish, I soon noticed that the tide had turned, so calling to my sister I started to return to the spot where we had left our mother. But we found our way barred, time after time, by deep channels of sea water: hollows in the sand unnoticed by us had been filled by the incoming tide. Detour after detour we made, seeking some hollow shallow enough for us to wade across. As the tide was now coming in fast I became very anxious, and thankful indeed we were to find a place where the depth allowed us to get across, though it was nearly up to our middle. Being rather wet we lost no time in returning home, but we had thoroughly enjoyed our picnic by the shore.

As the schoolchildren had acquitted themselves well at the recent examination by an inspector of schools from Aberdeen, I proposed to give the whole school a picnic at the sea-shore. I had been increasingly pleased with their progress. Speaking nothing but Gaelic at home, their English, both spoken and

written, as learned in school, was practically free from any col-
loquialisms so difficult to deal with in schools of children speaking English only. Their vocabulary was admittedly limited but
was correct and good, and as I encouraged private reading
among the elder pupils, their vocabulary became more extensive. With a few exceptions I insisted upon the whole of the
instruction being given in English—these exceptions applied
to the very young whose instruction was bilingual, and to the
testing in Gaelic of the effectiveness of the instruction in English.
I often wondered to myself if purely English-speaking children
would acquit themselves as well as these children did if all their
school instruction were given in, say, French: reading, writing,
grammar, arithmetic, history, geography, and the rest. Some
years after leaving the island I learned of the success of many of
my former pupils there, some of the girls became head teachers
and qualified nurses, some of the boys doctors, head teachers,
captains and mates of seagoing ships.

I think that I have already made it clear that Gaelic was the
sole language talked among the people of the island, with a few
exceptions. Of course, the priests, the doctor, the harbour
master, the factor (estate agent), the storekeeper, the hotel
proprietors, and post-office officials spoke both English and
Gaelic, but very few others. Some of the full-grown men had
been to the east coast fishing (Aberdeen, Yarmouth) and had
picked up a little English, but, as may well be imagined, not
of the choicest; but generally speaking, these were very shy of
using it on the island, though one or two whom I met were very
proud of 'airing their English'. I remember meeting one of these
on the road as my sister and I were taking an evening walk.
'Halloa, Mister Rae!' said he raising his peaked cap. 'A (blank)
fine (blank) evening!' etc., etc., etc. Meanwhile my sister was
tugging at my arm to get me away. As we passed on she said:
'What terrible language that man was using.' I explained as
best I could and told her that he must have picked it up among
some fishermen on the east coast, quite sure that he was speaking the purest English.

We arranged to hold the school picnic on Kilbride farm
where Prince Charlie had rested and hidden, and whence we
were obtaining our milk and butter; I had permission to close
school for the day. Sandy here proved invaluable: obtaining

supplies of food, including fruit, cakes, and sweets from the shops by the pier, and taking them with other things in his cart to the farmhouse the day before. He also arranged for a piper to be with us. The weather still held fine, and we started off from the school next morning in a long procession down the road, the piper leading the way, and the school-children following in fours, smallest first—about a hundred and fifty of us. Reaching the farm after about a two-mile walk we assembled on the sloping ground near the little bay before the large farmhouse. Seating themselves on the hillocks and rocks scattered in the vicinity, the children were supplied with fruit and sweets by the teachers, while I went to see the farmer's wife about the milk supplies, and the later tea, as previously arranged. When this had been done I returned to the children, where the pipes were playing and many of the older children were dancing reels, the rest of them clapping hands and laughing—it was a happy scene! Afterwards the piper selected a few boys and girls who danced the 'Highland Fling', and I was surprised at the agility and lightness of foot they showed. Next I found that a number of boys had brought their 'chanters', and the piper held a competition to ascertain the best player. It was amazing to me to see and hear how well these lads played, and as I watched their easy but rapid fingering of the notes and listened to the variety of tunes I felt that they were natural players. The teachers seemed to take it as a matter of course, and when I expressed my surprise they told me that the families to which these boys belonged had been noted as great pipers for many generations; indeed, there was scarcely a house on the island where you would not get one or more pipers in the family.

Beginning with the little ones we now held the various races, and the other usual school sports, ending with tug-of-war contests, teams of bigger boys opposed to each other; and when the girls wanted a match against each other, they pulled nearly as well and as strongly as the boys.

It was now time for a good meal, which all had, seated in classes on various hillocks. Their rapidly working jaws soon showed how ready they had been for it, and their bright eyes and happy faces expressed their pleasure. Fortunately there was no lack of supplies and soon they had eaten and drunk to contentment. They were dismissed to play for a time, with a caution not to go far away; meanwhile the teachers and helpers repaired to the farmhouse where a substantial meal had been prepared for us. While taking our meal and conversing I stopped now and then to listen to the shouts of the children and wonder if they were getting into mischief; but not wishing to appear fussy, I each time resumed my meal. However, at last I left them at the table and went outside the house. Not a child was in sight! I could hear their voices some distance off, but could not locate the sound: even when I stood on a high hillock commanding a good view around I could see no sign of them. Hastening to the house I summoned the teachers, and told them. We all hastened outside. A mist was coming in from the sea, partly obscuring our view and making it more difficult to locate sounds, though we could hear the shouts of the children. One of the teachers had gone down to the little bay now shrouded in mist. She called me and said: 'I believe they are out there! They must have been paddling when the mist came on!' I darted to the house for my school bell. Now this was a large one, for I used it to assemble the children in the playground before school, and it had to be a loud one so as to be heard at some distance in rough weather. I had trained them to come to me immediately as soon as they heard me ringing the bell, next to spring up to the attitude of 'attention' at two strokes of the bell, and then form up in classes at one stroke of the bell.

Going to the edge of the sea in the little bay I began ringing the bell loudly, all of us meanwhile eagerly and anxiously looking out to the misty sea. One by one, then in twos and threes, then in groups, the children emerged from the sea and the mist to where we stood a little back from the shore. I prayed that none would be missing while the group grew larger as others came from the sea and joined it. Stragglers now began to appear from the mist; but I constantly rang the bell till even stragglers ceased to come in. The crowd of children stood as they usually did when summoned by the bell, quiet and calm, as I strove to be, despite my state of mind, for I felt myself directly responsible should any be missing. My feelings may well be imagined as I gave the signal to spring to attention, next that to form into classes, then counted each class separately to check each class-teacher's counting. It seemed too good to be true when all our figures tallied and not a child was missing. I formed them in single file and counted the whole school again myself and found that the number of children agreed with the number we had brought to the farm. It appeared afterwards that some of the children began to paddle in the little bay when we left them for our meal. Others followed, the bigger venturing further out into deeper water and evidently the whole school had joined in the paddling. Those further out saw the mist coming, and waded towards the shore but the the mist advanced so rapidly and enveloped them so quickly that they lost their bearings and all sight of the shore. It was then that they heard the familiar sound of the bell close at hand, so joined by the others they waded to where the sound came from, and mustered for assembly as usual. Sandy offered to stay and clear up. Accepting his offer, as the mist was thickening fast, we formed in fours, as in the morning, and marched back towards the school to the skirling of the pipes. Parents of children whose homes were *en route* met us and took charge of them, smiling at me in thanks; the rest of the children living north of the school left us near my gate and my anxiety about them was dispelled, for the mist seemed to have risen clear of the ground and was seen shrouding the tops of mountain and hill.

I was filled with gratitude to Providence for sparing me from what might, so easily, have been a tragedy. It was a lesson to me never to leave children unattended while under my charge.

My feelings of joy and gratitude to find the children all present in school next morning, looking well and happy, was somewhat clouded by my hearing sad news. It transpired that early the previous afternoon the wife of a crofter of the neighbouring township had gone down to the western shore with a bucket for some white sand to sprinkle on her earthen floors. She had not returned at sunset, so her husband and others went to search for her. Her drowned body was found later cast up by the tide. It was surmised that the tide had turned while she was filling her bucket; the mist that we had experienced had come up suddenly and she was cut off by the tide. When I thought of those channels in the sandy hollows of the western shore that had menaced my sister and me some little time before, I visualized only too well the predicament of that poor woman in a mist at probably the same place.

I now began to understand a little the attitude of the people,

Uist-born and others, towards the sea. I often spoke to them of bathing and swimming in its clear waters, and expressed wonder at their not indulging in these pleasures. These remarks were always met with a slow shake of the head, or a threatening fist stretched out towards the sea—their feeling regarding it seemed a mixture of awe, fear and anger. With a landsman's ignorance of its power I often eulogized on its beauty and immensity, and remember someone saying to me: 'Ah! Those who know the sea best fear it the most.' Yet these Uist men are the bravest and the most daring of all fishermen, and make the finest sailors in the world, I am told.

Chapter Twelve

FATHER ALLAN was a lover of bagpipe music and he often invited different pipers to his house to play for him. He was a typical Highlander; he told me that he was born at the foot of Ben Nevis so his love of the traditional pipes was not to be wondered at.

I noted how his eyes lighted up at the music of a strathspey, and, at a pibroch, his rugged weather-beaten countenance became suffused with colour and he drew himself to his full six feet height at its warlike strains. Much as I had enjoyed the sound of the pipes at times, I must confess that I was not able to appreciate the music of the pibroch. It was supposed to be a musical poem telling of the beauty of hill and dale, of gentle love, joys, war, of battles, victory, defeat, and sorrow. The Highlander to whom the airs are familiar is naturally stirred by the music of the pibroch: but to me, a native of the Midlands of England, it struck me as being rather long and tedious.

Among the pipers who played to Father Allan there was one whom I saw only once or twice. He was a peculiar looking man with almost lint-white hair, smooth hairless face, was of squat figure, and spoke no English. There was no doubt about his ability as a piper. His speciality was the pibroch, and as he played the others seemed to listen to him in awe—I believe that he read and wrote music for the bagpipes and was a composer himself. I heard afterwards that he subsequently carried off many valuable prizes for pipe-playing at the various annual Highland gatherings held in many parts of Scotland.

Happening to speak of him to my mother and sister when Catriona was present, the latter said: 'Ah! He is the seventh son.' We asked her to tell us more: so she told us the following tale with every indication that she implicitly believed it to be true.

1 The author and his wife fishing for trout, 1894.

2. Garrynamonie school as the author knew it.

3. Garrynamonie school group. *Left to right, back row,* Baby Joan and Joyce Rea, Miss O'Sullivan, Catherine Martin, the author, Donald MacIntyre, Mary MacInnes, Miss Milner; *front row,* Kate MacInnes, Christina MacInnes, Harry Rea, Ewen Steele, and Donald Steele.

4. Ewen MacLennan, playing the pipes, Eriskay, 1899.

5. Haun, Eriskay, 1899.

6. Father Allan McDonald and waulking women on Eriskay, 1899.

7. Pollachar Inn and Standing Stone.

8. Lochboisdale and Pier.

9. Lochboisdale. Boisdale House is on the right.

Living on the island was a family who had always been famous as a race of pipers. This family consisted of the father, the mother, and seven sons. The father and his sons were all fine pipers and in great requisition for special weddings, dances, and so forth, with the sole exception of the youngest son. He could not play even the chanter, much less the bagpipes. His father and his brothers did their best to teach him, for it would be a disgrace to the family to have a son who could not play the pipes. All in vain! He seemed utterly stupid, with clumsy fingers and no idea how to use them; so one after the other they gave him up in despair, loath as they were. The poor fellow took it very hard that he could not play; when he went to the parties and dances and saw how welcome were his brothers he felt that the people despised him, especially the young women. Soon he gave up attending these affairs and used to wander alone on the hills with his chanter in his pocket. Sometimes in some lonely spot he would take it from his pocket and try to play, but found he could make no headway. Early one evening he had been roaming the hills disconsolate, as he knew that his brothers were going to a special dance that night. Feeling tired he lay down on the hillside and dozed off to sleep.

How long he slept he did not know, but he wakened suddenly to see a short man in brown clothes standing at a near-by rock and gazing at him. Leaving the rock the little man came towards him telling him not to be afraid for he wished to help him. Then he said that he knew all about his trouble, and told him to follow him. Rising from the ground he followed the little brown man round the rock where he had first seen him. Here was the opening to a cave in the rocks. Beckoning him to follow, the little man entered the cave, followed by the young man. A passage led from this cave deeper into the hill-side. As they proceeded along this passage voices could be heard, then the young man heard the playing of bagpipes getting louder as they progressed. Quite suddenly they came to a large lighted chamber in which a number of people were dancing to the music of the pipes—they were all small men and women no taller than the young man's companion, and all dressed in various shades of brown. Seizing the pipes from the piper who was playing, the little brown man continued the dance tune then branched off into others so full of trills, runs, grace-notes, wonderful airs, that the young man felt he had never heard real piping before. Without warning, the player pushed the bagpipes into the young man's hands with the injunction: 'Play!' Unheeding his protests that he could not play, he shouted at him again: 'Play!' while thrusting the chanter into his hands and the pipe-piece in his mouth. To his surprise and delight the youth, who had been so forlorn, found himself fingering notes with ease and confidence, and tunes and airs came to him spontaneously. As he played on, the joy of it made him feel that he wished he were playing for ever.

Suddenly all went dark, the bagpipe set was snatched from his hands and soon he felt that he was alone. Gropingly he found his way from the chamber, along the passage to the cave and, looking out, saw the stars shining. Leaving the cave he commenced to descend the hill-side when it occurred to him to go to the place where his brothers were attending the dance. When he arrived there he found the dancing in full swing and one of his brothers playing. Entering, he found a quiet corner as was usual with him on the rare occasions he attended such affairs. The reel having ended, other couples took position on the floor for another dance. A mad desire to play the pipes again now seized him. Another of his brothers was preparing to commence playing when his youngest brother approached him and took them from him. Ignoring the other's protesting: 'Don't be a fool!' he commenced playing joyously. His brothers and those who knew him were astounded; and, as he played on, they heard such airs and melodies that they had never heard, nor dreamed of, before. On and on he played, the dancers, becoming exhausted, sat down while others took their places. When at last he ceased playing and it was realized who had been playing, he was accused on many sides of having been secretly taking lessons for a long time from some great master; even his brothers thought that his previous apparent stupidity had been pretence. He was henceforth *the* player of the family; but his brothers bore him no ill-will, for his wonderful skill commanded their respect and admiration.

Poor Catriona! She so evidently believed the truth of this story that we forbore from laughing at or criticizing what she had told us, and my mother was particularly fond of hearing her stories.

I had been waiting the arrival of my fishing-rod and the other tackle that I had ordered, and one evening the package arrived at my house. With what eagerness did I open and examine the contents and with what interest did my mother and sister watch me open each packet while I dilated on the purpose of its contents. I well remember going out into the garden and fitting the rod together, fixing the line and reel while the others looked on admiringly as I whirled the rod in the air trying to make the line describe figures of eight above my head. I spent most of the rest of that evening practising with full cast of three flies, endeavouring to drop the tail-fly gently upon some distant mark such as a small flower whose head I tried to whisk off with a twist of the wrist. After practising for some time, during which I managed to hook my sister's dress, some clothes hanging on a line, and the various garments I myself was wearing—it was slow and intricate work to disentangle the barb of the hook from the cloth fibre without much damage to either— I attained some degree of skill in making the flies fall lightly where I wished. With the intention of trying my luck at the near-by loch before breakfast next morning, I put the rod and tackle away but left two casts of flies soaking for the night in a saucer of water.

I was at the loch-side soon after six o'clock next morning, rod, landing-net, and tackle all complete. Standing on a jutting rock I made a cast well out towards the middle, then trailed the flies lightly and gently towards me, reeling the line in a little towards the end of the cast. Just as I was raising the flies from the water almost at my feet a fish made a dart at the tail-fly, a March Brown. Jerking my rod, I missed him; so stepping well back I cast again close to the shore. I saw a swirl in the water and struck lightly with a turn of the wrist. I had hooked him and he was off with a rush. He fought well, but I was careful and had him in my landing-net very shortly. He was a little under a foot in length—a beautiful spotted trout. In about an hour I had six or seven but none as large as the first—one, the smallest, gave me most trouble, for I had hooked him through the tail—I suppose that I struck late and, as he turned away the hook caught his tail-end. But he had tremendous power for his size and till I saw him I thought that he was a very big fish. I was a proud man when I handed them over to my sister, who fried them for breakfast, and their delicate pink flesh made delicious eating.

Of course, I was anxious to show my fishing outfit to my angler schoolmaster friend without delay, so set off soon after tea that day. He grunted and we immediately set out for some sport. Instead of making for one of the nearest lochs he led the way across some marshy land, keeping to the hollows and now and then glancing round rather furtively, I thought. Descending some rocks we came suddenly upon a fast-running stream of sea water as the tangled weed on the shores denoted. 'We can't do any harm fishing here,' my companion said. I asked him what he meant and he told me that he had been warned not to fish without obtaining permission. It seemed that the proprietor of the hotel at the pier had the fishing rights on lease, and reserved them for the anglers who stayed at the hotel during the season. My colleague said that this was a tidal stream from the sea so no one had a right to interfere with us here. We set to work but our bag was poor—he hooked several good fish, sea-trout, but the thick seaweed hampered our playing the fish and all the big ones got away among the seaweed, and they broke and lost us several casts of flies; those we caught were small enough to enable us to force them away from the thicker weed and to tire them out—these sea-trout were very different from the loch-trout, their scales being of silvery whiteness and the flesh like that of salmon but more delicate in flavour. Disappointed as I felt at my friend's news of the restrictions I enjoyed the evening's sport.

We talked over the situation at home that night and I decided to see the hotel proprietor. My sister's vacation from France was fast drawing to a close so I proposed that she and I should go to the hotel the next day—we would order a vehicle to fetch her from my house to the hotel on the day she was due to leave the island.

We naturally had much to talk about on our six-mile walk to the pier so that we did not feel the distance—indeed we both had found that walking about the island did not fatigue us as as much as one would expect. I can only suppose that it was the pure air. I remember someone saying to me: 'You will find that the air here feeds you.'

Arriving at the hotel I ordered tea, which was served in the coffee room. While we were taking our meal there arose quite a commotion outside and we heard many excited voices. My sister paused and said: 'Listen; they are talking French.' Leaving the table, we went out into the hall. A crowd of men was assembled outside the door, talking in loud voices, some in Gaelic and others, who looked like foreign sailors, in another language. The proprietor was standing on the doorstep looking very nonplussed. He told us that a boat-load of strange looking sailors had just landed at the pier but could not speak a word of English or Gaelic and no one could understand what they were saying. My sister addressed them in French, and the look of joy and of relief on their faces was evident to all. She soon was able to tell us that they were the survivors of a French barque which had sunk in the Minch the previous night, and they had put into Lochboisdale for help. The proprietor of the hotel had them taken round to the kitchens to be fed and entertained. Before we had finished our tea he came in to thank my sister, saying also that he had telegraphed the French consul who would arrange for their speedy repatriation and that he himself would see that they were suitably lodged meanwhile.

The saying ' 'Tis an ill wind . . . ' was verified here, for the proprietor was so grateful for my sister's help as interpreter that he not only gave permission to fish but insisted upon our being driven home in an hotel trap. In recognition I ordered a case of whisky from him, and engaged a trap to fetch my sister from my house on the day she sailed from the island. I also bought from him some casts of flies which he stocked for the convenience of the angler guests staying at his hotel. On our way home I stopped to tell my schoolmaster friend what had transpired, and he was more than pleased.

I was with my friend again next evening, and we fished two lochs near his house with little or no success: he landed one less than a pound in weight, but I had scarcely a rise to my flies. The evening was calm and bright so the fish were shy. While we were fishing in the second loch I saw a tall dark figure leaving the road, crossing the rough ground, and coming towards us. It was Father Allan, who had seen us and came to see how we were getting on. We told him of our want of success; so telling us to wait for him while he borrowed a rod, off he went. He soon returned with an enormous clumsy-looking rod about eighteen feet in length. This formidable looking weapon caused us some amusement, but laughingly he told us to follow him. We crossed over the rough ground and then the road on to some boggy land; following him we carefully picked our way for a quarter of a mile over this, which he called 'the moss', and came to a small loch lying in a hollow. This loch was very small, less than two hundred yards long and from sixty to eighty yards broad, and near the shores was very shallow. The middle part of the loch was occupied by a long low island. Father Allan began to look for bait, lifting up stones and capturing bright red worms which he put with damp moss into an empty tin tobacco box. Baiting his hook, he gave a mighty sweep with his rod and dropped the bait near the island. Almost immediately it was taken and he hauled out a nice trout about a couple of pounds in weight by the look of it. My colleague and I moved casting our flies well out towards the island, and the fish rose at once. Father Allan put a piece of cork as a float on his line, rebaited his hook and cast out again, sat down, filled his pipe and sat smoking while he watched us. I forget now how many fish we caught, but I remember that it was a good 'bag'. But a most remarkable thing was that all our fish, including Father Allan's, were of just the same size, colour and general appearance. In all my fishing I have never had a similar experience. We all three discussed this matter afterwards, but could come to no satisfactory conclusion as to the cause of the extraordinary similarity in these fish—I think, that if we had weighed them then, we should have found them all to agree in weight almost to within an ounce.

The following evening we had a somewhat alarming occurrence at my house. We were all in the sitting-room at the tea table, engaged in quiet conversation over our meal, when there was a loud but muffled explosion. I ran into the kitchen and there was a roaring sound in the chimney—it was on fire. Telling the others what had happened, I went outside. Men with spades in their hands were hurrying from all directions towards the schoolhouse and shouting to each other. Some clambered over the garden wall and began hurriedly to cut large sods from the ground; two climbed on to the house roof with damp pieces of turf, and clapped these on the top of the chimney pot which was belching forth dense smoke and fire. Others were carrying sods into the kitchen where there was an alarming sight: the whole of the fireplace was a red-hot mass, while piled on and around it were heaps of burning pieces of what, to me, looked like tar; every moment these heaps were being added to by fresh lumps of red-hot matter falling from the chimney. How we fought that fire! The red mass now reached up to the mantelpiece and out into the room; and there we were carrying shovels full, and buckets full outside, fighting our way through the heat and smoke till we had somewhat got the upper hand of the glowing mass, and the whole of the front of the fireplace, higher than the mantelpiece, was shut in by the damp turf. Buckets of water were fetched and thrown time and again on to the sods, while other full buckets were taken to the roof and poured down the chimney, the sods on top being replaced each time. At long last the whole had been completely drenched, the air had been excluded from the chimney with sods, and it was considered safe to leave it till the next day. These fine willing fellows would take no thanks: I had worked along with them, so with a grin and a clasp of our hands they went home. But in what a mess was my kitchen! Nothing could be done that night to remedy the state of affairs here. My hands were blistered, my hair and eyebrows singed, and I was glad that I had recently got rid of my beard. My mother had been against my cutting it off; but I found it somewhat inconvenient and I certainly felt cleaner without it. My only qualm was due to the fact that my colleague's beard had grown nothing like as long and strong as mine.

I was down in the kitchen several times in the night to see that all was safe. The next day the stone house-wall next the chimney was still hot to the touch, and it was a day or two before the kitchen could be cleared. To make sure of clean chimneys I got a man who was accustomed to the work to come and clean them. We were amused at the method he used. He brought with him a coil of thick rope and some bunches of coarse heather. He quickly mounted the roof carrying these with him, and was soon astride the chimney stack between the chimney pots and engaged in tying pieces of heather to the rope at intervals. He then dropped an end of the rope down the kitchen chimney and lowered it through his hands. I was outside watching him and when he shouted to me: 'Go! Pull!' I went into the kitchen, saw the rope's end, so pulled. Hauling away, I first came to one bunch of heather followed by a downfall of brown soot and lumps of a tarry substance; after more hauling, other heather bunches, followed by further soot and lumps, appeared. He hauled at the other end and up it went, and down I then pulled it; so up and down we pulled till I ached. At last down he came from the roof to inspect the result; he seemed satisfied and pulled the rest of the rope through into the kitchen. Coiling the dirty rope and heather round about him, he remounted the roof and chimney stack, and the whole process had to be repeated with the other chimney. By the time this second chimney had been finished I was in a parlous state: head, face, arms and clothes were covered with soot and that sticky substance, and I ached all over—'we live and learn'!

It was about this time that, during one of Father Allan's visits to the school and my house, he confided to me that his bishop had consented to his going to live on Eriskay, the small neighbouring island, among the poor people who had been displaced years before from South Uist and whom I had visited previously in his company. Only occasionally was he able to get over there to say Mass, and the people sorely felt the need for a priest among them. Though it was a whole day's undertaking, many of them came to our island in small boats, if the weather permitted, and journeyed many miles to Father Allan's church rather than be deprived of hearing Mass.

I was much concerned at the thought of his leaving us; yet I could only admire his self-sacrifice and devotion. His heart evidently was with these poor fisher-folk, and he felt the need to go and minister among them. *

* Fr Allan McDonald took down two versions of the story of the man who got his power of piping from the fairies; one is printed in the *Celtic Review*, V, 345. The man was known as Domhnall Ruadh Pìobaire; he was a McIntyre, and descendants of his were living in South Uist in Rea's time. One of them, Fr Allan says, was a great great grand-daughter, Janet MacNeil of Cachaileith, Smercleit, who was born in 1810.

Chapter Thirteen

THE summer was waning, and the annual school holiday was now due, so we discussed the advisability of my accompanying my sister as far as England on her journey to France. My mother needed some comforts not to be obtained here on the island—certain articles of furniture and of clothing I wished to obtain—so we decided that I should go away for the first fortnight of my holiday. My mother felt that it would be better for her to remain rather than undertake the fatigues of a double journey. It was arranged for Catriona to look after her for the short time I should be away, and I knew that I should be leaving her in good hands. So I well provided them with funds, and when the trap from the hotel whirled us off to the pier, I left home in good heart and with hopes of the future.

It was early evening when we went on board the steamer. Soon after we left the harbour, the sea became choppy, with some fog, and, though my sister was a good sailor, I advised her to retire to her berth. After seeing her comfortable I went up on deck to look round. Several passengers were about, among whom I noticed a middle-aged clergyman. Some chance remark caused him and me to chat together. Soon we were engaged in conversation. He said that he knew me, or of me rather, that he was the Established Church minister of the island and lived some ten miles north of my schoolhouse. I found him to be a most delightful companion. He had travelled a great deal and had a first-hand knowledge of the world's many peoples, hence he was singularly free from any of the narrow petty prejudices and bigotries one so often meets with. We conversed well into the night, principally on books, metaphysics, and life in general.

During our conversation I had noticed the fog become denser, and that the ship slowed down at times almost to a standstill, then crept cautiously on. It was about midnight and we were still on deck, when looking upwards I exclaimed: 'Look at the moon!' At that moment there was a shout of several voices from the bridge, and the course of the vessel was abruptly altered amid some excitement among those on deck. What I had taken to be the moon overhead was Barra Head light: we were close to that enormous rock upon which is built the loftiest lighthouse in Great Britain, whose light warns ships for thirty miles around from this dangerous rock which constitutes the southernmost outpost of the Outer Hebrides—680 feet high: no wonder I thought it was the moon appearing through the mist. In the fog, we had passed by Castlebay, the next proper port of call as we crept along the rocky coast, and we had now found ourselves at perhaps the most terrible spot to be found in the British Isles. Had the fog not then lifted as it did I almost tremble, even now, to think of what might have happened to us.

As the fog lifted the wind rose rapidly, and by daylight it was blowing a gale. The lifeboats had been lowered and lashed securely to prevent their being washed away; men were busy fastening heavy planks in position to protect the bridge and other parts of the vessel from heavy seas. No other passenger excepting myself seemed to be on deck—the minister had retired long before. I suppose there must be something fascinating though appalling in a storm at sea. I had ensconced myself in a comparatively safe place between the funnel and a deckhouse which had a strong rail clamped to the wall of it. Here I had a certain amount of shelter from the seas that came aboard; while I watched, hour after hour, the mounting waves and the behaviour of the ship as they struck her, I could not analyse my feelings as I gazed around: there was a mixture of awe, exultation, wild joy and fascination in it all; yet, strange to say, I do not remember that I had any fear. As the gale, which was from the south-east, increased it met the incoming tide from the western ocean and I watched with interest the waves mount higher and higher, saying to myself: 'That is the highest one yet!' I remember looking out for those that were higher than the top of the highest of our masts and thinking, after one had broken and swept over us: 'That was a beauty!' I had my arms fast hooked on the deckhouse rail and ducked my head on my chest as each deluge came; nor did I mind getting wet through for the novelty and the grandeur of the scene gave me a strange feeling of exultation. The force of the wind must have been terrific for it tore off the tops of the high waves as they mounted. The worst of the storm was felt as we approached Skerryvore lighthouse which marks a reef of rocks lying twelve miles out from the island of Tiree. Here the waves were tremendous; and, as they struck, the vessel seemed to stop and shudder with the force of each blow—this was when, I confess, I for the first time began to feel some fear. Suddenly amid this welter of wind and waves I caught a glimpse of a large sailing ship scudding before the gale. Again and again she came into view and I noted how well she rode the seas; whereas we, meeting another wave before we were well out of the last, were tossed, rolled about and deluged, the sailing ship seemed to ride each wave gracefully, racing up one, down again into a hollow, then up the next. Soon she disappeared in the distance, to my regret for she was a beautiful and an inspiring sight.

I was by now rather tired and hungry after so many hours amid the turmoil. Once only had I seen anyone on deck except the captain and his mate, who had remained on the bridge throughout; this was when the steward once managed to reach me in my refuge after many ineffectual efforts to get along the sea-washed, rolling, and pitching deck. He shouted in my ear: 'No breakfast. Nothing till shelter.' As I watched him make his way back, making short darts from point to point where he had to hold on to save himself from being washed away, I was thankful that I had not tried to leave my place. At last we passed the islands of Tiree and Coll, and reached the lee side of them, where the sea, though rough, allowed the ship to ride on a more even keel. I was soon able to leave the place where I had sheltered so long, and felt the relief from the tension I had been under. When we were abreast of Ardnamurchan Point I got below to the cabin and changed my wet clothes. I then found my sister, who was delighted to see me; she had been in her cabin the whole time, but did not wish to have such an experience again. It was well after mid-day when breakfast was served; though we were now in relatively calm water, cups or plates would suddenly shoot across the table and deposit themselves in someone's lap, as the vessel lurched. But we were thankful for the meal and made light of any inconvenience. I remember the captain telling us that he had sailed those seas for thirty years but had never seen such a 'sea on' before. He also said that there was not another ship in the fleet could have survived such a battering. We arrived at Oban having taken twenty-eight hours, instead of ten hours, on the voyage. As we were being warped to the quay I heard the captain call to the skipper of an out-going craft: 'It is hell outside!' We were too late for the train to Glasgow, so my sister and I stayed at an hotel that night and glad we were to get a good night's rest after our trying voyage.

Next morning we left early for Glasgow. I will not dwell on the enchanting scenery through which we passed on this journey. I had travelled through it at night the last time, so it was new to me, this, perhaps the most glorious train journey in the British Isles.

We spent most of the rest of that day and all the next making purchases in Glasgow. Some luxuries and immediate comforts we sent off by parcel post to our dear mother. We purchased some furniture: tables, comfortable chairs, and an American organ among other things; these were to be sent by one of two cargo boats that sailed weekly from Glasgow to South Uist—I knew that the pier-master there would look after them for me and keep them safely in the store of the pier till I arrived. These carefully selected purchases afforded me a considerable amount of pride and delight, for I anticipated how proud my mother would feel that I had paid for them all out of my earnings. Having seen them safely despatched and the freight charges duly paid, we took train for the Midland city where were the homes of my relatives. My elder brother, whom I had apprised of the time of our arrival, met us at the station and insisted upon our going to his home. My sister's time was short, so she spent the next day in buying clothing for my mother and some for herself; the next day we, my brother and I, saw her off for Paris. We then went round the shops to get for myself some articles of clothing that I wanted or thought would be useful on South Uist. As we walked along the streets I noticed that quite a number of people turned and stared at me. I asked my brother what made them stare so. 'It's your face,' he said. 'What's the matter with it?' said I. His answer was: 'It is so brown and tanned.' I felt somewhat embarrassed for I had not realized this; then, as I looked around, I remember the sallow complexions of dwellers of the city.

The rest of the time remaining to me I spent among friends and relations, who were unanimous in saying how well I looked. Two days before leaving I bought presents to take back with me to Uist. I had already spent a great deal on clothes and furniture so that these presents were not as handsome as I would have wished. The day previous to my leaving I felt that I must make presents also to my brother and his family, and they were very pleased with them when I presented them that evening. But when I went to bed that night I had a bit of a shock, for on counting my money I found that I had a little less than ten shillings left. This did not disturb me much as I had inquired at the railway station and was told that by changing trains at Carlisle and also at Stirling I should arrive in good time for the boat leaving at six o'clock next morning, Friday, for Uist, where I was due to arrive about four o'clock the same afternoon. My brother's wife was putting up some food for me to have on the train, and by using care I should have sufficient money for any necessary tips, and for food on the boat—I could just about manage it and no one need know how little money I had left myself. I slept well, and my brother helped me next day with my luggage and saw me off by train, the railway officials telling us both that I was due at the seaport at 4.45 a.m. the following morning but that I should have to change trains at Carlisle and Stirling.

It was a very pleasant journey compared with that I last took in winter time; my two or three fellow travellers were very affable and we all conversed freely with each other. At Crewe another traveller joined us. He was a very nice young fellow, in age in the late twenties, I should think; I quite took to him, and when we were left alone in the compartment at Preston we soon became quite confidential. We told each other much about ourselves. He was from Manchester, and was to change trains at Carlisle, where we should part company as he was going to Dumfries. He told me that he had married an English girl against his parents' will, and he and his wife were living in Manchester. Hard times had come upon them, so he was going to try for reconciliation with his parents in Dumfries and was now on his way there. Of course, he had my sympathy and I wished him a happy ending to his mission.

We reached the busy station of Carlisle late at night. There was the usual rush of porters, the opening of carriage doors, and the seizing of passengers' luggage. One seized mine with: 'Where for? Stirling! Right! This way.' Another took that of my travelling companion with: 'Dumfries! Right! This way.' We followed our respective porters as they hurried off laden— they disappeared, then mine reappeared saying: 'Wait here a minute,' and disappeared again. Soon both porters came back with a railway official, the station-master. The latter said: 'I am sorry, gentlemen, but I am afraid that you cannot get on tonight. This is the first of the month and there has been another alteration of the time-tables.' I protested that I was bound to catch my boat leaving Oban at six o'clock the next morning, but was told that it was impossible. We were in a quandary, but my friend was not so badly placed as I for he could reach his destination easily by train next morning whereas my next boat left port the following Monday and it was now Thursday night. With but seven to eight shillings in my pocket, my thoughts may well be imagined! I consulted with my friend as to the best thing to do that night and he said that there was no thing for it but to put up somewhere for the rest of the night and that he knew of a suitable place. I asked if it were cheap and he answered: 'Of course! You know I cannot afford anything else just now.' So leaving our luggage at the station, which cost us something, I followed him out into the streets. He stopped outside an hotel some distance from the station, and we entered. I was alarmed at the size of the place and wondered what a night spent there would cost, for my friend did not know the actual low state of my finances. To make sure, I went to the hotel booking-office and asked the price of a bed for the night. 'Five shillings and sixpence without breakfast,' was the reply. 'I shall not want breakfast as I am leaving by an early train. Please have me called at five-thirty,' said I, and I paid for my bed there and then.

I left my friend, and went to bed feeling very perturbed and wondering what I should do, for I had now less than two shillings left. I lay awake pondering how to meet my difficulties. Youth generally is sanguine and venturesome, and I remember thinking to myself: 'I have Friday, Saturday, and Sunday to get through before going on board the boat. I am young, strong, and healthy and have warm clothing. There are plenty of hills covered with heather around my particular Highland seaport, and doubtless caves: why not spend the time there! The little money I have will buy sufficient bread and I can find water. I shall be all right.' So, having settled this, and looking forward to it as an adventure, I went off into a deep sleep.

Leaving the hotel early in the morning, I walked along the different streets of Carlisle till I found a modest-looking coffee house. Here I had a cup of coffee and a roll which cost only twopence—I felt now that, with care, I should manage to make my money last out for food. It once occurred to me to find a pawn-shop and raise something on my watch, but a certain amount of pride and, perhaps, stubbornness in me made me dismiss this from my mind. I planned to leave Carlisle by some train which would enable me to arrive at Oban in the evening, which would give me time to purchase food and to find some cave, or other place, for sleep, before darkness came on. The rest of the morning I spent about Carlisle: the castle and the anglers on the River Eden occupied most of my attention and time. Later in the morning I approached the railway station and, having found that my train left very shortly, I regaled myself with another roll and a cup of coffee, which cost me fourpence. I determined to eat no more that day for I had more than two days to provide for. Fortunately I had previously provided myself with a good supply of tobacco to take back with me and I found this helped to assuage my hunger.

After reclaiming my luggage and ascertaining that I had to change my train at Dunblane instead of at Stirling, I set off on my railway journey which was supposed to take eight hours but took over ten. When we reached Oban it was long after dark and outside the station by the pier was pitch-black darkness, while to make it worse, rain was falling in torrents. My plan and my resolution were dissipated for I knew that I could not see a yard before me outside the town and that everything would be sodden. I was at a loss to know what to do. Suddenly an inspiration came to me. I already knew that there was a Catholic bishop living in the town; so, late as it was, after nine o'clock at night, I said to myself: 'I will go and see the bishop; will tell him who I am and of my difficulty.' I reached the house, rang the bell, and the door was opened by a middle-aged woman, probably the housekeeper. 'Can I see his Lordship?' said I. 'It is very important.' 'Who are you, and what is your business!' she asked. I told her who I was and where I was teaching. 'Oh! There is a priest here from your island. Would he do?' she now asked. I told her that he would do just as well, and she left me waiting in a small room. Providence was good to me for this priest I had met several times on South Uist, a dear gentle old man. He listened to me with sympathy and said: 'Of course! Of course! Wait just a minute.' He returned very shortly, and put five pounds in my hand, asking if that would be enough. I told him that two or three pounds would be plenty; but he insisted on my taking it all, saying that I could repay it after he returned to South Uist. I left him after thanking him, and receiving his blessing and direction to a decent hotel.

After my vicissitudes, how welcome was the comfort of the hotel—the food seemed luxurious after my day's subsistence on two cups of coffee and two rolls! I used some of the money next day on the purchase of some delicacies and fresh fruit to take to my mother—these I had nailed up in a wooden box to be easy to handle. How different was the voyage back to the island compared with my last crossing! The weather was beautiful, with a clear sky and fresh breeze from the south. We stopped at several islands, Coll, Tiree, and Canna—I thought the last island the most beautiful I had yet seen: green, white sands, gentle hills, and a peace reigning over all. We passed between Rum and Skye, the former a mass of dark mountains with a seemingly inaccessible coast; the latter island, with the Coolin Mountains towering in pinnacles and rising almost sheer from the shore, presented to me a sight unique in grandeur. I was interestedly watching the water flowing down the mountain-sides, for, when it reached the edges of the cliff, it did not fall into the sea, but was lifted up and up by the wind into feathery veils which obscured the slopes of the mountain-sides. A voice at my ear said: 'You are lucky! One does not often see that.' I turned and found it was the purser. He told me that this sight was rarely presented, only to be seen when the wind was in a certain direction and there had been much rain.

Soon after, there was some excitement among the passengers who lined the rails—they were looking at what seemed to be a school of fish which seemed to be trying to race our steamboat;

close beside us these fish raced, leaping along from wave to wave and forging ahead of us. Some of the crew joined us and told us that they were young dolphins. There was then a shout from the bridge and the sailors pointed ahead saying: 'Look! Whales!' We saw fountains of water being spouted as large as and some larger than our ship. We saw one large whale turn suddenly and head straight for us at right-angles amid-ships. The monster came at us full tilt on the surface. I remember thinking: 'If he hits us, we shall capsize!' Within a few yards of the side of the ship he dived right under us. We rushed to the opposite rail, and in a few seconds he rose. I shall never forget the vast white churning of the water all around, nor the loud 'Sweesh, shshsh!' we heard as he rose to the surface just a few yards away from us on the other side, and then he passed on.

Owing to the many calls the ship had made on her way, we did not reach Lochboisdale till four o'clock the next morning. I found all my purchased Glasgow goods safe in the pier-master's care. Leaving some of my luggage with him till I sent for the rest of my belongings, I strapped the box of groceries on my back and with a bag in each hand started on a six-mile walk to my schoolhouse. Having the box strapped on my back, I could only rest on the way by stepping into a ditch and resting my loaded back against the bank. However, I reached home eventually and having found my mother was all right and glad of my return I soon retired wearied out, and slept long and soundly.

Chapter Fourteen

THE island market! This was held on a fixed day towards the end of the summer and was chiefly for the sale of the surplus cattle of the island. Its venue was some ten miles north of my schoolhouse at a place about midway between the extreme south township and that of the northernmost. For more than a week before this event, heterogeneous sets of passengers landed at the pier by the different steamships calling there, both mail boat and cargo boat—cattle dealers, drovers with their dogs, itinerant Jews with their wares, tinkers, gipsies and various others. This invasion was quite an event which the natives viewed with mixed feelings which accorded with the various avocations of these strangers—on the whole, they were shy and suspicious of them.

I do not know where the bulk of these visitors to the island were domiciled while on the island; I believe some found quarters at the larger and better houses near the pier, others at the township near my colleague's schoolhouse, and I saw the tents of some gipsies pitched by the hill-side road where I had had my experience of 'will o' the wisp'. These latter people were rather a nuisance, in our district at least, with their importunity to buy their wares, and their begging; the native people were very suspicious of them and kept a wary eye on their fowl, locking them up for security. A Jew visited my house with a bag of jewellery, clocks and watches; he did his utmost to persuade me to buy an expensive gold watch and chain, at the same time telling me of the different people on the island who had purchased such from him. I bought some small article to get rid of him.

Later, my schoolmaster friend came to see me. Among others, my late visitor, the jeweller, was mentioned and my friend knew of him. The Jew had secured lodgings at one of the slate-roofed roomy houses near his school, at the house of Angus McA - - - who could speak a little English, and whom I had previously met. The Jew had tried in vain to sell Angus a gold watch. 'How much?' said Angus after looking at it. 'Ten pounds,' said the Jew. 'Ach!' said Angus. 'Two-and-six plenty!' I afterwards asked Angus how he, who I knew disliked Jews, came to allow a Jew to stay at his house. 'Ach! The money is verra seldom' said he—'scarce', I expect he meant.

Angus was not of a trustful nature, so he had another bed put up in his own room so that he could keep his eye on his lodger! The day previous to that on which the market was to be held a case of cheap clocks for the lodger arrived at Angus's house from the pier. Before retiring that night the lodger opened the case, wound the clocks, and placed them along the walls of the landing outside their bedroom door. In the night Angus woke to see his lodger sitting up in bed muttering to himself; he then saw him slip quietly out of bed, go to the door, and stand listening. Angus was now wide awake, and in a high state of nervousness as to what his lodger was after. Stretching an arm from the bed he reached for the poker that he kept in readiness near the head of the bed, clutched it and held it down by his side. He watched the Jew open the door gently and creep softly from the room; but the latter shortly returned and sat down again on the side of his own bed. Through half-closed eyes Angus continued to watch him. Again his lodger went out, then returned muttering to himself a little, and glancing across at the other bed. This stealthy going and coming was getting on the nerves of Angus; and when, after a more lengthy absence than before had occurred, the lodger again appeared at the door, Angus sprang to his feet in the bed, poker in hand, and lashed his bed with it, at the same time shouting: 'What's ahl up! What's ahl up!'

The terrified lodger tried to explain to his infuriated landlord that he was anxious to have all his clocks in good going order next day ready for selling at the market and he had only been visiting them to see if each was ticking correctly. I am not sure whether Angus believed him or not, but I believe he still had a suspicion that robbery or murder was intended.

I have previously mentioned that the 'market' was held

105

chiefly for the sale of cattle. These cattle of the island had been of special interest to me; the cows were rather small compared with ours; very shaggy, and practically all of them were black or brown. Their supply of milk was not copious but was of a rich brownish quality. I often, of an evening, met a small herd of them being driven along a road with the bull bringing up the rear. The latter were huge creatures with enormous heads and shoulders covered with long shaggy hair like a mane, and armed with long formidable wide-spreading horns. Though so wild and fierce looking, they were remarkably quiet and docile unless excited. Indeed, I had sometimes seen a herd of ten or twelve cattle coming towards me, the huge bull last, but could see no one driving them. Stepping aside as they passed me I have discovered the drover behind the huge bulk of the bull— a little boy or girl of five or six years of age in the infant division of my school, holding a piece of ragwort with which he or she would now and then strike the bull on the hind-quarters to hasten its step. Sometimes, when inquiring from these little children their reason for absence from school on the previous day, I was met with the answer: 'Please, sir, I was herrding the bool'*—which meant that they had been engaged in keeping the bull from the cornfields. And I could but smile when I compared their sizes, driver and driven.

Throughout the day and evening preceding that on which the 'market' was held, there might have been seen, at intervals, passing my house: herds of three or four cows and a few stirks in the charge of a man and his dog, solitary cows driven slowly along by women, a recalcitrant stirk with rope attached being coaxed or bullied into pursuing the proper road, carts each containing a young calf with the mother cow walking behind, all presenting a most unusual sight, and all trending north.

My friend, the innkeeper at Pollachar, at the extreme south end of the island, was going to drive to the 'market' in his trap and promised to find me a seat in it. So soon after nine o'clock on 'market day' morning I espied the trap waiting at the end of the short road that led to my gate from the main road. Without delay I mounted the seat behind and we started. There was a most animated scene on the road: men seated on horses and

* On 30th May 1890 Rea noted in the school log book that 'the attendance fell much lower this week owing to the commencement of the herding season'.

ponies with a piece of sacking for saddle and a rope as bridle, even women old and young similarly mounted, we passed on the road, besides pedestrians trudging laboriously along, young and old, men and women, and all dressed in their brightest clothes. As we passed we waved or called to those whom we knew, and received a smiling look or a wave in return—all seemed in good humour.

I had never been as far north as we drove this day, so I was interested in the character of the country through which we passed and which grew grander and more wild as we proceeded north. On our right, range after range of hills and mountains were massed; lochs and running streams filled the hollows and I thought of the good trout fishing these should give. To our left the land was undulating and in some parts almost flat, but it was mostly clothed in fields of gently waving oats and barley, and beyond this again we caught glimpses of the placid ocean when we reached any elevation on our road. Rounding a hill we saw before us a large valley; the steeply descending road passed between two large lochs and beyond these again, on gently rising ground, lay the site of the 'market'. I picked this out at once for there was a great concourse; people, vehicles, booths and tents. As we descended the road we came into full view of the two highest mountains of the island rearing their two thousand feet almost from our very feet. The craggy peak of one seemed to bend over a little like a person's head bent forward over his chest; I was told that this was the home of the eagles and inaccessible to man.

Arrived at the market stance, I was free to look around while my friend unharnessed the horse from the trap to which he afterwards tethered him. On the rising ground on either side of the road were scattered the cattle, ponies, and horses, either in groups or singly, but under the charge of their respective owners. Here and there market-stalls, tents, and booths had been erected. But what a miscellaneous collection of vehicles and of people was there: traps, old-fashioned and new, dog-carts, phaetons, governess-carts, wagonettes, besides carts both large and small, and many nondescript vehicles! Mingling among the crowds were the minister whom I had met on the steamship, with his family, priests, the factor or estate manager and his clerks, the banker, the proprietors of the two hotels, the doctor, the schoolmasters and schoolmistresses with their assistants from the different schools, the lawyer, the policeman, a number of farmers with their families from the large farms, and the crofters with their grown-up sons and daughters. Indeed, they made a miscellaneous crowd, but practically all were imbued with the holiday spirit: for this was the one day in the year when all the people of the island might expect to meet.

The business of the buying and selling of cattle was virtually over when we arrived; but I came across a crofter, an old acquaintance, who was arguing with a cattle buyer about the sale of the former's horse. He wanted £20 for it and the other's highest offer was £19. The crofter said that it would be a disgrace to him and his horse to sell it for less than £20. At long last the prospective buyer said: 'How would it be if I give you £20 for it, and you give me a pound back?' This was immediately accepted. This episode both amused and interested me, for the buyer must have understood the Uistman's psychology. The crofter was satisfied that he had sold his horse for £20!

C - - - , my schoolmaster friend, and I made the acquaintance of our fellow teachers from the other schools of the island; and, though we all naturally discussed professional matters, we had quite a merry time in the refreshment booth, and at the various stalls. I was introduced to many new acquaintances too among the priests, the large farmers and their families, and received many invitations to visit them. To my surprise I found it to be the vogue to buy sweets which were sold in abundance at the stalls: there was quite a variety of kinds, but the old-fashioned conversation lozenge seemed to be in great demand among the young people. Everybody seemed to eat sweets, and I smiled to see great heavily bearded men chumbling and swallowing them with gusto. Before the afternoon was spent all the sweets were sold and the people including ourselves were armed with huge bags of sweets to take home with them. As the afternoon wore on the crowds began to thin, for those who had far to go on foot started early on their journey home. Soon horses began to be harnessed to vehicles and so, with many good-byes, smiles, and good wishes to those we left behind, we started on our return south in the trap.

The journey, after my novel but pleasant day's experience,

was most enjoyable. The names of those large farms, now on our right, with those of their respective tenants, were designated to me and, as we passed the few townships, children lined the banks beside the road. To these we threw handfuls of sweets for which they joyously scrambled. My friend stopped his trap by my house before dark and, with a smile, thanks, and 'Good night', we parted, he to drive to the inn, and I to recount to my mother the day's happenings.

Chapter Fifteen

THE trout fishing that I had done up to this time had been rather desultory; the loch near the schoolhouse (Loch nan Capall I learned to be its name) was the scene of my local efforts in that way and good sport I had, though the weight of the best fish never exceeded two pounds; my other efforts in this line were made in the company of my schoolmaster friend and Father Allan among the lochs in their vicinity; our favourite rendezvous was Loch Dùn na Cille, a long rocky-shored loch which communicated with the sea.

Feeling that I had now attained to some degree of skill in the art of fly-fishing, I set out one morning to try some of the other lochs of the south end of the island. My first essay was at the loch near the miller's house about a mile from my house and situated not too far from Kilbride farm. It was a large loch with several shallow sandy bays on the northern and the eastern sides, but the other shores were high and rocky. I worked along the north shore, then the east, casting far out into the deeper water as it was shallow nearer in. I had been patiently casting for some time without result when I saw a fish rise to my flies. I drew my line gently in and recast to give him another chance. He rose; I struck quickly, hooked him, and away he dashed in full career. He was a good fish and gave me a good fight, for he afterwards weighed nearly four pounds; but he nearly got away when I was landing him. After he was thoroughly exhausted, as I thought, I drew him in to the shallow water of the bay where I had been wading. He lay quite passive, so I unhooked the landing-net to slip under him; but he recovered, darted between my legs, and dashed off again into deep water. I shall never forget my predicament, for he had run between my legs from the front, so that I now had my back to him and my efforts to throw a leg over the taut line behind me were unavailing. Fortunately this was his last rush, and I was able to negotiate a leg over the slackening line. I drew him in, netted, landed, and killed him with a knock on the back of his head. As he lay dead on the grass I, somehow, felt admiration for the gallant fight he had made: this was tinged with a little regret for his death, but I thought to myself: 'Well, old chap, it was odds on you: but you lost!'

I had had enough of shallow water, so went round to the high rocky shore where there was deep water. Making my way out along a pile of rocks that jutted some distance into the loch I jumped on to a high flat-topped stone from which I could be at an advantage in casting. My first cast was successful, and as I struck, a big fish leapt into the air—I had hooked him! What a dance he led me! Mad rushes he made hither and thither; he shot clean out of the water and slapped at the line with his tail; this only to be succeeded by a rush straight at me where I stood on the high rock. I was at a tension the whole time for I had the utmost difficulty in countering his tactics: I had to keep a firm, steady, but gentle strain on the line except when he made his leaps out of the water, when I dropped the rod point for a loose line, raising it again to resume the tension as he dropped back into the water, and reeling in my line as fast as possible when he rushed towards me. Yet I had to use the utmost care for I knew the slightest jerk would break the fine-drawn gut of my fly-cast. I do not know how long the fight lasted—it seemed ages before there were signs of his giving in. At last he was thoroughly tired out, and, as I drew him gently towards the rock, I confess that I, too, felt tired. He was a beauty, but so exhausted that he lay on his side at the foot of the rock without a kick left. Reaching for my landing-net, I discovered to my dismay that it was not there—I must have dropped it some-where on my way without noticing the fact. I dare not relax tension on the fish; so I knelt carefully on the rock gently reeling in the while. Leaning over I tried to reach for him; but the surface of the water was well beyond my hand. There on its side lay the fish, the largest I had yet hooked. Reeling my line in till the tip of the rod was just below the edge of the rock, I lay flat, rod in my left hand, my right reaching down to seize him under the gills. Reaching my furthest till I was in peril of overbalancing, I found my fingers about six inches from the fish. I thought: 'If I can raise his head a little from the water I may be able to reach his gills.' So holding the shortened line taut in my right hand I laid down the rod with my left, transferred the line again, lay flat on the rock and gently raised his head with my left. Gradually his head rose, desperately I reached till my fingers nearly touched his nose! Another inch or two will do it! I tried to raise it this inch or so. Oh! horror! I saw the hook tear through the skin of the upper lip of the fish by reason of its own weight—it was free! Even then it lay on its side still exhausted. I now experienced the chagrin of seeing it recover, right itself, and, with a flap of its tail, swim off at its leisure. For a few minutes I was almost beside myself with disappointment at losing this big fellow. I remember standing up and stamping with anger at myself for being without the landing-net—I called myself all kinds of names. Then I sobered, took my rod, hunted for, and found the net, then left this loch in high dudgeon.

Reaching the loch near the sea where the farmer and I had together seen a trout leaping, I found a worm, baited a hook with it, fixed a piece of cork on the line as a float, made a cast out, sat down, and after washing my hands, ate some sandwiches. I had finished my meal while keeping an eye on my improvised float, and was having a smoke when my float bobbed. It rose again, then disappeared and I struck. Away it went—'A heavy beggar!' thought I as he bored deep down deep in the water. Try as I would I could not get him to show himself for some time. At last far out I saw his head appear. It was a very ugly one and I thought it must be a bull trout. After a little I began to have doubts about its being a trout at all. It was very strong but had not the dash of a trout. I reeled in till I had it at the side. There was no trouble in landing it, for it was a conger over four feet long and it squirmed along as I pulled. I had a large clasp knife which I opened intending to decapitate it; but its neck was thicker than my wrist and it kept coming at me with open jaws. I was somewhat at a loss as to how I should deal with it. Then looking round I espied some rocky ground and manœuvred the brute on to some fairly level rocks. Picking up a big heavy piece of stone I advanced towards my formidable capture with the purpose of bashing its head in. But more easily said than done! Each time I approached it reared and darted at my legs. I was wearing knicker-bockers and stockings so that my legs were very vulnerable. I must have presented a comical spectacle to anyone looking on as I danced around the brute with the rock in my hands and looked for a likely chance. An opportunity occurred before long which I seized, and I dashed the rock on the conger's head which was smashed flat. Feeling that I had had enough for that day I returned home, not feeling very proud of myself.

Next morning it was blowing half a gale with rain driving before it. But I was feeling so disappointed over losing my big fish on the previous day that I determined to have another try at that same loch despite the weather. No persuasion could prevent my venturing out. When I again reached the rocky shores of the loch I found the water in great waves, swirling over the rocks. Nothing daunted, I cast my flies out as well as I could over the heaving water; it was difficult to keep the cast in the water for the wind whipped the line out as though it were a cotton thread. But what was that I saw at the top of that wave as my flies were blown from the water? A large fish! Letting out more line I allowed the flies to sink well before bringing it in jerks towards me. I saw a fine fellow rise in a wave after a fly, then another and another. The water was so wild that they missed it. I tried again with more patience so as to give them a better chance. I hooked one. I had six others after him one after the other, all of them as big as or bigger than the one I had lost the day before.

I fished this loch on other days, but never caught so many big fish there in a day, for the larger fish were shy. But I suppose it was only the large and powerful fish that could combat the waves in stormy weather to go after flies. They were easily netted after being hooked, for the boisterous waves battered them and I could easily bring them within the ambit of my net. Less than half an hour was the time I was at the loch and I had seven fish, none under six pounds in weight—the quickest 'bag' of fish I ever remember getting.

Of course, I was very wet and blown about so did not stay for more. I was now quite reconciled to my failure of the preceding day, and arrived home in triumph.

Chapter Sixteen

THE annual school holiday extended over two months. All hands were required on the crofts—crops had to be cut, gathered, carted to homesteads, and stacked; potatoes to be 'lifted', or in other words, dug up, carried home and stored for the winter; while the peat was gathered into snug compact stacks beside the houses which, in many cases, had to be re-thatched ready to withstand the gales of winter. Some of the young men went out in boats and caught fish, which were brought home and salted as food for the winter.

Late one afternoon I saw five young fellows whom I knew getting a boat ready for an evening's saithe fishing. At their invitation I joined them, got into the boat, and out to sea we sailed. Lying at the bottom of the boat were the rods—clumsy-looking affairs, a kind of lightweight clothes-prop. To each rod was attached a strong brown line, and a large hook with a white feather tied to its shank. Soon we were well away from the coast and out at sea. Three reefs were now made in the sail so that our speed slackened down and we were moving gently along. Making fast the helm, each man seized a rod in each hand, cast the lines overboard and held the top of the rod well under water. After a little while, as they had no result, they replaced the rods in the bottom of the boat and made full sail for other fishing ground. Arrived here, the procedure was as before and each man stood at the boat's side holding his two rods in the water. A shout! A rod lifted, and a saithe about the size of a large herring was dangling on the hook. Sweeping it inboard, the fisherman unhooked the fish, thrust a spare rod into my hand as other shouts and cries arose, and we all were soon swinging fish in as fast as we could—you simply put the point of the rod under water, trailed the line, felt a tug, gave a short jerk, and swung a fish into the air; lifting him in you slipped the hook out, dropped him in the bottom of the boat and carried on again. Before long the bottom of the boat was rull of wriggling, writhing or jumping saithe, my hands and clothes were covered with blood and fish-scales and I began to feel rather nauseated, so desisted from the execution, but the others continued and were quite as excited as ever.

I think that what followed must have been due to this excitement or to their youthful lack of caution. A fog had been stealing upon us unnoticed and it almost reached us before they were aware of it. Before they had stowed their rods and made sail towards shore we were so enveloped that I could not see the mast-head. We sailed on and on for a long time with no sign of the shore. Course was altered several times and still no sign of shore in whatever direction we sailed. Darkness came on but the fog persisted, so the sail was furled and we just drifted on waiting for the fog to clear. But hour after hour passed and we could not tell where we were or whither we were drifting—maybe out into the ocean.

With a landsman's ignorance and inexperience of the dangers and terrors of the sea I do not remember feeling any fear, only an interest in the experience as I gazed around us and looked at my companions' stolid countenances. How many hours we had been drifting I cannot remember, but it was far into the night when a light loomed at us for a moment out of the fog. The men sprang for the oars and rowed desperately in the direction of the place where we had passed the light. Almost immediately it was picked up, and nearing it, we found ourselves in a small rocky bay. Climbing ashore some of us approached the light and were amazed to find that it came from a powerful lamp standing in the window of the porch of my innkeeper friend's house at Pollachar. This window looked straight out to sea and at night he always placed a powerful lamp in it as a guide to those at sea.

My imperturbable companions, after anchoring and securing the boat, began sharing the fish, putting them into sacks as they did so. They called these fish 'saithe'. This done, one of them gave me a sack—my share, eighty-three fish, I remember him telling me. I laughed and told them to share these among them. I knew my way, so shook hands all round and started for home which was less than two miles away.

My mother was not anxious at my absence and late return for she always encouraged me to be quite independent in my goings and comings; as to where I had been or what had happened to me while away, she never questioned me but left me to tell her what I would—she trusted me, and I in return trusted her and perhaps told her more than I would otherwise have done.

One morning, a Thursday, two days after my saithe fishing experience, Father Allan called at my house. He was accompanied by a friend, a doctor from Glasgow, who had been spending a holiday on the island. They were on their way to the small island of Eriskay, which was to be the scene of Father Allan's future labours. With them they had a large closed can containing live trout in water with which they intended stocking the only loch that the island possessed. Father Allan invited me to go to with them, and we had great fun carefully carrying the tin can of trout in turns, peeping at them occasionally on the way and replenishing the water at intervals. In the bay beside Pollachar inn we found a boat waiting for us in charge of the old ferryman and his son. We did not delay, as the doctor's time was short, for he intended to return that evening to catch the next steamer from Lochboisdale.

On reaching Eriskay we all three made direct for the loch to give the trout their liberty—they were in lively condition and darted from the can as soon as we placed it in the water. From there we visited the schoolhouse, and I learned that Mrs Robertson, the schoolmistress, was leaving and going to live in her native Edinburgh,* also that a dance was being given in the school that evening at which a presentation to her was to be made. Father Allan then led us to the site of his new house and church,† and we found it perched on the top of the high rock overlooking the sea, near which he and I had scaled the cliff face. I remarked on the exposed position, but he drew himself to his full height, raised his arms, and exclaimed: 'What could be grander? Exposed to the four winds of heaven!'

* She had come to Eriskay in 1884, the first Catholic schoolmistress appointed there.
† The house was built in 1891; the church in 1902.

Already the building had commenced: the foundations were in the solid rock, some huge stones and boulders, placed in position for walls or lying near, were ready to be roughly dressed. We learned that these poor fishermen of the island were building their priest's house and their church with their own hands, making cement from burnt shells and sand, using balks of wood from the cargoes of timber ships thrown on the sea from wrecked or distressed vessels, and that they devoted the proceeds of twenty-four hours' fishing at regular intervals to provide funds for the purchase of other necessary materials unobtainable from the resources of the island.

While the doctor was being shown Prince Charlie's landing place I went down to the store by the 'Haun', or haven, to have a chat with Ewen MacLennan the storekeeper. He was a very pleasant affable young fellow, intelligent, fairly well educated, speaking good English, and was about twenty-eight years of age, I should think. He introduced me to his sister Marion who kept house for him, a very pretty girl aged about seventeen years. She had been educated at a High School in one of the Scottish cities, but she seemed very happy here with her brother. He was really the agent or manager of this store, which belonged to a man in a large way of business, and who owned quite a number of stores scattered about the islands. He bought cargoes of fish, cured them, and despatched them direct to places abroad; he also supplied the London market at Billingsgate with large fresh lobsters—indeed, some of the lobsters I had seen caught here were tremendous fellows with claws nearly a foot in length. The agent at this small island store bought the catches of fish from the men and paid for them in cash or in goods, whichever they preferred. I happened to refer to my having heard that the proceeds of a day's fishing were regularly devoted to the costs of the church buildings. He corroborated this, saying that every other Friday's catch was sold for this purpose; then he added: 'But it is a very strange thing, that that special day's catch is always a bumper. I cannot understand it; for no matter how badly the fishing may have been going, they always seem to make a good catch on that day.' This man was not a Catholic, and he was puzzled. I then purchased one or two articles and left the store soon after.

While I had been talking to the storekeeper and his sister

we had heard the sound of the wind rising. Before I reached the schoolhouse where I was to meet Father Allan and the doctor from Glasgow, the wind had increased to a gale against which I found it difficult to climb to the schoolhouse. These gales often rise quite suddenly, and may drop again just as suddenly; but their duration is uncertain: some last for only a few hours, others for three or four days, or maybe for a week. We all had dinner together at the schoolhouse and then went down to the 'Haun', or harbour, to see if we could get a boat to take us back to South Uist. It was too rough and wild to attempt it, so we reconciled ourselves to waiting, in the hope that the weather would improve towards evening. The doctor was extremely anxious to catch the steamer next day so that he might be present at a very important meeting to be held in Glasgow on the Saturday following, and this was the Thursday. At intervals during the afternoon and evening we went to see if it were possible to cross the sound, but were told that it was too dangerous. Eventually it was decided to wait till the morning when there might be better conditions, and that a make-shift bed would be made up at the schoolhouse for the doctor.

The dance was held that night in the school, despite the weather, and all seemed to enjoy it and to make little account of wind and rain. Immediately before the last dance the presentation to the retiring schoolmistress was made with many expressed good wishes and regrets at her departure. The last dance, called 'The White Cockade' after Prince Charlie, was very much like our 'Sir Roger de Coverley', yet was different. The girl dancers formed a rank with the same number of men forming another, both ranks facing each other. As far as I can remember the girl at the top of her rank, and the man at the bottom of his, advanced towards each other between the ranks and performed evolutions similar to those of the 'Sir Roger'. But at the end, when these two returned to their original places, the girl danced across and down the line behind the men. Without stopping on the way she placed a white handkerchief on the shoulder of the man of her choice as she passed. He left the rank and followed, meeting her at the bottom where she waited for him; together they danced out of the door. The dance now proceeded as before; and, as each girl departed from the dance with her chosen cavalier, the number of dancers became less and less till all had gone home and the dance was over. I had never seen the dance before: but I thought it a very pretty ending to the night's amusement.

There was no abatement of the storm; and when we went to the 'Haun' next morning, we found a group of fishermen watching the seas—they knew that Father Allan's friend, the doctor, was desperately anxious to get across that morning to South Uist. 'I would give a hundred pounds to get across so as to be at my meeting tomorrow—it is very important that I should be there,' I heard the doctor say to the group of men. Father Allan interrogated them in Gaelic but they only looked at the raging seas and shook their heads. 'Couldn't they attempt it with their biggest boat?' cried the doctor. Father Allan said he would send for MacIsaac, the old experienced ferryman, who knew every rock and shoal and was well known for his daring and skill, for if it were at all possible to cross this man would do it. The doctor said he would submit to the verdict of this ferryman, but he was walking up and down in much agitation all the time we were waiting for MacIsaac. The other men drew back when the old seaman arrived, and remained apart while Father Allan and the doctor explained to him the extreme importance of getting to South Uist without delay, the doctor being most lavish in promises of reward. MacIsaac listened without a word, looked long at sea and clouds, then turned to the doctor and said calmly: 'I don't want your money; but I will try if you like. Are you prepared to die? We *may* get across in the biggest boat, but I doubt it.' He coolly turned aside and took a pinch of snuff. All these details were so distinctly imprinted on my then youthful mind that I have the scene vividly before me as I write, and I still feel the tension of that moment—the doctor turned on his heel, saying: 'Oh, if it's like that! I don't want you to throw away your lives'; so we returned to the schoolhouse.

The storm continued throughout the day and night, and all the next day, Saturday, until on the Sunday afternoon intimation came that it was now possible to attempt the passage. We hastened to the 'Haun' where a number of men were waiting with the largest fishing boat ready to make the trial. MacIsaac, the ferryman, was in charge and he stowed us under a kind of half-deck forward so as to protect us from the seas; a small piece of sail was raised and away we flew before the wind. The planks above us saved us a good deal from the waves that broke over us. In what seemed to me only a few minutes I peeped out, and to my amazement found we were close to the shore of South Uist. Not a moment was lost; the boat ran into a sheltered bay, we three were helped ashore, the men raised the sail, and out again they were sped in the direction of the island of Eriskay which we had only just left. When we reached the inn at Pollachar early in the evening, a trap was made ready to take the doctor to the hotel at Lochboisdale. We managed to get the four of us into the trap—I was to be dropped at my house and Father Allan near his place. As the latter had said: 'You need to be prepared for at least a three weeks' stay when you cross to Eriskay!'

Chapter Seventeen

I HAD much admired the home-spun cloth made by the people of South Uist—it was soft, warm and of a very durable texture. No two patterns of the cloth seemed exactly alike as probably each person wove according to her own individual taste; but the result was that many cloths were of a very pronounced type. Wishing to obtain some of quiet pattern for myself, I consulted Catriona on the matter. She said that she and her mother would be delighted to make a 'web' of cloth, about twenty yards I think. Their hand-loom was small so that the width of the cloth would be a little less than thirty inches and it would take them the whole of the winter to complete the web.

The wool was obtained from their own sheep; it was then washed, disinfected, dyed and spun with their own hands. We were very interested: Catriona brought us various coloured threads that she had dyed, blues, browns, and greys of several shades—she obtained the dyes from the water lilies (so abundant on some lochs), lichens, mosses and even seaweed which she boiled in iron pots. Having selected grey threads of different shades and two blues, and deciding on a soft grey as the main colour, we said that they might set to work. My mother and I were invited to see the cloth as it was being woven, and we were delighted with the texture and its tasteful appearance—a soft quiet grey with just a suggestion of blue: when afterwards it was made up into clothes (which I wore for many years), it was very much admired by my friends and relations in England; they endeavoured to get it matched but with little success.

On the whole of South Uist there were only two tailors, one living at the north end and the other at the south. It was the custom for these men to be away from home for weeks at a time. If a family had woven cloth ready, they sent for the tailor and he would go to their house and stay there till he had made their clothes—in some cases they consulted with him beforehand as to the style and pattern of cloth to be used. Donald Gillies was the tailor for the south. He visited the school sometimes, and I found him very interesting. He had learned his trade in Glasgow and, as far as I could see, was doing well on South Uist. His forefathers were tailors, he told me, and his grandfather used to be the only tailor on the island, living in the middle of it near the place where the annual market was held. Donald Gillies had a crippled leg and used a crutch, but he travelled about on his pony; it was surprising to see the agility he displayed in mounting and dismounting, and how confidently he rode along, crutch under arm. He was full of anecdotes and stories, and he much amused my mother and myself with their recital. One of the stories was of his grandfather's father, Alexander Gillies, who was the sole tailor of the island at that time. This story ran something as follows:

Alexander Gillies lived near the middle of the island and was the only tailor for the making of clothes for the men of the island. When a family had cloth for this purpose they sent for Alexander, who went to them and stayed till the clothes were made —not infrequently the people consulted with him before commencing to make a web of cloth, for they relied much on his judgement as to pattern, colours and texture. Sometimes his services were required many miles to the north or the south, so that he was frequently away from his home for weeks at a time. Among those for whom the tailor made clothes was a family consisting of a widow with her two grown-up sons. They lived at a lonely house high up on the slopes of wild Ben More. A taciturn family, dark and gipsy-like in appearance, they had little in common with the other people of the island, and kept themselves aloof as far as possible. Tailor-like, Alexander had always particularly noticed the clothes of the two sons and wondered at their fine texture and finish. On the rare occasions of his being summoned to work at their house his wonder had increased and some suspicion aroused, for not only were the texture and the colouring quite different from that of any cloth made on the island, but the width of the cloth was much greater than could be made with native hand-looms. Pondering over this he determined to be more on the alert at his next visit.

Alexander waited patiently till their next call for him, and at last he was summoned to the widow's house to make two suits for her sons. Arrived at their thatched cottage in the afternoon he received a surly acknowledgment of his greeting to the two sons working on their plot of ground—this family were squatters or people settled on ground to which they had no title. But no one had interfered with them in this remote spot. Entering the cottage Alexander seated himself on the settle by the peat fire. The woman appeared shortly and without a word brought two pieces of cloth for his inspection. In accordance with his plan he found fault with the cloth, colours and texture, and said he was busy and must leave the work till later on. The widow protested and said she would be able to get more for the next day quite easily. This was just what the tailor had expected and he determined to find out whence she obtained her cloth. Vigilantly he watched that she did not leave the house, and when they all retired to rest at night he was still on the watch though he pretended to sleep almost at once.

Well into the night Alexander thought he heard someone moving about, so slipping out of bed he peeped into the kitchen where he had heard the movements. By the aid of the firelight he saw that it was his forbidding-looking hostess, and he watched her closely. He saw her cross to the dresser and take from a drawer what looked like a piece of black velvet, and a small pewter plate. Scarcely breathing he watched her close the drawer carefully, and move silently to the middle of the floor; then she placed the piece of velvet on her head—it was a cap. She stood there and commenced a rhyme, turning the pewter plate in her hands the while. It was a short rhyme of four lines she repeated, Alexander watching fascinated. To his amazement when she had repeated the rhyme three times and reached the last word of the fourth line, she rose in the air and passed right through the roof of the cottage. Mystified but determined to find out more, Alexander went back to bed, trying, as he sank into slumber, to repeat the words of the rhyme he had heard.

The family were about next morning, and after a meal the woman produced two other pieces of cloth. Now the tailor could only remember a part of the rhyme that she had three times repeated the previous night, so he dissembled, praising one of the pieces but pretending to find a flaw in the weft of the other. He said that he would set to work that very day upon the suit and perhaps she could obtain another piece in the place of the piece he had pretended to find faulty. He was hard at work making the suit throughout the day, often repeating to himself as many words of the rhyme as he remembered, and he felt that if he could hear her repeat the whole of the rhyme once again he could memorize it.

That night the procedure was a repetition of that of the night before, but he had learnt the rhyme after he had heard it repeated the three times more by the woman; and after she had disappeared as before, he went to sleep repeating the rhyme to himself, quite satisfied that he had thoroughly and correctly memorized the rhyme.

Next day he professed complete satisfaction with the cloth produced by the widow and continued his labour upon the clothes, often repeating to himself the widow's rhyme. When all was quiet that night and the people of the house wrapped in sleep, he rose from his bed, stealthily dressed himself, and crept to the dresser in the kitchen. Taking the velvet cap and the pewter plate from the drawer he placed the former on his head and turned the plate in his hands as he had seen the woman do. Very carefully he repeated the rhyme, once, twice, then as he completed it for the third time, he felt himself rising and immediately after lost all consciousness.

When he came to himself he found by the light of the moon that he was in a large room which had tables down the middle, and the surrounding walls fitted with racks holding rolls of cloth—he was in a cloth store. The night was still and all was silent: so he went round the racks of cloth examining the various cloths as well as he could by the dim light. Many of them he admired for their texture and finish, and from some of these he cut suit-lengths to make clothes for himself. After rolling these pieces tightly together to take away with him, he, velvet cap on head and pewter plate in hand, began to repeat the rhyme for the first time; but at the end of the first line he paused, for the beginning of the second line had escaped him. Recommencing the rhyme he got stuck again as before at the end of the first line. Time after time he tried without any more success. He then sat down and thought, and soon found that he could remember a few isolated words of the other lines; but repeat the whole rhyme he could not. Time was passing and he became anxious—the doors were securely locked and if he could not remember the rhyme he would be caught. But his anxiety over his dilemma only served to defeat his efforts at exercising his memory, and his thoughts became more and more confused; ultimately he felt beaten and resigned himself to his fate.

Morning brought the arrival of the people of the factory and the discovery of Alexander Gillies, the tailor, with the suit-lengths of cloth he had cut. Of course, he had little or nothing to say, and all the previous thefts of cloth were attributed to him; in consequence he was put under arrest and confined in Tolbooth prison, for he had been found robbing an Edinburgh cloth factory.

The laws in those days were harsh, and often the penalty for stealing was hanging. One can imagine the state of mind of the wretched tailor as he lay in prison awaiting trial; though he had been able to retain the cap and pewter plate, his anxiety and confusion of mind had banished all memory of the words of the widow's rhyme—all he could do was revile her, and his own foolish curiosity as to how she had obtained the cloth. The day of his trial arrived, and, in view of the total amount of cloth that had been gradually stolen from the factory, he was found guilty and sentenced to be hung—his protests were useless for he was judged to be a stranger, a rogue, and a thief, and his death would act as a warning to others.

As he lay in gaol awaiting the day of his execution he was in despair, and his only hope, though of the faintest, was that he might recall the rhyme—desperately he tried and sometimes a few of the words returned to his mind but with all his efforts he failed to recall the complete rhyme. The day of execution arrived and he was led out to the scaffold erected in the market place, for public execution was supposed, in those days, to act as a deterrent to possible evil-doers. A large crowd of sightseers had surrounded the scaffold when Alexander stood near the gallows. An official read out aloud to the crowd a list of the supposed crimes of the poor tailor, who was then asked if he wished to say anything before paying the penalty of his crimes.

Poor Alexander advanced to the edge of the scaffold with the intention of warning the assembly against the dangers arising from the exercise of too much curiosity, then, before he could utter a word, the words of the rhyme came into his head. Plucking from his bosom the black velvet cap, and putting it on his head, he pulled the plate from his pocket and began to turn it, saying the rythme through correctly while turning it. The onlookers stood amazed as he rapidly repeated the rhyme a second, then a third time, but they were then more amazed to see him rise in the air, higher and higher, and then disappear.

'A good story, Donald,' said I. 'How much of that story originated in your own head?' Donald was indignant and said: 'It is true, for Alexander arrived at his own place after disappearing for some weeks from the widow's house among the hills; and the piece of the scaffold on which he had stood came with him. If you don't believe me you can go to Milton where Flora Macdonald was born, and there you will find a bedstead which was made from that very piece of scaffold. Prince Charlie slept on it while staying on this island.' We did our best to mollify poor Donald, for he was evidently very proud of this adventure attributed to one of his forefathers.*

* This story belongs to Gaelic folklore. See *Stories from South Uist*, p. 101, where Angus MacLellan tells the same story of a crofter from Kintail; he learnt it from Allan MacDonald, Peninerine, South Uist.

Chapter Eighteen

MRS ROBERTSON, the schoolmistress from Eriskay, with her little daughter, had left with the intention of settling among her relations and friends in Edinburgh. A young schoolmaster in London had been appointed to take up duty in her stead, at which I was delighted, and I looked forward eagerly to his arrival. The building of the house for the the priest was nearly completed,* and Father Allan was eager to go and live among, and minister to the poor island fishing folk. One Sunday I found at Father Allan's house on our island a new priest, who was introduced to me by Father Allan as his successor. He was a tall dark man with a gentle kind manner and I took to him at once: indeed, he softened my regret for Father Allan's imminent departure. Soon after I had resigned my post at Garrynamonie School, I learnt that this gentle but heroic priest had given his life for his flock: a severe epidemic of fever broke out and when the people, panic-stricken at the number of deaths, feared to tend the sick, Father Rigg devoted himself to waiting personally upon the patients, nursing them, feeding and comforting them with unsparing and unceasing devotion till the epidemic subsided. Then he who had saved so many lives, weakened by his indefatigable efforts and want of sleep, fell a victim to the fever and died.†

The thought of soon having a young colleague from England aroused in me feelings of great pleasure, and when I heard that he was expected to arrive at Lochboisdale by the afternoon's boat on the following Monday, I was full of joyful anticipation. Monday came and we kept a good look-out in the afternoon for

* In 1891.
† Father Rigg died on 15th August 1897; Father Allan wrote a Gaelic elegy on him, as did Donald MacCormick and Donald Patterson.

any stranger on the road. Night came and the postman; I asked for news of the new schoolmaster and was told definitely that he had not come by the boat. Feeling very disappointed, I nevertheless determined to be patient and to expect him by the next boat, as his train might have been late for the first. All Tuesday and Wednesday I had someone on the look-out but could gain no news of him—the postman told me on Wednesday night that no one had heard anything of him since he left London six days before. When Thursday came with no news of him I was anxious. Early on Friday morning I had been scanning the main road to the north when I saw a solitary figure appear on the skyline about a mile and a half away. With the aid of a field-glass I made out the figure of a stranger carrying a large package or portmanteau, and I hoped it would turn out to be my new colleague. At intervals I went out again to see if he were still approaching my school on the hill: his progress was slow but undoubtedly he was approaching. When he was nearer, my doubts as to his identity disappeared—a London man! Smartly cut and well-fitting clothes, white starched shirt and collar, stylish homburg hat! Running out of my gate and across the brae I jumped from the high bank on to the road before him, extended my hand and said: 'Welcome!' He dropped his heavy portmanteau on the road and shook hands. 'I have been looking out for you all the week!' exclaimed I. 'Where have you been?' 'All round the map!' said he.

Taking up his baggage in my hands, for he had walked the six miles from the pier and was tired, I said: 'Come along, and you can tell me all about it later.'

After a good meal we talked—or at least I led him on to talk, for I enjoyed listening to the familiar English accent. He told me that he had left London on the previous Friday night reaching Glasgow on the Saturday morning. He had intended taking a train from there to Oban, the railway terminus whence I myself had gone on board the steamer during my first journey north—this steamer left at six o'clock on the Monday morning for Lochboisdale. While in Glasgow he heard that a steamer left the Clyde every Monday morning for Lochboisdale so he saw no necessity for going further than Glasgow by rail. He spent the rest of the weekend there enjoying the sights of this great Scottish city, and on the Monday morning went on board the S.S. *Dunara Castle*. The shipping of the Clyde, the glorious scenery of Bute, Arran, and the Argyllshire coast so entranced him that it was well on in the day before he inquired for the time they were due in Lochboisdale. 'Early Friday morning,' was the reply! Friday, and he had expected to be in Lochboisdale that afternoon, Monday!

The *Dunara Castle* was a cargo boat calling at nearly all the islands of the Inner and the Outer Hebrides, even at St Kilda, and our Lochboisdale was almost the last port of call; so my friend arrived in port early on Friday morning when no one expected him. We arranged for him to stay with us till the next day. Much of mutual interest we found to discuss, and it was very late that night when we retired to rest. Next day he and I walked south to Pollachar inn, where I introduced him to my friends. The ferryman from Eriskay happened to be there; and this was fortunate, for I knew that my new friend would be now in good hands. Shortly after, I saw him off in the ferryboat, and started for home.

Nearing my house I heard gunshots at intervals, and wondered. Soon I located the origin of the sound; two men were beside the loch shooting at wild duck. I stood and watched them as hiding behind rocks they worked their way alongside the loch; then came a flurry of birds on the wing, shots, and a dog would dash out into the water, swim out, and return carrying a bird in his mouth. After watching a little, I continued my way home and saw a dogcart from Lochboisdale hotel standing near my house. As I approached my gate there came towards me a young lady in tweed sporting costume—short cloth skirt, well-fitting jacket with belt, tweed hat in which was stuck a black cock's feather, and strong brogue shoes. 'Are you the schoolmaster?' said she. On my acknowledging the fact she asked if we could supply some hot water, as her father and his friend were shooting in the neighbourhood and they would soon be returning to her for lunch. This was contained in a small hamper to which she pointed, at the same time apologizing for troubling me. Asking her to wait a moment I consulted with my mother, who at once invited her into our sitting-room; I carried in the hamper, and the table was soon laid and chairs placed ready round it.

While we waited for the sportsmen, my mother, Miss D - - -

and I conversed. Her father was a clergyman from London, and his friend was a celebrated doctor from Edinburgh—they had rented the shooting of the south end of our island and were putting up at Lochboisdale hotel. Very soon afterwards they appeared, so I explained the situation, and they came in to lunch without delay. They were very pleased with their sport, and after lunch we all sat and enjoyed an animated conversation. The keen professional eye of the medical man noted the delicate state of health of my mother; he was most sympathetic and kind to her. When they departed I found a brace of duck behind the front door: evidently left in acknowledgment of our little act of hospitality.

I had heard that during the week Father Allan had gone over to Eriskay and was settled there.* Wishing to see him and my young colleague from London again, I went over in the ferryboat the next weekend. The priest and my schoolmaster friend were at the 'Haun' when I landed; they had come to meet the ferryman, who had been to our island to fetch the mail bags which came overland from Lochboisdale to the inn at Pollachar. Both welcomed me, but Father Allan soon went off visiting the different houses, after inviting me and my friend to dinner with him at his new house so recently erected.

I accompanied my friend to the post-office for he was anxious for letters. The post-office was just an ordinary thatched house, and Dougall MacMillan the bearded postmaster was dressed like the fishermen. That my companion and he were already good friends was evident: it was: 'Dougall, have you any letters for me?' and a few joking words spoken in English by Dougall as he handed a few letters and parcels over to my friend. I carried the parcels as the latter read his letters on the way to his schoolhouse. 'Good old London!' he exclaimed once or twice, and I said in joke: 'Let's go to the "Tivoli" tonight,' at which he made rather a wry face.

When we duly arrived at the priest's house for dinner we were surprised to find the table set outside against a wall on the lee side of the house; while a large bucket stood on stones and contained the fire. In explanation our host said, as though it were to himself a matter of small concern: 'I cannot have a fire in

* This took place in January 1894. As chairman of the school board he continued to visit Garrynamonie school until April 1894.

any room of the house, for the wind blows down the chimneys and drives the smoke and fire into the room. So we will have dinner here, for you will be cold in the house without a fire.' Before many weeks had passed, a system of cowls was fitted to the chimneys, and the smoke nuisance abated. *

Early in the afternoon we three went for a walk and on reaching an eminence I noticed a large boat in full sail about three miles away coming towards us from Barra. On my calling attention to it Father Allan said: 'That will be the fishing-girls returning from the fisheries on the mainland; I know they are expected today.' We stopped there a minute or so to fill and light our pipes, and I happened to glance out again towards where we had seen the boat. There was no sign of it. 'Where's the boat?' I called out. Not a boat was in sight. Father Allan said: 'Something has gone wrong!' and we hurried off for help. In an incredibly short time boats were launched, and a search for the missing boat commenced, and was continued throughout the rest of the day and all that night. The boat and its occupants were never seen again. It was surmised that a sudden short unexpected squall of wind had struck and capsized her and she had sunk like a stone.†

I the better understood now the attitude of inimical fear of the sea that I had sensed at times among the people.

* But was never entirely got rid of.

† Mr Donald MacDonald, M.A., tells me that this fatal accident took place on the feast of the Epiphany, but he is not sure in what year. Two men and two women were lost. The cause was a sudden strong gust of wind off Ben Stack.

Chapter Nineteen

ANDREW MACELFRISH, the clerk of the school board had intimated to the head teachers of the several schools that, should they wish to hold evening classes for adults during the coming winter, arrangements for doing so would be made.

I and my schoolmaster friends consulted together, and, having agreed on our respective curricula and arrangements, we notified the clerk, and each of us began to prepare for opening 'A Night School'.

At once I announced to the children in school during the day that evening classes would be held for their brothers and sisters who had reached the age of eighteen years, and that I invited all prospective evening school pupils to attend a dance at the school on the following Friday evening. I shall never forget that dance! I had engaged a special piper who came from a distance but who was very popular at all weddings and parties—he was said to be the best player of reels on the island. Donald the piper arrived in a small pony trap. (The name 'Donald' was very common: indeed, I once had seven 'Donald Macdonalds' in my day school at a time.) All was ready for the dance in school: the benches were ranged in double rows round the walls of the main room, lamps were lighted, and a classroom had been prepared for refreshments. It was a dark night so I could not conjecture how many had assembled outside the walls, but I could hear subdued voices in the darkness and, occasionally, the scrape af heavy boots on stones.

I took Donald into my house to 'sort the pipes', as he said. He told me that he had not been to bed for three nights, as he had been playing at three weddings and had just come from the last one, which had taken place on a neighbouring island. On my suggesting a rest he laughed, and said: 'Ach! That's ahreet, Mr Rea; I shall do fine!' at the same time wiping his mouth. I took this as a hint, so poured out a small dram of whisky and was going to add water when he said: 'Never mind that. I like it dry,' and tossed off the neat spirit.

When he had put his pipes in order he started to play, stood up, marched out of the room, through the hall, out at the front door, and round to the school door which some hand opened for him, the pipes, with ribbons flying, blaring a march. Still playing, he advanced into the school, followed by a motley crowd of young men and girls who had been waiting outside in the darkness. Up and down the middle of the floor of the main room he marched, playing away, while the crowds of young people filled the benches, men on one side of the room, the girls on the other. When all seemed there, the piper halted at one end of the room, still playing the march which he had commenced in my house and had continued playing without pause till now.

Suddenly the air he was playing was changed into a kind of wail, and immediately all the young men sprang from the benches to the floor and formed a long line down the room. While the wailing air of the pipe was continued the men looked deliberately along the line of girls on the benches, and then hooked a finger to the girl of their choice, who demurely came from the bench and stood on the floor facing the man who had beckoned. Several times it happened that a girl showed reluctance to respond to the man's invitation, and to my surprise he would dash across and haul her out of her place, she sometimes looking finally quite dishevelled. The piper seeing that each at last had a partner immediately changed to a rousing reel tune. At once more than a hundred pairs of feet shod in heavy boots were thudding on the floor in some step of the reel, but all in time: all faces devoid of a smile, serious as though dancing was a business, the men looking upwards, and the girls with down-cast eyes. The rhythm of the tune changed with an increase in time. With a loud yell the men now danced together in pairs— they whirled and sprang in a mad dance till, when they were pouring with perspiration, Donald slowed down his tune; it died away and the dancers were glad to rest—Donald knew his work!

I was utterly ignored by the company: all were absorbed in

the pleasure of dancing in a large room with a good floor, and to the music of Donald's playing; and, when he shortly recommenced, the floor was soon filled and another reel was danced. Hour after hour passed and reel followed reel almost without pause till I wondered that they were not exhausted, especially the piper; but, they danced on, apparently as fresh as ever. I fancy they had danced fourteen or fifteen reels on end when I approached Donald and put my hand on his shoulder. He stopped playing and I asked him to tell them in Gaelic that there would be an interval for refreshments. He did, and while tea and cake were served to the girls in the classroom, the men fared similarly in the main room. In half an hour the piper began to 'tune up' and the dancers returned, keen to resume; but I now took the opportunity to address them briefly regarding the evening school, and invited them to enrol on the Monday evening following. At my request Donald repeated in Gaelic what I had said; but, though they all appeared to listen, there was no response by word or look.

The dance went on into early morning, reel succeeding reel as though there were no other dance, and I strongly suspected this to be the only dance they knew. After many more dances Donald suddenly ceased playing, stood up and said something in Gaelic at which all flocked out of the school.

I now took Donald to my house for refreshment, and left him while I went to the school to put out the lights and to lock up. When I returned to the house he was missing though I saw his pony and trap at the gate. I waited, but he did not appear, so I searched around the buildings by the light of a lantern, but there was no sign of him. Assuring myself that the pony and trap were still there I went into the house again and sat down to wait. I must have dozed, for how long, I cannot say, but I woke at hearing some sound outside. Thinking it might be Donald I went to the gate. Dawn was breaking and I saw the pony-trap still there waiting. Then I saw a figure staggering towards me—it was Donald! He had evidently been imbibing somewhere and could scarcely stand. I went to him saying: 'Donald! Donald! Where have you been? Come into the house and I will make some coffee.' 'Wheest! Mr Rea. I'm ahreet,' he answered; but when he reached the trap and tried to get in, he stumbled and fell on the floor of it. I went forward to help him up, but the pony started off, with Donald on the floor and the door of the trap swinging open. Standing at the gate I saw the trap bump over the ground across the ditch on to the road, and then I heard the fast clatter of the pony's hoofs along the road, the sound dying quickly away in the distance. 'Poor Donald!' I mused. 'No sleep for four nights! No doubt someone gave you whisky and it's no wonder that it overcame you. But I wonder what will happen on the road to you, the pony and the trap!'

Two days later I met the pony-trap on the road which led to the pier, and Donald was driving. Pulling up, he hailed me cheerily. I went to him and said: 'Donald, how on earth did you get home from the dance?' 'Oh! Fine!' said he. Then he bent down and said: 'You see I met three good companions on the road and they saw me right.' 'I am glad,' said I, for I had been anxious. 'Who were they?' Donald straightened up, saying, as he did so: 'Father, Son and Holy Ghost.' He flourished his whip and off he drove quite happily.

Through some of my early talks with Father Allan and others I had learned that many of the young fellows from Uist went to sea as ordinary ship's hands, but made little or no progress owing to their lack of opportunity for receiving instruction. With the wish to help I had sent for text-books and instruments; for many months I had been seriously studying the science of navigation and had found the subject most congenial. I also seized every opportunity that offered of learning as much as possible of the theory and practice of seamanship so that, by the time the question of evening classes arose, I had well covered the advanced stage of the subject including nautical astronomy. In consequence, in drawing up my curriculum for the evening classes, I included navigation as a special subject for the men, with needlework for the girls.

To my surprise, when I opened the evening classes on the Monday and told them of the proposed curriculum, the utmost enthusiasm was shown among the men on my reference to the subject of navigation. I found that quite a number of them had been on long voyages but none were qualified to act as able-seamen or to take the wheel of a vessel—they did not thoroughly understand a ship's compass. I showed them the one I had provided for teaching purposes, binnacle and all; I took it to pieces and briefly explained its construction and working. I was delighted with the keen interest aroused in every man present, and thoroughly enjoyed answering their questions on the subject. The following evening many more men joined the classes; these were of a different type from those who had attended the dance in the school—older, more serious and respectful in their demeanour, and I judged these to be sailors of experience who were anxious to learn more of the science of their calling. The progress made by the class in this subject amazed me, and I had to extend the syllabus. The general keen interest was sustained throughout the winter's session, and before the close some of the older sailors said that they had learned enough to enable them to take the examination held in Glasgow for granting the Mate's Certificate. As a matter of fact, I heard later that quite a number of these men gained the certificate and were serving as Mate on board ocean-going vessels sailing from Glasgow. They were all fine fellows and deserved whatever success they attained.

Most of these young men pursued the herring fishing round the coasts of the islands. They generally worked in crews of five, six or seven. When opportunity served a crew would club their money together to buy a second-hand boat and nets. If it were a crew of five and the total cost were, say, £40, they would subscribe according to the means or desires of each; perhaps one gave £15, another £10 and the other three £6, £5, and £4. At the end of the season all profits were shared among them, according to the number of shares each held, in this case, forty shares among the five men giving 15, 10, 6, 5 and 4 shares respectively. As the herring from these waters fetched a high price, the shares often represented a considerable sum of money.

The presence of whales always denoted herring, the shoals of which they pursued. * Whenever herring were reported many of the young men attending my class would be absent an evening, and they generally sent word that they had gone after the herring. I, of course, understood, and would ask them next evening what success they met with—we always had the spirit of mutual help. One day herring was reported, so I expected a depleted men's class that evening. The wind began to rise in the afternoon, and by the time the hour for opening the evening classes

* The whales 'pursued' the plankton on which both they and the herring fed.

arrived a furious gale was blowing from the north-west. Very few pupils from the south townships arrived, and the few who did were very late, for they had to battle against a fierce head-wind. After opening school I had occasion to go round to my house to fetch a book and had great difficulty in preventing myself from being blown past my house door. Securing my book I braced myself so as to meet the wind on my way back to the school. Such bracing was not necessary—the wind, as strong as ever, was blowing from the opposite direction, south-east. I was blown right past the school door, across the playground and up against its north wall. I regained my breath and crawled on my hands and knees to the schoolroom door.

The gale had subsided by morning. The ground for fifty yards around as far as the main road was strewn with slates torn from the roof of the school and house.

When school assembled next evening an atmosphere of restraint and quiet prevailed over all, and I sensed that something was wrong. Looking round I saw that most of the absentees of the previous evening were present; then I missed a few of the men, including perhaps my best student, Donald Macdonald, a fine fellow in every way, a man about thirty, stalwart, with quiet manners, very intelligent, and looked up to by the whole school. I asked where he was, and the answer was: 'We don't know!' Alexander Campbell, a big red-haired man, who with his brothers owned a fishing boat, then stood up. He told me that his boat along with others went out the previous day to catch herring on the east side of the island. A north-west gale sprang up in the afternoon, and they ran the boats into a deep inlet of the sea, and recast their nets there. Macdonald and his crew of four cast their herring nets near Campbell's boat intending to stay there the night and ride out the gale. Suddenly the wind dropped, and then blew at full force from the south-east—they were on a lee-shore; so they cut their nets, ran for the open sea, and reached home after a night of peril. Macdonald's boat had not returned by morning, so the other boats had been out all that day searching for it, but had found no trace. Campbell said the last he saw of the missing boat was when he cut his nets adrift, and saw Macdonald and his crew trying to haul their nets on board to save them. Those five evening school pupils I never saw again. After three days had been spent in searching and the sea had calmed, the outlines of a boat were seen lying in twelve fathoms of water. A diver descended to the boat and discovered four bodies entangled in the nets. That of the skipper, Macdonald, who was a powerful swimmer, was missing. A month later his body was found on the shore of one of the islands of the Inner Hebrides. Poor Donald Macdonald, we all missed you sorely and grieved for your loss!

The neighbours related that Donald had been most averse to going out with the boat that day, but he was overpersuaded by the other men, so being the skipper of the boat, he at last reluctantly consented. Whether his reluctance was due to mistrust of the weather, or to the fact that he was due that evening to visit the girl whom he was to marry, was never known. The girl lived with her father and mother, and it was the custom for Donald to visit her on a certain night every week, an appointment he had never failed to keep. If he should be late he always knocked at the window with three sharp taps. Before setting out for the fishing this last time he saw her and promised to return as soon as possible that night, saying he would be sure to visit her at the house however late his return.

When the storm arose she became anxious, and more so as night came on and the wind increased in strength. She and her parents sat all evening listening to the howling of the wind; suddenly they heard Donald's three sharp taps on the window. The girl hastened to open the door to welcome her lover, but no one entered, for no one was there. With lanterns they searched round the house without finding anyone. Her parents retired to rest, but the girl sat all night waiting for the lover who never came.

When the full particulars of the tragedy reached her, the shock was almost too much for the poor girl. I know she was ill for a long time.*

* This happened in 1906–07. The school log book reads:
5th November: 'The Evening Classes commenced this evening—51 present. Very few of the older pupils are in attendance—most of them are prosecuting the fishing which has had a record season, locally, this year.'
21st November: '68 on Evening Classes rolls, but more expected if fishing ceases.'
23rd January: 'Evening Classes conducted as usual this week; but the attendance has decreased—perhaps a report that a boat's crew containing five of last season's pupils of this school, from S. Lochboisdale had been lost at sea, and of which no trace had been found from Monday up till tonight, may account for this. There is gloom on the whole district.'

30th January: 'Exceptionally bad weather. The worst fears regarding the boat's crew of five young men (formerly pupils of this school) have been realized—the sunken boat has been located, and two of the bodies, those of Angus Gillies and Hugh MacDonald, have been recovered.'

The name of the boat was the *Cheerful*, and the accident took place near the island of Stuley. The body of the skipper was found afterwards on the Isle of Skye. He had been warned by a seer not to go out on that night, so Peggy MacRae tells me.

Chapter Twenty

TWO of my brothers were sergeants in a line regiment stationed in the Tower of London, and at the schoolhouse we learned that they intended spending their Christmas leave with us in our island home. Soldierlike they regarded as mere details the discomforts of the long winter journey north. Arrived at Oban after a day and a night of railway travelling they found the mail boat disabled by the winter gales, so boarded a tugboat from the Clyde that was making a trip to South Uist. Fourteen hours on this powerful but small vessel—constantly washed by the heavy seas. With the only shelter the captain's tiny cuddy, in which three persons formed a crowd, did not serve to lessen their ardour. They found that the only other passenger was a little white-haired old man, the Bishop of Argyll and the Isles, on a visit to the missions in the Outer Hebrides. Crowded together in the tiny cabin and pitched about by the rolling vessel, these three kept cheerful nevertheless, and contrived to pass the time with interest in each other and the recounting of their various experiences.

My brothers arrived at the schoolhouse late at night, wet and hungry, yet bright and cheerful at the prospect of spending their brief holiday with us in our new surroundings, all so novel to anyone accustomed to English town life. Our household was a merry one that night with no shadow of the future to dim our happiness. Now the bones of the elder of these two soldier brothers lie in the sands of Egypt near Omdurman!

In the night the wind rose to a gale, but its booming did not disturb any of us, for my mother and I had grown used to it and my two brothers were too tired to give any heed. But I was afforded some amusement by the latter the next morning after breakfast. A strong steady wind was blowing from the south-west, so I bet that they could not get round the gable end of the schoolhouse. They accepted the challenge at once. I laughed at their ineffectual efforts: the moment they reached the corner of the house the wind met them, and they went staggering back till brought up by the garden wall. Time after time they tried, and it was amusing to see their different tactics—one would go to the corner then make a mad dash to get round; the other tried to crawl round on all fours, but all their efforts were in vain. We retired indoors, they laughingly acknowledging their powerlessness against a Hebridean wind.

As the morning advanced, the gale increased, and we saw men throwing ropes over the roofs of their cottages and hanging great stones from the ropes to prevent the thatched roofs from being blown away. Before long a hurricane was blowing, and from my house on the hill we saw the giant rollers of the Atlantic rise higher and higher, mounting behind the hill of the island off the western shore, up, up, higher still, and we, watching, speculated as to whether these unbroken rollers would rise as high as the hill on the island, at least a hundred feet in height; but soon the long line of sea not only rose as high as the hill, but mounted far higher, and we saw the whole sea-line behind the island rise till it seemed almost to reach the clouds. Then we saw what I had never seen before, nor did I ever see it afterwards: the wind whipped off the top of these rollers, and this water was twisted about and whirled upwards to the clouds above, till there appeared from south to north along the horizon for many miles a continuous line of columns of water being swirled up into the black clouds—water-spouts!

It was a full week before the seas subsided; Uist people told me afterwards that it was the worst storm they could remember.

One of the evenings Catriona's brother came to see me. He told me that a friend of his intended marriage, and I and my two brothers were invited to the 'Réiteach' or 'Contract'. I had but a very vague idea of what this term meant, so judging it to be some kind of island ceremony we accepted for the next evening, Sandy saying that he would call for us. The invitation had come from a widow whose family, consisting of a son and five daughters, ranged in age from eighteen to thirty years; the intended bride was the youngest daughter of this family.

I was rather interested, as well as amused, at learning that the Uist people were very careful as to what family they married into. I was told that the Mac - - X - s were sly, the Mac - - Y - s were wild, the A - - - - s bad tempered, the Mac - - Z - s were liars, and so on, and no one would marry into a family whose ancestors had ever done a bad turn to theirs.

Sandy duly called for us the next evening, and I with my two brothers accompanied him across the braes to the widow's house. With solemn decorum we were motioned to take seats on a bench beside a long table, near the end further away from the fireplace. At this end of the table sat two men, one brown-bearded about fifty years of age, the other, seated beside him, considerably younger, and clean-shaven with the exception of a dark moustache. Round the fire were gathered the widow and her family, and at the end of the table near them sat a huge man whom I knew well, the brother of the widow. I felt rather ill at ease for there seemed to be two camps, Sandy, I, my brothers, and the two silent men at our end of the table forming one group, while the others formed a whispering group near the other end.

Then there came a dead silence which seemed to be a signal, for the bearded man at our end stood up and, in a mixture of English and Gaelic, began a eulogy of the younger man beside him. He spoke of his companion's strength, his skill with a boat, of his knowledge of farming, and his success as a fisherman; he praised the man's parents and forefathers and their achievements. He then intimated that his friend asked for the hand of the youngest daughter in marriage, and wanted to know what would be given along with her in the way of dowry. He then sat down, and the widow's brother stood up and eulogized the girl, her family, her qualities, honest, clean, kind, and so on. Then followed a contest between these two men as to what would be given with the girl, one trying to obtain as much as possible, and the other endeavouring to part with as little as possible. As far as I can remember a bargain was made at last that a stack of corn, a calf and some fowls should be given with the girl.

All this time these two men had held the field, and no one else had spoken a word: the would-be bridegroom had sat with bent head and downcast eyes throughout, while I and my two brothers had sat and listened with very mixed feelings. At this stage the widow's brother left the table and joined the group at the fire, whence there then ensued much emphatic talk but in subdued voices; we sat at the table in silence. Eventually the man from the group at the fire returned to the table and announced that the girl refused the offer of marriage, but that her eldest sister would be willing to accept it. The spokesman at our end bent down and consulted the would-be bridegroom, who looked up for the first time, nodded, and said: 'Ach, aye! It's all the same.' Immediately all came and stood round the table; a bottle and a wine-glass were produced; and, in turn, each drank to the health of the pair who in due course were to be married. We three brothers wished them every happiness, shook hands all round, and left for home talking over this experience of a 'Réiteach' or 'Contract'.

My brothers were great football players, one of them played in his regimental team; they had brought a ball with them on their visit to the island, but the weather had been too wild for football. When the first good day came, the ball was fetched out and blown up in my sitting-room, our united efforts with our lungs producing a fairly tight ball. We adjourned to the garden for a game, but a smashed window pane soon made us desist. We then went on the brae in front of the schoolhouse. Sandy espied us and stood there grinning. We invited him to join us; but he had never seen a football before and was nervous. I kicked the ball towards him and told him to kick it back; he walked to it, looked at it, and stood and grinned again—I don't know if he thought it would hurt him if he kicked it, but he stood there looking most embarrassed while we stood laughing at him. I went to him and gently kicked the ball two or three times with my toe; then I put it by his feet and told him to do the same. Very gingerly he touched it with the toe of his heavy boot. 'Good!' said I, retreating a few steps. 'Send it to me'; which he did but very gently. After he had watched us three giving the ball some hefty kicks he gained courage and joined us, we played a two-a-side game, with Sandy most enthusiastic but observant of the rules about handling the ball. I saw two young fellows at a distance furtively watching us; so I called to them to come over to us. They came very sheepishly for they had never seen a ball like ours; but I suppose they thought: 'If Sandy can do it, so can we,' and they were soon thoroughly enjoying the game.

It was holiday time, so, as the ground of the braes was uneven and rocky, we proposed to have a game next day on the hard sandy levels of the machair, where Sandy and the two others promised to meet us early the next afternoon. My brothers and I became very busy in the preparation of goal-posts—these had to be light enough for us to carry down to the machair. We had them all ready in time, and we three sallied forth, bearing the poles and ball. After descending from the house on the hill, we before long came in sight of the machair, its level sands stretching for miles along the western seaboard. The machair seemed deserted, but we soon espied three solitary figures, evidently our three football companions of the previous day, waiting for us. Reaching them we set to work pacing out our pitch and fixing the goal-posts. No one else was in sight, so we chose our teams of three-a-side and kicked off.

We had been playing for about five minutes when a number of figures appeared on the machair advancing towards us; more and more appeared on the sky-line coming from various directions, scores of them. Sandy had given the ball a mighty kick towards the opposite goal and dashed after the ball, when the foremost of the newcomers rushed forward and reached it first. He picked up the ball, ran with it, then kicked it in the air. My younger brother trapped it as it fell, and we hastily chose and arranged our two elevens from those of the newcomers. They seemed to understand Sandy's explanation of the game, and that no one was to handle the ball but the one in charge of the goal. The game restarted and all went well for a few minutes till the newcomer players became excited—then they would rush at the man who had the ball, catch hold of his coat and hold him, while another player of his side got the ball: the opposing men then rushed at this player and rolled him over while he lay clutching at the ball. By this time more men had arrived on the scene, and seething with excitement they joined in the game. My brothers and I stood aside shaking with laughter, for there were now fifty a side at least; some were tearing about the field looking for the ball or rushing at each other, while in another part of the field a mass of men were rolling over each other, one of them wildly clutching the ball; if the ball came into sight again the excitement waxed furious, and the whole hundred or so of men would dash after it, throwing each other down, tearing at each other, all in a mad effort to get the ball. Fortunately the ball came towards me, and I put my foot on it, held up my hand, and called out: 'A mach!' ('Go'). Perhaps hearing me pronouncing Gaelic sobered them, for they all stopped and I told them quietly that the game was over. Several helped with the goal-posts, and we reached home thankful that no casualties had occurred.

News travelled fast on South Uist. The next day was Sunday, and as we proceeded on our favourite walk to church in the morning, we passed several groups of men chatting away in Gaelic as they walked along. Several times I heard them say 'Fooot-baal' and I guessed that they were discussing the episode of the previous day. Outside the church were more groups of men from its immediate neighbourhood talking together as was their wont before service commenced; again we heard the words 'Fooot-baal'. Father Rigg was at his house door and invited my brothers and me into his house. He had heard of our having a football, and said that he had been very fond of the game in his college days; so he made a suggestion that we should bring a team from the south end of the island, and he would provide an eleven to give us a game on the machair after service in church on New Year's Day.

The few days intervening gave us time to choose eight other young fellows and to coach them in the rules of the game, with also a little practice in their respective positions, my brothers and I playing forward. On New Year's Day we found that Father Rigg had been as good as his word, for he had not only provided goal-posts but had had them erected and also provided flags on sticks to mark out the playing pitch. In his team were two other priests from further north, a college student on vacation, two clerks from the factor's estate office, the young accountant from the bank, and four stalwart young fishermen. He had obtained as referee a captain of the Cameron Highlanders who was staying at the Lochboisdale hotel.

When we arrived on the ground we were surprised at the number of people already assembled, practically all men, young, middle-aged, and aged, from all parts for miles around. While the crowds were being cleared from the playing pitch I noticed my old friend MacKay, the retired schoolmaster; we shook hands and he sniffed as much as to say 'What new-fangled idea is this!' Then arrived Father Allan, who had crossed from Eriskay, and who insisted on helping our team from the south. He was chosen for our goalkeeper and right gallantly did he perform.

We had a delightful game; the crowds remained outside the playing pitch; the teams played to the referee's whistle, and it was a lesson in restraint to the many young fellows who had followed us from our end of the island. The game ended in a victory for the south by three goals to one. Of course, we had an advantage in that we three brothers had often played together and understood each other's play; so, if my brother on the left wing were tackled by several opponents, he swung the ball to me in the centre where I made ahead for goal, and, if pressed, I tapped the ball to my other brother on the right wing, thus combining our play; whereas the opposing side were individualists who, though good players and full of energy, wasted much effort. I saw my old schoolmaster after the match and he sighed as he wagged his sage head and said: 'Ach, aye! But you and your brothers understand the game,' and off he went without further word.

Rather tired after the football match and the walk home, we enjoyed a good meal and a rest with a talk afterwards. I was rather pleased at the way the sport of football had been received by the local people; so I began to make plans for encouraging the boys of the day school, and the young men of the evening school, to develop a taste for healthy sport. One of my brothers had taken a first class certificate at the Aldershot School of Physical Training, consequently I sought his advice. After much discussion we evolved suitable courses for me to adopt. In the way of apparatus I decided to get a joiner to make a set of parallel-bars in accordance with my brother's specification. Also both my brothers promised to send me footballs, sets of single-sticks, boxing-gloves, also a few other items.

We were retiring to rest late that night when there were sounds of my garden gate being opened, and also of steps on the shingle with which the garden paths were covered; there was a knock at the door. It was a pitch-black night so that when I opened the door I could see nothing at first. Then a man's gruff voice said something in Gaelic and, by the reflected light from the kitchen, I made out the heavily bearded faces of two big men. 'Here!' said one, thrusting something into my arms,

and the other thrust something else at me; they then disappeared
without further word and I heard the gate shut behind them.
I called to my brothers to bring a light for I could not tell what
the men had brought. To our surprise we found that they had
thrust two huge black lobsters upon me, the largest we had
ever seen.

It was late and we did not know what to do with them for
the night. Then one of us suggested the largest wash-tub from
the outside of the house. Having fetched it, by careful manœuvring, and amid much laughter, we managed to get the formid-
able-looking creatures into the tub. I was awakened in the
morning by cries and a commotion downstairs. Hurrying down,
I found the girl who brought the morning milk from the farm
dancing on her bare legs around the kitchen. She was terrified
at the two lobsters which had escaped from the wash-tub and
were careering round the kitchen—as I have mentioned before
in an earlier chapter, theft was practically unknown on the
island, so no one ever thought of locking doors at night, so if we
were not about in the early morning the girl always came in
and placed the milk on the kitchen table. When my brothers
and I had got the fearsome-looking crustaceans back into the
tub, the girl was able to join with us in a good laugh.

None of our saucepans or pots was large enough to take even
one of the lobsters, so we had to borrow a large cauldron from
Catriona, and even this would take only one of the shellfish.
We had considerable fun in getting it into the vessel of boiling
water. First one would try to lift it with a large pair of tongs
while its huge claws groped around, but it was heavy and it
would slip back into the tub; then the others tried, all keeping
a wary eye on the creature's formidable claws, but no one succeeded. Luckily, on going outside, I saw Sandy working on his
croft and I enlisted his help. He came into the kitchen with a
grin on his face. 'Ach! I'll soon sorrt him,' he said; and, stooping;
he seized one of the lobsters with his two big hands just behind
the creature's head, quickly carried it to the cauldron and
dropped it into the boiling water. A kind of screech came from
the lobster as it plunged into the water which made me, for one,
feel rather squeamish. By the time it was cooked, the shell had
changed in colour from a deep blue-black into a bright red and
the fish looked most appetizing. Our largest dish would not

hold it, but that did not matter as the claws alone were more than sufficient for our dinner. I have always been averse, and am so still, to eating shellfish, but I always remember that delicious fresh lobster—as my brothers remarked: 'No chance of ever getting a lobster like that at Billingsgate.'

Though there had been frequent storms during the winter, the climate of the island was quite mild; during my two winters there I had seen snow only twice, and that was on the top of Ben More, up some two thousand feet—the local people had exclaimed at seeing this, and remarked: 'See! She has on her white petticoat!' and they regarded the phenomenon as quite an event. The mildness of the climate was due, so I was told, to the proximity of the Gulf Stream to the Outer Hebrides. I found it to be cold only when the wind blew from the north; and then I realized the difference of latitude, and how much nearer to the Arctic ice-fields I was than when living in the Midlands of England. The air was very pure and healthy. Two doctors, retired from the navy, had taken a farm on one of the adjacent islands, and they declared that the air was the purest of any that they had ever analysed.

One calm night my brothers went out into the garden, and called me to join them, and, on my doing so, one of them said in an awed voice: 'Isn't it wonderful!' The word was justified. All was perfectly still; not a murmur came from the sea, no cry of bird nor bark of dog was heard, and there was a complete silence. Overhead the sky was a canopy of deep cobalt-blue. There was no moon, but myriads of stars shone so brightly in the clear air that by their light the whole landscape around us stood out in every detail to the south: the hills, the lochs, the road down to the sea, the sea itself with its islands placid and dark, the crofters' cots, and the inn by the shore. The stars did not appear to be *in* the sky but hanging from it like globular lamps, so that I remember my impulse was to raise my arms and to clasp my hands around them, as would be the urge had they been beautiful scintillating diamond balls. Silently one of us fetched our mother to share in the beauteous scene; she was soon as rapt as we were.

On our looking north there was not a star to be seen, but a huge black curtain of brooding cloud lay across the horizon for many miles from east to west, shutting out all beyond. As we watched wonderingly, a wave of light crossed this dark curtain like a beam from some gigantic search-light sweeping from east to west, a distance of, perhaps, fifty miles; again and again this light wave swept backwards and forwards across the black cloud; then the top edge of the dark curtain of cloud became tinged with crimson as though an enormous fire were burning behind it and were reflected at the top edge. Streaks of light now flashed upwards and then downwards on the black barrier of cloud; brilliant streamers of coruscations in different colours next appeared, till the whole brilliant spectacle resembled a mammoth fire-work display, but far transcending in splendour any such human effort.

Gradually as we gazed in silence, the brilliance of the lights began to wane, whilst the whole curtain seemed to pulsate; fainter and fainter became the manifestation, the waves of light fewer and slower, till at last they ceased altogether, and nothing remained but the silence, a dark cloud, and the star lamps in the dome of the sky overhead.

We had seen the Aurora Borealis, the Northern Lights. All the world around us was wrapped in a mantle of calm as we silently entered the house and retired for the night, hushed by the marvellous phenomenon of nature we had witnessed.

Our holiday was nearly over, and my brothers' leave was running out when we received an invitation to attend a dance at the Lochboisdale hotel. As the invitation was written in the third person, on notepaper addressed from the hotel and signed by the hotel proprietor himself, I assumed that the affair was organized by him. Consequently I was curious as to the kind of evening we should spend, especially as I had never before attended any but the dances held in my own school for the benefit of the young people of our neighbourhood—incidentally, I should explain here that the behaviour at these school dances was now vastly improved since that which had inaugurated the opening of evening classes.

When we arrived at the pier hotel after our six-mile walk from my house, we found quite a number of vehicles there; the horses had been removed from them, and were probably in the stables, of which the hotel boasted not a few. All the hotel windows were lighted up and we three brothers were cordially received at the entrance hall by Mr and Mrs Bain, the proprietors. With very little delay we were shown into the long dining-room by their son, Duncan, and here we found quite a number of the guests had already arrived and were occupying chairs placed round the walls of the room. It was a very fine room, well carpeted, about sixty feet long, and had a lofty ceiling. A number of the guests were present whom I knew, and I introduced my brothers to them: the clergymen and their grown-up families, the banker, the factor or agent of the proprietor of the island, with their wives, also the doctor and his sister.

Several farmers from the large farms were there too with their grown-up sons and daughters, also the accountant, and the clerks from the bank and the estate office, besides others. The gallant captain of the Camerons, our football referee and one of the heroes of Dargai, was present also, and he looked fine in his kilt as he came forward to welcome the three of us. Altogether some thirty or forty guests were present; and, after a general introduction, dancing commenced; and well the assembly looked: the captain and several of the men in their tartan kilts, my brothers in their blue and scarlet uniforms, and the light-coloured dresses of the ladies giving a gay brightness to the scene. Though the only music for dancing was supplied by a piano—several ladies willingly presiding there in turn—I was happy to dance again the polka, the waltz, the quadrille, and the lancers, which were the dances in vogue when I had first left my native city to come to the Hebrides. At intervals, refreshments of cakes, sandwiches, oatcakes, cheese, coffee and wine were served by hotel servants from a long buffet which stood at one end of the room, and a few Scottish songs were rendered by lady guests. We three brothers were pressed to contribute items, and my elder brother who had a good baritone voice searched the music copies lying on the piano, and then rendered 'Cleansing Fires' in fine style. All I could do was to recite from Shakespeare—I think it was 'Wolsey's Farewell to Cromwell'— I remember Captain M- - - saying, as I afterwards sat down beside him: 'I would rather lead my men in a charge against the enemy than give a recitation.'

During a longish interval the men adjourned to the smoke-room. My brothers were engaged in the general conversation, so Duncan Bain and I sat in a corner and talked of local matters.

He had bought a row-boat from a Norwegian ship recently anchored in the harbour. He was very proud of it and invited me to go with him for a row in the loch whenever I liked. I had always been fond of sculling on the park pools of my native city, so I gladly accepted and promised to join him some fine Saturday.

Dancing was once again resumed, and it was kept up till the early hours when the company began to disperse, all expressing appreciation of the pleasurable time they had had. As the various vehicles were announced to be ready for their respective parties, my brothers were much amused, for each vehicle was called a 'machine', whether trap, wagonette, or governess-cart; it was 'Mr - - - , your machine is ready', each time. We three had a lift in one 'machine'* to the cross-roads, and we were then half-way home; when we reached it we were tired out but happy. My elder brother was not too weary to announce that he should go to the pier again next day. He had noticed a baker's shop near the hotel, and said that a change from our usual scones and oatcakes to 'loaf bread' would be good for us. Off he went soon after breakfast the next morning, and he returned some time later with a couple of new loaves. For the rest of his stay with me, whatever the weather he never failed to fetch two loaves on alternate days, though this meant for him a walk of twelve miles. I, of course, had long ago become accustomed to oatcakes and scones, which my mother always enjoyed; but I certainly welcomed the change to 'loaf bread', to the gratification of my brother.

In our talks together I had mentioned to my brothers that Father Allan was a great archaeologist. I had seen many fossils in his house: stone and bone combs, pins, stone spear and axe heads and other things he had found among the sands of the machair, relics, he said of the Stone Age.† He contended that the islands were of igneous formation, for he had found seashells, besides other marine signs on the tops of the mountains, which fact showed that at one time these rocky mounds of earth had once been below sea-level. My brothers showed interest and proposed a ramble along the machair and the shore in the hope of finding something of archaeological value.

* The term is still used in Gaelic.
† What became of this collection is not known.

We had searched along the sand for about two miles without finding anything in the way of fossils,* when I noticed a very disagreeable smell for which I could not in the least account. As we advanced, the strength of the odour increased till, as we drew near a huge bank of sand probably cast up by wind and wave, a number of ravens and hoodie-crows swept into the air from behind the sand-bank. Rounding the latter we came in sight of an immense form lying just beyond. At once we judged it to be a whale, but the stench from it was so intolerable that we did not venture to approach nearer! There was a strong breeze blowing from that direction, so we made a detour and got to the windward of the creature. From here we were able to get quite close, for the strong wind blew the smell of the animal away from us. We were now able to inspect it without discomfort. It was evidently a whale that had been cast upon the shore by some huge billow, but how or why it died we could not ascertain, for we could see no wound. My brothers, after pacing from its head to its tail, calculated it to be about eighty feet long, of which nearly a third formed the head. It lay on its side, and I remember the loose upper jaw fell sideways so that the interior of the great mouth was exposed to our gaze. This looked to be of enormous capacity, but I do not remember seeing any teeth; in fact, I did not approach very close to it for obvious reasons; so that, apart from noticing the huge interior of the mouth and the apparent absence of teeth,† I have but little more recollection of it.

Notwithstanding the obnoxious smell from it I was very glad that my brothers saw what they had never seen before, a whale at close quarters. They were to return to London in two or three days, and this experience would be something worthy of relating to their friends.

* More correctly artifacts. It was not 'fossils' they were looking for, but prehistoric implements.
† It would have been a whalebone-whale, toothless in any case.

Chapter Twenty-one

THE Uist people were a hardy race, but during the winter I had often felt sorry for the school children who, with a very few exceptions, had nothing to eat from when they left home in the morning till they returned in the evening. Often they were wet through before they arrived at school, and remained all day in their damp clothes, for it would have been an impossible task to have dried all their clothes by the fires.

When I heard that a cow belonging to a neighbouring crofter had broken its leg and was to be shot, I had an idea. Beef or mutton was very seldom used by the people; the animals producing the meat were kept till the annual market, and then sold to dealers who took them to the mainland of Scotland. In the way of meat our food consisted principally of fowl, eggs, and fish; the fowl were very cheap, the current price at the stores being sixpence per fowl, and that for eggs was sixpence a dozen; fish, when in season, cost me nothing, for, being plentiful, the people would not hear of my paying. Sometimes I bought a lamb for five shillings, which was the current price when they were plentiful, and its owner would take no more nor no less, neither would he sell you less than the whole live lamb. This latter was very embarrassing, for I had no sooner intimated that I wanted one than a man would arrive at the back door next morning holding a lamb by a cord and he would kill it there and then in the back garden. After I had assisted in the skinning, cleaning and the cutting of it into joints most of my appetite for roast lamb had disappeared. What remained after we had eaten fresh meat for a few days was salted down for future use.

My idea was to buy a portion of the crofter's cow when slain, salt it down and make soup from it for the school children. In answer to my inquiries the owner sent word that the cow was killed and I could have half of it for a pound. I bought the half and the joints were salted and put into barrels. Knowing well the pride inherent in the people and their independence I refrained from the semblance of charity. It was announced to the day, and also the evening classes that I proposed supplying a basin of hot soup to the school children at mid-day during the rest of the winter; that a concert and dance would be given in the school to raise funds at once, and each family with children in school could buy a shilling ticket. The idea was taken up enthusiastically, all families I think bought tickets. The affair was a success, the songs were chiefly rendered in Gaelic both by men and women, and after the dance it was proposed to repeat the social evening later on if further funds should be needed.

Without delay I obtained dozens of new basins and spoons and two large pots. Under the supervision of my mother in the house ten of the girls in the top class prepared the soup, two at a time for the five school days. We had plenty of vegetables, for the children brought a few potatoes each day and some brought carrots, turnips and onions. When these were cut up very small as well as some meat, a little barley and lentils added made an appetizing and nourishing soup. The first distribution* of the soup was amusing: I had told the children that if any of them cared to have some at the mid-day interval they were to go into a certain classroom. Whether from pride or shyness it was hard to judge but only a dozen or so went into the room. Two big

---

* On 13th March 1908 according to the school log book. On 12th February 1909 the log book records that 'The hot soup distributed at mid-day has been most beneficial to all the children and it is still being continued'.

The log book records that: On 29th November 1911 'The managers gave Friday also as holiday there being an Entertainment in the building to find funds for establishing a School Soup Fund' and on 22nd December of the same year 'A basin of hot soup has been given to the children at one p.m. yesterday and today and the effect on the children is most marked'.

22nd December 1911: 'A basin of hot soup has been given to the children at one p.m. yesterday and today and the effect on the children is most marked.'

8th January 1912: 'Severe frost with wind-driven snow showers today—parents took charge of children to and from school: only sixty-nine children were present. Soup was distributed which was much appreciated by those coming from a distance.'

On 29th March 1912: 'The weather remains cold and showery. Soup has been distributed three times this week as usual.'

5th April 1912: 'The weather continues wet, and soup has been distributed on Monday, Tuesday and Thursday.'

boys helped me to serve and give out the soup; not a child began to eat, though 'Grace' had been said, they sat still, spoon in hand and basin before them, with eyes cast down—presumably they were unaccustomed to eat in company and were shy. So I filled a basin for myself and began to eat, remarking how good it tasted: they were all looking at me quite solemnly. 'Come along, Mary,' said I to one of the girls after a mouthful. 'You see how good it tastes.' Obediently she put her spoon into her basin and took a little, shyly glancing sideways at the other children. 'Good!' said I. 'Try another spoonful.' She did and the others then tasted some and before long all the basins were empty. The next day there were more children in the room at the interval and by Friday the room was filled. The following week I had practically the whole school partaking of a basin at mid-day. Later I was gratified at seeing the effect of the good nourishing soup upon the children: they had become brighter, more alert, smiles were more frequent, and they certainly looked more robust.

Gradually I had been gathering books together for a school library: my friends gave me second-hand books that they thought suitable, and my brothers who had returned to England sent me some for which I had asked them specially. I kept all the books in the vestibule of my house which as I have before mentioned was fairly spacious, and there they were directly under my eyes. After numbering and cataloguing them I announced to the evening classes that I had books for private reading at home, for those students who liked reading might come to my house afterwards for books. Hitherto any reading in English done among the people consisted of the perusal of odd newspapers, often weeks old. Nearly a dozen of my best students accompanied me to my house after class for the purpose of selecting a book. Carefully studying the characteristics of each student as far as known to me, I selected for that individual the book I thought most suitable. I told them to wait till I had supplied books to all of them for I had to give them some instructions. When the selection was over I gave them the usual conditions on which books are lent: care of them, clean hands when using, not to tear the leaves, and so on; then I told them that they might have them two weeks for reading. During my little address on these instructions I noticed looks of growing astonishment on their faces, and when I concluded by telling them that they could have the books for two weeks only, they stood and stared at me in open-mouthed astonishment. I asked: 'What is the matter?' They looked at each other for a minute then one of them almost gasped out: '*Have we got to bring them back!*' Three or four handed me back their books and left without further word; but to the remainder I explained the reasons for the making of such conditions for a lending library. These seemed a shade dubious even then, but they took their books home with them after I had recorded their names and their respective books. Thinking over the matter later I concluded that their chief difficulty lay in the fact that the only home reading in their experience was that of the newspaper, to the reading of which no conditions were attached and when read it could be torn to light their tobacco pipes.

Perseverance brought reward, and before long quite a good proportion of the evening-class pupils became home readers of books from the library; some few became indefatigable readers and would come for books frequently from miles away, sometimes at inordinate times, but I never refused them and was glad that interest was aroused. I was pleased on the whole at the care taken of the books, though occasionally some part of a page had been torn from a book, but, considering their advance in knowledge and the love of reading, I did not make much account of such happening.

My brothers kept their word and sent me physical exercise apparatus for the young men: two footballs, small size and full size, sets of boxing gloves, single-sticks complete with wicker-basket hilts and head-guards, and also sundry other articles. The local joiner had made me a satisfactory set of parallel bars not too heavy so that two men only were needed to carry them about. I arranged to use these for the recreation of the young men on Wednesdays after evening school. The first Wednesday night's recreation nearly produced a serious accident. The parallel-bars had been carried in and occupied a space in the middle of the schoolroom floor, the benches having been moved back to the walls so as to leave the middle part of the floor clear from end to end.

I explained to the assembled men that the object of the exercises on the bars was to make them both physically and mentally

156

more alert and to gain for them a greater control over themselves and their muscles, but that this could be accomplished only by going steadily through a carefully graduated series of exercises proceeding in course of time from those of the very simplest character to much more difficult exercises. My coat, waistcoat, collar and tie removed I alone went through the first set of six exercises on the bars; they were of the simplest character: the first was to walk smartly along between the bars without touching them; the next the same excepting that before emerging from between the bars the hands grasped the further ends and a jump forward was taken; the third exercise was the same but when the ends of the bars were grasped a high vertical jump was made and the body was held upright and still with rigid extended arms and hands grasping the bars, then a jump forward cleared the bars. By the time I had been alone through the six exercises the eager looks on the men's faces showed how keen to begin they were. Forming them in a file I led the way, remaining near the bars to watch each man as he took his turn at a signal from me. They went through the exercises very well on the whole, some of course, performing somewhat indifferently, but they all thoroughly enjoyed themselves and were amused at bringing into play muscles of which they were not previously aware. As they asked me to let them see some of the advanced exercises on the bars I told them that I would show them a few but that they must not attempt them for a long time till they had by many exercises gained better control of their muscles. I finished with the back-lift exercise in which with hands grasping the bars the feet and legs are raised backwards till the whole body is inverted vertically overhead, and the rigid arms walk along the bars to the other end when with a slight spring a landing is made lightly on the two feet. I had just made my landing when I heard someone shout 'I can do that' and from the group rushed a powerful man who sprang to the bar with rigid arms, swung his legs backwards to throw them over his head and came to the floor with a fearful crash and lay there. I was horrified for I feared that he had broken his neck, but he was only stunned and he recovered consciousness after a while. This incident served to bring home the instructions and advice I had given and it showed them the necessity of self-control. At the same time I felt it to be a lesson for me too, that I must proceed with more care and caution in the introduction of innovations among the young people.

The recreation class was more serious and earnest at the next meeting and the parallel-bar work was devoted towards perfecting the performance of the six exercises taken before. The apparatus was taken away and then securely fastened across the bars with padlock and chain to prevent promiscuous use and possible accidents. I now introduced the single-sticks and taught them individually the chief cuts and guards in very slow time, with myself in opposition to each at first, then with two others, feet to lines, opposed to each other. They soon became very adept and I promised fencing matches for the next meeting. At that assembly, after revising all that had been taught previously, I donned a head-guard, after fitting my opponent with one, and each with toe to our respective lines, we fenced so as to illustrate the cuts and guards they had learnt. All went well and others then took our places and they all performed very creditably. I blame myself, for I now allowed two couples, equipped with the single-sticks and head-guards and provided with chalked-out toe lines, to engage in separate bouts simultaneously. I do not know whether it was due to excitement or to temper aroused by being hurt, but, quite suddenly, after fencing quite skilfully in a seemingly friendly manner, each pair began to slash at each other in great fury: the guards they had been taught were ignored and they dealt each other tremendous blows indiscriminately on body, limbs and head and such was the force of their blows that, in a few moments, the tough wood sticks were reduced to splinters with little remaining in their hands but the hilts. They then desisted, glared at each other for a minute, removed their head-guards, gazed at the shreds of stick, and looked sheepishly at me. I could see that they were now cooled down and ashamed at losing control of themselves, so I laughed and said: 'The head-guards saved four heads from being broken.'

I think it quite needless to say that I did not now think of producing boxing-gloves and that I determined to keep these very much in the background. But I shortly afterwards found an occasion when I thought they might be useful. I had always discountenanced fighting and quarrelling among the children; nevertheless, I happened upon a quarrel between two of the biggest boys who had just begun to fight in a corner of the play-ground. I ran to the house for the boxing-gloves before they saw me and they were hard at it when I returned a minute after. On seeing me they stopped but glared fiercely at each other. I said: 'All right, you shall fight it out but you must wear these', and I fitted each with a pair of padded gloves. Perhaps a doubt that they could hurt each other with these on their hands lent fury to their blows, for they fought with surprising ardour and strength, but little damage was done and they stopped at last, exhausted. I said to them: 'You have both had enough, haven't you? Now shake hands and be friends.' They did so and grinned at each other while the boys around looking on laughed aloud, and from that time quarrelsomeness seemed to disappear. I was able to introduce school football and the fairness of its rules seemed to appeal to the boys who played both with zest and enjoyment but with due observance of a penalty for unfair play.

Mr MacElfrish the clerk of our school board had his offices at Loch Maddy, about forty miles away on North Uist from which communication could be made by crossing the inter-mediate island of Benbecula. At low tide it was possible to make the forty-mile journey on foot by means of two fords which separated the three islands. This journey overland was fre-quently made to and fro by the inhabitants of the islands who would put up for the night with hospitable crofters *en route*.

Letters from the clerk to the schools on our island were often sent overland by this route, but, as the crossing of the fords owing to the tides was sometimes hazardous, communications between the clerk and the schools were more often brought by the steamer calling at Loch Maddy and Lochboisdale. Postmen collected the letters at these two places and delivered them at the respective destinations. Our local postman's house and croft adjoined the school property and three times a week he called at my house early in the afternoon to collect my out-going letters and generally returned in the evening with the incoming mail. In February I had received from the clerk of the school some forms and documents, and, before filling them in, decided to consult my colleague, Mr Craig.

Leaving my house one evening I set out to visit my friend Craig at his schoolhouse at Daliburgh three miles away to the north. The weather was bad, but, clad in my oilskins and being

young and vigorous, I thought little of this and started off quite
buoyant in the anticipation of seeing my friend. A strong northerly wind was blowing, but for the first hundred yards along
the road I was sheltered by the banks on either side of me. Then
I emerged into the open and was struck by a furious icy blast
and I thought that my face was cut to pieces, for the wind was
full of frozen rain and seemed to cut like splintered glass and
leaden shot. I was blinded and bewildered for a moment, but
held down my protected head and tried to struggle on. But it
was useless: I was battered, whirled about, and torn by the ice-
laden storm, and half-blindedly staggered against something.
Gropingly I felt it and knew that it was a friendly peat-stack; in
a moment I was round it and crouching on its lee side in fear.
I had often read, and had been told, of the terrors of a blizzard
and now I realized its deadliness. After a little while I worked
myself along the partially sheltered side of the peat-stack and
stumbled over an obstacle. I felt it with my half-frozen hands:
it was the crouching figure of a man who like myself was shelter-
ing from the elements. Audible speech was impossible owing to
the noise of the tearing wind, but gradually it dawned on me
that this man was the local postman who two hours before had
left his house (not two hundred yards away) to fetch the letters.
He had been, for years, the postman for the south end of the
island, strong, reliable, honest, and never-failing in his duties—
and in two hours he had only managed to travel two hundred
yards! I now felt how puny, after all, are the physical capabili-
ties of man and wondered whether we two would be able to
reach our homes that were so near, while the possibility of reaching them in safety seemed so remote. We, cold and numbed,
must have been behind the peat-stack an hour or so waiting
for a lull in the storm to enable an attempt to be made at returning home. Well we realized the danger in such an attempt
—battered, beaten, bewildered, blinded, and whirled about
in the blizzard we should fall and be frozen. Time and again we
would put out a hand from the end of the stack to ascertain if
the wind were still as heavily laden with ice or was as fierce. At
last a lull came and holding hands we dashed out from behind
our shelter. The recollection of how we reached home, or of
how long it took us to do so, is very faint—I have now vague
memories of our being wrenched apart, then crawling along on

all fours, of blindly seeking for each other after rolling down some declivity, of lying exhausted, then struggling on again, and of finally finding ourselves against the school wall, and, both of us, practically home. I have one vivid recollection: that seating myself in a chair I at once thrust my feet on the fire and smelled the burning leather of my boots some time before any feeling was restored to my feet. The direction of the wind changed in the night and the next morning a warm gentle wind was blowing from the south-west. My companion in the peril of the previous night was none the worse for the experience and by mid-day had completed his ten-mile journey and had delivered all our letters.

During the morning of Friday of the following week I came into the house to fetch a certain book of reference. I had passed through the glass-panelled door which gave access from the vestibule to the hall when I fell at the foot of the stairs and became unconscious. I remember nothing till I opened my eyes and found myself lying on the camp-bed in my sitting-room. I recollect my saying: 'What time is it?' and looking round saw my mother in the room, also the doctor. In answer to the question the former replied: 'It is seven o'clock, Sunday evening.' I felt in full use of all my faculties and was incredulous of my having been unconscious for fifty-odd hours. However, the doctor told me not to be alarmed but that I had been attacked by the new kind of influenza which had recently come from the East. Aided by him I got to my bedroom and into bed. He told me not to worry but I should be out of school for a week or so— I was back in school again in a fortnight.

I was still in bed on the Saturday following my seizure, and late in the afternoon my mother came upstairs to tell me that three of my young friends, Mr Craig, with Mr MacQueen from the estate office and Mr Law from the bank at Lochboisdale, had called to see how I was. She did not think it wise for them to come up, so she was going to give them their tea in the sitting-room. After some little time had passed I heard them leave the house. Shortly afterwards my mother came to me and said that they had had tea and were gone but were coming back again. It appeared that during their tea they had asked if I were having whisky and milk. On being told that I was having milk but no whisky, they insisted that whisky and milk was the finest thing for influenza; so, after tea, they said they would go on to the inn at Pollachar and fetch me a bottle of whisky and would soon be back.

It would be between five and six o'clock in the evening when they set out for the inn less than two miles away. It was a fine clear evening and I told my mother that probably they would be back at the house about eight o'clock. She went down stairs again saying that she would have supper laid ready for them on their return. Two hours passed; three hours, and more, with no sign of the return of my three friends. Several times my mother went out into the garden in the hope of hearing their voices, or their steps on the road; though it was a calm night on which sounds carried far she could hear nothing and all was still. At half-past ten I would not let her wait up for them any longer and begged her to retire for the night. She promised to go to bed at eleven o'clock if they had not then returned, which she did.

After she had retired, I lay listening for a long time but all was quiet, and at last I began to doze. I was aroused by hearing a dog barking in the distance. I dozed off again and slept some little time. My slumber was broken by my mother coming into the room. She stood by my bed and said: 'Oh, what shall I do? Mr Law has come and he is drunk.' I was out of bed and had put on some garments in less than a minute. My mother protested, but I insisted on her remaining upstairs. Candle in hand, I descended the stairs, and found my friend lying on the floor of the sitting-room. My mother had evidently lighted the table lamp, for by its light I saw the poor chap looked very untidy, with his clothes soiled and torn as though he had fallen on the road. As I bent over him he opened his eyes and said: 'I've come at the peril of my life; at the peril of my life!' I said: 'All right, old man, just lie here on the hearth-rug and sleep till the morning.' I made him as comfortable there as I could with cushions and rugs and, blowing out the lamp, left him going to sleep and muttering: 'At the peril of my life!' I told my mother that I had left him quite comfortable and that he would be all right. We then retired and were soon fast asleep.

I was awakened in an hour or so by hearing bumping sounds. Wide awake I listened but all became quiet again. Shortly after I heard the strange sounds again. Fearing that they might waken my mother, I took a lighted candle and crept quietly downstairs and looked into the sitting-room. There was not a sound, but the sitting room was empty—my friend Law had gone! Going to the door leading into the vestibule I peered through the glass panels while holding the candle above my head. I saw at once that the double front doors were shut, then I distinguished a form, that of my friend MacQueen; he was huddled in a corner of the vestibule with his head on a box of books, clutching a stick, but fast asleep. On looking around further I saw my friend Craig lying flat on his back on the floor. The light of my candle must have disturbed Craig, for he raised his head slightly, looked at me through the glass of the door, and placed a finger on his lips to enjoin silence. On my opening the door quietly, he said: 'Wheesht! I have brought you the whisky,' and, still lying on his back, began to feel in his pockets. While he was doing so I noticed that he was wearing a new suit made of a light-coloured homespun cloth, but one arm of the coat was black with mud of which there were patches on the trousers—the suit looked ruined. Raising an arm he held up to me an unopened bottle of whisky saying: 'There you are; now go back to bed; we are all right.' I took it, and he lay back again and went to sleep. Everything had been done so quietly that my mother was not aroused as I ascertained before going into my room. They were not there in the morning, but it transpired that each arrived home safely before daylight. They came and apologized to my mother the following evening. My friend Craig said to me afterwards: 'We did not have much whisky at the inn, really; only a glass or two while we talked. After a time I looked at my watch and said: "We must be going, or we shall be late getting home." We then had a parting glass with the landlord and started off quite all right. As we were going up the road Law said: "We shall be late," and he started to run and fell into a ditch at the side of the road. I was standing laughing at Law when I fell into the ditch on the other side— I remember feeling water trickling down my back and then I forgot everything till I found myself at home. It must have been that last glass that did it!'

I do not think that anyone ever learned of the episode with the exception of us at the schoolhouse and themselves and I never heard it referred to by anyone after!

Chapter Twenty-two

MANY and curious were the remedies suggested to my mother by various persons as a cure for my illness. Perhaps the most curious of all was one that was said to be a certain cure for rheumatism. The patient was to be stripped, and then wrapped from head to foot in the skin of a freshly killed seal with the fat adhering to the skin next to the patient's body; at the end of three days, the skin might be removed and the patient would be cured. My mother received all the suggestions with politeness, but said that she would rely upon the doctor's advice and treatment, together with my good constitution. She was justified for, within a week or so, I was back in school again and thoroughly recovered.

Remembering my promise to go rowing with Duncan Bain of the Lochboisdale Hotel, I set off the first fine Saturday in order to redeem my promise. I found him ready and willing to go; he had had his boat repainted and varnished and was very proud of it saying how light and steady it was. On our way to the boat we called at the bank to see if Mr Law would accompany us. He was delighted to see us and we went down to the slip where the boat was moored. It was much like to the ordinary fourteen feet double-oared boats used on our city pools and we enjoyed our row about the large expanse of the loch, I and Duncan each wielding two oars. Law, who was at the tiller, then suggested that we should go out through the loch mouth into the Minch. As the weather was fine and calm we did so, and our frail craft was soon out on the heaving sea. Twice, as I rowed, I thought that my left oar slid off something just below the surface of the water, but I put it down to my imagination. Then I definitely felt something with my oar, and the boat itself slid on to something then off again, while immediately after a huge long grey body showed itself beside us. Law shouted out: 'Look! A whale! Row back for your lives!' We got the boat round and headed for Lochboisdale as hard as we could row, where we landed without mishap.

Duncan invited us to the hotel for tea. We had finished and were talking over our scare when we heard the loud excited shouting of many voices. We went out of doors and saw a number of men on and about the pier running about, gesticulating, and shouting. Before we reached the pier some had jumped into boats and were pulling out into the loch and others were preparing to follow. Next we heard firing and, by the time we had reached the pier more men were arriving as excited as the others. On inquiring what the commotion was about we learned that schools of whales had entered the loch chasing after herring. The scene that followed is indescribable: more and more boats put out crowded with men who were armed with guns, axes, spears, even spades, and there ensued a spectacle of wild, indiscriminate slaughter of whales, large, small, old and young, all valuable for their oil and whale-bone; dead bodies of whales were soon floating about in the water mingled with blood and oil. It was now getting dark but by the light of torches the slaughter still went on, till, feeling nauseated with such carnage, I bade farewell to my friends and went home.

About this time my colleague, Craig, and I received forms and schedules from the school board office in Loch Maddy together with the intimation that government inspectors were coming shortly to examine our evening classes. We duly prepared the documents, the inspectors came and inspected the classes, expressing approval of the work especially approving of the subject of navigation in my school, and of agriculture in that of my friend. They further suggested that we should prepare a syllabus of hygiene as a very suitable subject for teaching in the schools. As neither my friend nor I held diplomas in these subjects, we were advised to take the Advanced Science and Art Examinations of the Board of Education and an examination centre on the island would be arranged for. Having already a fair knowledge of, and a predilection for our respective subjects we commenced preparing ourselves for the examination.

Later it transpired that Craig's school was selected as the examination centre. We heard that there were only three men examinees, ourselves and the headmaster from a large school on another island, a university graduate. Craig was taking the agriculture and hygiene papers, myself navigation and hygiene, and the graduate was taking the three subjects. It was with some feelings of deference for the third man that we two awaited him at the schoolhouse on the examination day. He arrived at the school and introduced himself to us as we appeared outside. The school board members who were to superintend the examination had not yet arrived, so we three men adjourned to Craig's house for a while. Our new colleague seemed to make light of the subjects we were to take saying that navigation was only mathematics, agriculture a matter of chemistry, and hygiene was easy to read up. By this time the other people had arrived at the school, the chairman of the board carrying a large officially sealed envelope containing the examination papers sent directly to him from London and which registered packet was not to be opened till we were all seated and ready to commence. I was somewhat diffident about going in and waited till the last. Instruments and a book of logarithmic tables in hand I left the house for the school when I heard excited shouts from the south and saw men running. A clattering on the road soon showed me what was wrong. Along the road came a horse in full career dragging a cart containing corn; men were running after it, for it had evidently taken fright at something and I saw the reins trailing on the ground as it dashed along. It was travelling too fast for the men to catch it up, which gave me an idea, for it was now from twenty to thirty yards away and coming towards me. I dropped the things I held, vaulted the wall and started to run along the road on the side that I had seen the trailing reins. I was a good runner, and, as I looked over my shoulder and saw the frightened creature near I put on a spurt. When level with me I ran at my very best pace beside it and snatched at the hanging reins. I held on still running, but slackening speed and bearing my weight back on the reins; this soon had the desired effect and it came to a standstill just before it reached the cross-roads three hundred yards past the school. The men had now come up, but I did not stop a minute for I was late. Hurriedly I returned, picked up the things I had dropped and hastened into school. Evidently all were waiting for me as the last to arrive, and were not aware of what had been happening on the road. I quietly seated myself, the sealed packet was opened, the printed question papers distributed and in a few minutes all the examinees were hard at work.

My little adventure before must have unsettled me, for instead of reading through all my questions first and then selecting those requiring the least time in answering, as I usually did at examinations, I plunged at the longest and most intricate of all the navigation questions. Before I had completed half the calculations required for the solution of this question, the university man who had filled his sheets of foolscap, throwing each aside as he filled it, was calling out: 'More foolscap, please.' My friend, Craig, looked across at me, and I am afraid that we both felt very small fry indeed as we had not then filled more than a quarter of our original supply. This did not serve to settle me and I was half-way through the next question on 'Day's work' when I noticed that the last four questions were easy to answer, requiring short answers which I could supply in much less time than I had spent on my first answer. I called myself many kinds of an ass, left the 'Day's work' question and hurriedly attacked these four last questions while hearing calls for more foolscap from another part of the room. 'Time is up!' was announced before I could finish, and less than half my foolscap was filled. All answer papers were immediately collected, packed up in special wrappers sent for the purpose, and this was then labelled and sealed. Both Craig and I felt very dubious about our chances of gaining the diplomas in view of the amount our graduate colleague had accomplished and we marvelled at the lightning speed at which he must have written. After a short interval and a rest, the examination in the other subjects followed, and, feeling more settled, I worked with more confidence. Though Craig and I worked steadily on, our answer papers combined did not equal in number those of our colleague at the expiry of the time allowed. When we left the room our friend was already started on the third subject, and we two looked at each other rather wryly as we retired to Craig's schoolhouse and I am afraid that we parted rather disconsolately when I soon after started for home. A month later the results of the examinations were published and I do not know which of us, Craig or I, was the more astonished at learning that we had both gained diplomas in our subjects, but more astonished still were we to find that our graduate colleague had failed to gain one.

Here I would like to make an interpolation. I feel that my narrative may appear rather egotistical at times. In autobiographical writing it is very difficult to avoid any apparent eulogy of oneself. But I would ask that it should not be forgotten that, as the only resident Englishman on the island and a schoolmaster, I was the cynosure of the natives as of the resident Scots, and throughout my sojourn there I was imbued with the spirit of doing nothing derogatory to the good name of my native land. I would therefore ask the indulgent reader not to judge me harshly if at times I err in apparent egotism on occasion.

The proprietor of our island was a Scottish knight. He owned much property, a castle with adjoining estate in the Highlands, a place in the south of England, and the greater part of the southern Outer Hebrides. His house on our island was large, fine and well built but he was not often resident there; but the grieve, the housekeeper and some servants were there all the year round so that the house should always be ready for him and his wife at short notice. Sometimes he would come for grouse shooting or trout fishing but only stayed a month or so at a time. Several times he came with some servants to the inn at Pollachar near my house and went out seal shooting with the landlord of the inn, who was a crack shot. I remember talking to the latter outside his door one day when he stopped abruptly with 'Just a minute,' went in, reappeared with a gun, raised it and fired out to a reef or rock lying at least five hundred yards away. Scores of seals slipped from the reef into the sea but one big fellow lay there still. 'I will get him later with a boat,' said he, and continued the conversation as before. To shoot a seal dead instantly, so that it is not able to slip from a reef into the water, is a feat of great skill. I believe that this vital spot is just at the base of the skull; if wounded anywhere else, though mortally, it will dive and entangle itself in the weeds so that it is not possible to retrieve its body.

The knight's estate agent of the Hebridean property, or the 'factor', lived at a fine house on a large farm situated about five miles north of my schoolhouse. I had frequently met him and he recently had asked me if I played golf. I answered in the negative and inquired the reason of the question. He told me that a professional golfer from St. Andrews had been to the island and had specially laid out an eighteen-hole course along the machair near his house, expressing the opinion that this part was a natural golf-link course, and if I cared to play, my presence would be welcomed. I accepted the invitation for the first fine Saturday asking if I might take with me also my friend, Craig, and was assured that I might; but doubt of his interest was expressed as his taste in sport seemed to be confined to angling. I was informed also that there was an ample supply of all golf requisites at the factor's house, so I naturally was relieved on that score.

Saturday being fine I went, and I called for Craig on my way to the factor's place. I found my friend at home but he expressed himself as being completely uninterested in the game of golf, his opinion of it was that it was a silly, stupid game. Using my utmost powers of persuasion I at last prevailed upon him to accompany me to the house, for I had never visited there before and he had. Our way lay north for about a mile and a half along the main road when we came to a wide gate guarding the entrance to what was evidently a private road. Beside the gate was a stout wooden pillar to the top of which was fixed a large locked box having an aperture in one side. This was new to me and I asked my friend why it was put there. He told me that it was for the factor's correspondence. The house was a good mile along the private road so the postman simply placed letters in the box as he passed along the main road; having a key of the box he could easily collect outgoing letters also; one of the estate clerks had the duty of removing the correspondence from the box and of placing therein any letters for the outgoing mail. I appreciated the idea and we passed through to the private road and my companion led the way. On either side of this road were fences separating it from fields extending north and south as far as I could see and dotted here and there with browsing cattle—evidently a large farm. Half a mile along the road we came to a well-built two-storeyed stone house, that of the factor's chief clerk, his wife, and two junior clerks, so I was informed by Craig. Passing on we came to a large white gate opening on to a typical farmyard. Beyond this stood a fine stone house, spacious and of many rooms as I judged from its numerous chimneys. The approach to this was through a very high arch formed by two whale jaw bones. Passing through I found that we were in a well-kept expansive garden surrounded by high stone walls. The factor then came to meet us and welcomed us to the house. Here we found quite a small party assembled; besides his wife and children were a young lady cousin from Inverness, two or three clergymen and the two junior clerks. Introductions over we selected clubs and balls, though Craig did not say that he did not intend to play; the factor led the way to the machair and the golf course. Craig and I watched them drive off from the 'tee', and our young friend, MacQueen, whom I have previously mentioned in this narrative, stayed behind to initiate me into the mysteries of golf. Pointing out the direction of the first hole and explaining its situation he drove off his ball which disappeared behind a distant bank of sand. He watched me try to imitate him and though my drive was not as hefty as his had been I had the satisfaction of seeing my ball reach, and topple over, the aforesaid sand bank. We went on to find our balls, Craig reluctantly following with a disgruntled 'Silly! Hitting a ball and then having to go and look for it! Absurd!' He followed us nevertheless and we easily found our balls. Not far beyond the bank of sand, right across our path to the hole, lay a long narrow loch about fifty to sixty feet in width. MacQueen made a fine shot, for he made his ball sail high over the water and land near the first hole. He watched me as I prepared myself to emulate the success of his stroke, but I foozled my shot and to my confusion my ball plopped into the middle of the loch. MacQueen told me to try the shot again with a fresh ball, placed it in position for me then went on after his own ball. Looking round at Craig I saw that he was watching me. So I held my club out to him saying: 'You have a try.' He demurred at first , and I then put the club in his hands and said: 'Go on, man!' He took it, went to the ball, looked a little undecided, then made a mighty swipe at the ball lifting it clean over the loch well on the way to MacQueen. Before I could say anything to him he was off full speed after the ball my club in his hand. Before I came up with them they had both holed their balls, and were starting for the next hole. Smiling to myself at my friend Craig's sudden and enthusiastic conversion to the game, I went for another club and ball, restarted, cleared the loch, and caught up to my two friends and we all three completed the round of eighteen holes thoroughly enjoying the game. Craig's conversion to it was complete: most evenings he spent on the golf links; and on many Saturdays when I called for him to go fishing I was told that he was playing golf, so I usually left my rod and tackle at his house and joined him on the golf course.

NOTE. The 'proprietor' referred to on p. 168 was Sir Reginald Cathcart, Bt. He was not the proprietor of South Uist, but the husband of the proprietrix, Lady Gordon Cathcart, who had inherited the estate in 1878. She lived until 1932.

Chapter Twenty-three

WHEN I had first left England to take my school in the Hebrides my younger sister was teaching in a Yorkshire school. Recently we had heard that her health was giving way, and I proposed that she should come and stay with us at the schoolhouse for a while. My mother would be glad of her company and I believed that the pure air we enjoyed and the spring weather would benefit my sister's health. My proposal was adopted and it was arranged for me to meet her in Glasgow, I being granted two days' leave of absence from school duty to enable me to do so. After an uneventful journey I arrived in Glasgow late at night. My sister's train was due there the following afternoon; so I stayed the night in a comfortable hotel.

After breakfast the next morning I strolled around the city amusing myself by looking in shop windows, observing the people and the traffic. One of the principal streets took me down to a bridge across the Clyde. I stayed here for a time, being most interested in the shipping and the busy life in the river. Happening to look up at others, engaged as I was, I saw that one of them looked familiar, so walked towards him. It was Donald MacPhee, one of my late evening class sailor students—and a good one too. 'Well, Donald,' I said, shaking him by the hand heartily. 'How strange it seems to be meeting you here!' He looked at me sheepishly and answered: 'No, sir, when we Islesmen come to Glasgow we can nearly always be found near the Broomilaw.' I asked him to take me to some place near by where we could have a cup of coffee and a talk. He appeared very awkward as we walked along together, hands in pockets, and shoulders sloping. However, he soon found a clean-looking coffee house, and we soon sat down at a small table with our coffee and some cakes. I asked him what he was doing in Glasgow. He told me that he always came to Glasgow when seeking a sailor's job on a vessel. Before this he had signed on as an ordinary seaman; but the navigation he had learned in my evening class had helped him to gain a Mate's Certificate. He said he was going to Greenock by the eleven o'clock train for he had been told of a sailing ship lying there which was short of a second-mate and he was going to apply. I was pleased; and, considering about when my sister's train was due in Glasgow and that I should have ample time, I said: 'I will come to Greenock with you, and see how you get on.' He looked surprised, gave a slow smile, but said nothing.

Having settled for our refreshment we went on the short journey to Greenock. Memories of the details of that journey are now somewhat dim, but I still have recollections of our walking along a quay-side, negotiating a way past merchandise and tripping over taut cables, of seeing ships, both sail and steam, lying afloat on the river beside the long line of quays. Donald led the way till at last he stopped and looked interestedly at a four-masted sailing ship warped close alongside the quay. On the bow I saw the ship's name—*Fairfield*. There was no one in sight on deck, so Donald, followed by me, descended a gangway. As he looked around I stood and watched him move about. What a change had come over him! Till now he had appeared apathetic of expression, almost slouching in his gait, hands in pockets and shoulders slumped forward. As soon as his feet touched the deck his face lighted up, his movements became quick, active and alert, hands out of pockets and swinging as if ready and eager to hold a rope—he was transformed, a different man from him I knew and I watched him as if fascinated. A born sailor and he was happy!

He came to me and said he would go below and look for someone. I stayed on deck while he was gone and gratified my curiosity, for I had never been on a sailing ship before. As I looked at the long and narrow deck, leant over the bulwarks and saw how close to the water the deck was, I marvelled that this thing on which I stood could weather the storms and gigantic seas that it must encounter on ocean voyages. Donald now reappeared and told me that the captain was ashore, but the first mate was on board and he was to see him in his cabin in a few minutes. I accompanied him below and he knocked at a door which brought a 'Come in'. Donald entered while I stood outside the open door and I saw it opened into a small, but comfortable, cabin. Seated at a table was a little thick-set man, blue-eyed with weather-beaten countenance. 'Let me see your papers,' he said to Donald, and at the same time he looked him over with a swift comprehensive glance.

Leaving them together I returned to the deck, as curious and interested as ever over what was to be seen there. I had been examining the various appurtenances, and was looking at the tall masts, my imagination busy as I viewed the ratlines for mounting aloft, when I was aware that the mate and Donald were near me engaged in apparently friendly conversation. From Donald's animated looks, and his quick critical glances at the various parts of the vessel, I judged that they were discussing sea matters, so I continued my occupation. At last they came towards me and the mate looked at me with indulgent smile and held out his hand. As I shook it I said, rather inanely: 'I have been looking around at your ship. How does she sail?' The mate answered: 'She doesn't sail; she drifts.' He then turned to Donald and said: 'The captain is ashore, but I can see you'll do, so come along and I'll sign you on.' Then he left us and went below. Donald told me, without undue pride, that he had secured the berth and they were sailing in a few days on a three years' voyage. He thanked me and asked me if I could find my way back alone. I reassured him, shook hands, and went ashore. The last view I had of him was his waving his hand to me as he stood on the deck looking, every inch, the sailor he was.

I never saw him again. Years after I was glancing through a newspaper when my eye caught the name *Fairfield*. There was just a small paragraph announcing that news had been sent from New Zealand of some vessel arriving there with the survivors from the sailing ship *Fairfield* which had been lost in the Antarctic; a ship's boat containing a few exhausted starving men had been picked up while adrift; these men were being cared for in a New Zealand hospital. That was all. Donald was not among them.

My sister's train arrived duly in Glasgow early in the evening and I was on the platform to meet her. She had not been in Scotland before and she was very animated at seeing quite new scenes and people. But, as we affectionately greeted each other, I could but notice how pale and thin she was; and I hoped she would gain much benefit from her stay with me in the Hebrides. After a comparatively comfortable and easy journey, though my sister was rather ill on the boat, we landed at Lochboisdale. The first to greet us was the landlord of the inn at Pollachar. He had brought his best trap and the horse, Jack, to convey us to the schoolhouse. His benevolent and honest face beamed with pleasure as I introduced my sister, shook him by the hand and thanked him; this was only one of the many kindly actions he never failed in showing towards me and mine. Others on the pier greeted us too; but those who were natives contented themselves with touching their caps and looking curiously at my sister who looked frail with her small frame and pale thin face. One of these remarked to me later: 'Your sister must have been hungry in England, sir.' I asked what he meant, and he put a hand to his face and pressed in his cheeks, by which I gathered that he thought her face was thin. 'Never mind, whateffer,' he said, 'the air here will feed her up; it is as good as food.' I laughed and refrained from asking him if he would care to feed on the island air alone; however, I knew that he meant his remark as a welcome to her.

During the drive home my sister was full of questions, showing her great interest in all she saw. At the cross-roads were waiting my friend, Craig, and his couisn. We stopped while they spoke kindly words of welcome; then we drove on home. When we reached the high point of the road where we had a full view of my schoolhouse my sister showed her delight and I could see how eager she was to arrive. Our companion spoke scarcely a word throughout, but I often caught him looking at her with a gentle, half-amused expression on his face. He would take no thanks from us on our arrival, but smiled at us and drove off south to his inn—a Nature's gentleman, I always felt!

Chapter Twenty-four

THE spring-like weather enabled me to take my sister out for many walks and within a few weeks I noticed a great change for the better in her health. She had now a good colour, was gaining flesh, and had more spring to her step. The hills, lochs, and the sea charmed her; we soon were climbing the hills together and I rejoiced as she advanced in health and strength. On one of our first walks we visited my friends at the inn at Pollachar. The innkeeper's wife and my sister became great friends at once, and afterwards it was not seldom that a bottle of wine, a fat chicken, or a roll of freshly made butter was sent to our house by this kindly lady. Unfortunately, about this time my mother's health began to fail and I was glad to know that she had the companionship of a daughter; but on her good days she always insisted on my sister enjoying the open air either alone or in my company. Sometimes my sister would visit Craig's cousin, who kept house for him, and though it was a walk of three miles each way, it did not unduly fatigue her. On Sundays we walked to church and back, which was still further. My sister's hair was much admired by everyone: it was of a golden colour and very luxuriant. Such hair is very rare; she wore it in plaits coiled on the top and the back of her head, and, when she was sitting, she sat with her head forward to support the weight of her tresses. Whenever I visited at the inn my sister's hair was invariably mentioned—'Wonderful! I did not think there was such hair in the world. Pure gold!' I remember my hostess saying.

One Sunday, on the way to church, we had reached the top of the hill that was half-way when we paused and looked below at the scene around us. On our left lay the large loch with the single island in its centre. 'Do people live on that island?' asked my sister. 'No, of course not,' said I. 'Why?' 'I saw a woman on the island washing on its shore one day last week,' she replied. 'I have seen her several times.' 'Perhaps so,' I remarked, 'but it seems a strange thing to go across to the island for washing clothes.' We resumed our way then and talked of other things. The next time I saw Catriona, I told her about what my sister had seen on the island and asked why a woman should go to wash over there, and was there a boat there? Catriona said: 'Is she sure that she saw this?' I assured her that she had seen it more than once. My questioner said nothing more for a moment and looked grave. 'There is no boat on the loch. That island is haunted. Only a few people have seen what your sister saw,' said Catriona, and she shivered. I decided to say nothing more about it to my sister, and hoped she had forgotten the incident or attached no importance to it. I was glad, as she might have been nervous and I had warned Catriona of this.

Looking north along the road from my house I saw a strange figure more than a mile away. It was coming along the road too fast for anyone walking yet it was not anyone on horse-back. As the object came nearer it dawned upon me that it was a man on a bicycle—a strange sight for our island! When the rider reached the foot of the hill on which the schoolhouse stood, he dismounted and walked, pushing the bicycle up the incline. Then I recognized him: it was MacQueen from the estate office. Of course, I went to meet him; so we stopped while I inspected his machine, and I asked him how long he had had it. 'Only a few days,' he said, 'but it is the first bicycle ever brought to the island,' he added somewhat proudly. Then he began to laugh and told me that the women were afraid of it, for if they saw him with it they scurried into their houses and quickly shut the doors. But the men had made a great tumult about it and had been to the factor complaining that it frightened the horses and cattle, and they wanted the bicycle banished from the island. The factor took the part of his clerk and told them that the animals would soon get used to it. As the estate agent for the whole of the estate in the Outer Hebrides the factor had great authority; so MacQueen kept his bicycle. He said that he was on his way to the farm of Kilbride and that he had found his machine very handy for getting about quickly. I watched him remount, and as he rode down the other side of our hill, I noticed the cattle stop grazing, erect their tails, whirl round, and rush pell-mell away, terrified at the new strange object skimming along the road.

My sister had improved out of all resemblance to her former frail self as she was when she first came to the island and she had developed physically by out-door life in the good pure air. One Saturday morning I took her for a visit to Eriskay. We fortunately found the old ferryman and his son with their boat lying in a little bay near Pollachar inn. He was proud and pleased to take us back with him to the island when he had collected the mail-bags waiting for him at the inn. My sister was delighted with the three-mile sail, and we soon landed at the 'Haun'.＊ Ascending from the south shore of the little bay we came in sight of the newly built church and priest's house. A tall black figure standing there began to descend the hill towards us as we climbed—it was Father Allan. His face broke into a kindly smile as he approached us and extended his hand in welcome. 'Come up to my house,' he said after I had introduced my sister. Then he turned to her with: 'It is a rough way up. We did make a road from here to my house, but the hens scratched it up,' and I saw a twinkle in his eye as he said it.

Father Allan's house was sparsely furnished with the sole exception of one wall of his sitting-room which was entirely occupied by his books carefully arranged on the shelves of a huge bookcase reaching from floor to ceiling and end to end of the wall. He was a great student and scholar, and master of five languages at least. I believe that his favourite studies were archaeology, philosophy, and philology. I had learned that he contributed papers to the Philological Society on the last-named subject, and that he attended the annual meeting. Of course, I had seen many of his books before, but my sister had not. Seeing how interested she was in his library our host told her to browse among his tomes while he took me round to see some of the improvements he had made outside. I had seen these, and we were standing near the edge of the cliff that we had scaled together on my first visit, and were looking at the various islands lying west of us, large and small, some inhabited, some not, when I recollected an incident that had occurred one night recently. I said: 'Do they ever send fire-balloons up from any of these islands?' Father Allan replied: 'No, of course not. Why

＊ The little harbour at the north end of Eriskay.

did you ask that?' I pointed across to one of the larger inhabited islands and indicated its northern part. I told him that I had been out in my garden a few nights previously, before retiring to rest, and stood for a moment looking across to the sea, when I saw a dull-lighted sphere hovering over that part of the island I had indicated. At first I thought: 'How curious the moon looks tonight!' But, as I was looking, I saw the sphere of dim light rise very slowly into the air. I watched it go up steadily, higher, higher, and disappear into the sky. I had not mentioned it to anyone until I asked someone who would probably know what it was. 'Oh, I have often seen it myself,' said my companion. Then he went on to tell me that sometimes when he had been roused in the night to go to the bedside of a dying person he had been too late, but he always knew he was too late when he saw that light. 'Sometimes I have been fetched in a boat to the dying person and when the boat has been perhaps half-way, I have said to the men: "You can put back, for we are too late," for I had seen the ascending light. I have never been mistaken yet over this.'

Feeling rather incredulous, I now told him of my sister and the woman washing on the island. His comment on this was: 'Some people have the gift of being enabled to see what is denied to the sight of others.' 'But,' said I, somewhat incredulously, 'how is it that we never see these things in the city?' The reply to this was: 'How do you know that everything that some people think they see in the city is real?' Nonplussed as I was, Shakespeare came to my aid and I thought of Hamlet and his 'There are more things in heaven and earth, Horatio, than are dreamt of in your philosophy', but I decided that it was best for me to leave such things alone.

The weather was fine and up till this time there had been a steady breeze, but this had now dropped, giving place to a dead calm. The result of this was the curtailment of our visit as it meant that the boat taking us back to our island would have to be rowed across the sound, or strait, instead of being sailed over. Also we should have to take the shortest crossing, which would entail for us afterwards a walk of over four miles instead of the short walk of less than two miles from the inn where I usually landed. Consequently it behoved us not to delay our departure and we went to the 'Haun' for a boat. It was early, so Father Allan said he would get a small boat with a couple of youths and he would accompany us across, for he would enjoy a little rowing. When outside the little bay, the two youths who had been rowing gave place to Father Allan and me. Shedding our coats we each took one of the long clumsy-looking narrow-bladed oars, and, though progress was slow, we two pulled the boat the rest of the way to the opposite shore. I was glad when we landed, for the heavy oar had made my arms ache and my hands sore. We watched them put off on their return journey with the two youths pulling well at the oars and Father Allan waving to us; then we turned towards home. Knowing well the lie of the land I suggested to my sister that we should cross over the range of hills and strike the main road about a mile south of the schoolhouse, thus cutting down our distance. We adopted this plan and taking our leisure over the climbing we were not too fatigued when we reached the top of the range and looked around us from the height. The land and sea lay like a vast panorama below; there was no wind, and no waves disturbed the placid surface of the westerly ocean: no ripple appeared to our sight on the eastern sea; all seemed to be wrapped in a perfect calm. No sail of boat nor ship, nor smoke from steamer could be seen by us on this beautiful Saturday evening; the sole occupant of the sea appeared to be a small boat which lay far out on the Minch, so far out that we had not noticed it at first. Much as we were enjoying the lovely scene we did not stay too long but proceeded on our way home down the hill-side. Eventually we reached the main road near the spot I had originally intended to strike it. Here we met a friend of mine, Colin Mac-Innes, the father of two of the children in my school. He was a most garrulous fellow and I was often amused at his use of the English language he had acquired during the short visits he had paid on the mainland. His wife had been ill and had been to a nursing home at a convent where she had undergone a serious operation; she had recovered and was home again. Colin had told me at the time of his wife's operation that she was at 'a crying house for black womans',* and I always inquired about her when Colin and I met. So, as soon as my sister and I reached the main road, Colin came forward and greeted us. As usual I greeted him with:'Hallo, Colin, how is your wife?' He doffed

* *I.e.* taigh eiridinn nan cailleachan dubha.

180

his cap to my sister and said to me: 'Well, Mr Rea, she is feeling very indelicate just at present, whateffer.' Of course, I did not look at my sister, but satisfied myself by saying: 'I am sorry for that, Colin. I hope she will soon be quite well again.' All this while he had stood cap in hand and he now replaced it; so we said a goodbye and continued on our way home.

After attending at church next day we called on my friend Craig and his cousin and found our chum Law from the bank at the pier was with them. He was telling them of four men who had gone out pleasure sailing in a boat the previous day and had not yet returned. It appeared that these men were fish-buyers from the mainland who bought cargoes of fish for export from the islands and were staying at the hotel. Early in the day the four of them hired a small sailing boat intending a few hours of pleasure sailing; they declined to have the boat's owner or anyone else with them saying that they understood and knew all about sailing boats, so, taking a few sandwiches with them, they had sailed out of the harbour. Twenty-four hours had since passed and they had not returned, hence some anxiety was being felt about them at the pier. 'I expect they will return all right,' said Law, 'they, perhaps, called at another port, and spent the night there.' With that we dismissed the subject and conversed on other things. During our talk I spoke of Colin MacInnes and his use, or his misuse, of English. We all, in general, had some amusing incidents to relate; Craig showed us a letter that he had received from a neighbouring parent of one of his pupils. It was written in red ink on a single sheet of cheap note-paper and was enclosed in an envelope. It ran:

'Dear Friend my son John Donald is to sick to be coming to school she have the meesel very bad etolovence [presumably "at all events"] please turn over will you pleas lend me your spaid yours truly Friend'—the name of the writer, which I omit, concluded the letter. He was a man of very little schooling and we said that the letter deserved some credit for it at least conveyed what the man wanted to say. Soon after my sister and I left for home our three friends accompanying us a part of the way.

As may be inferred from my narrative, our dear mother was unable to join in the long walks and expeditions of us two; she had had an accident to her spine many years before, and had been more or less an invalid ever since. She at first seemed to gather renewed strength after coming to the Hebrides, but of late she found exercise more and more exhausting. Nevertheless, she would never allow us to forgo any of our excursions and she rejoiced at the complete restoration to health of my sister. The latter was now quite strong and robust so as to be unrecognizable as the weakly being who had come to me only a short few months before. We three were seated at tea that same Sunday evening of our hearing about the four missing men when a knock on the front door was heard. A young lady stood there, while at the gate stood another holding two bicycles. 'Can you direct us to the hotel?' asked the one at our door from my sister who had answered the knock. I went to the door and told her the way and explained that the hotel was distant about six miles from the schoolhouse. She looked disappointed and said: 'Oh dear! and we do so want our tea.' Of course, I invited them to take tea with us and they were glad to accept the invitation. They told us during the meal that they were on holiday and making a bicycle tour of the Long Island; they, with their bicycles, had landed from the steamer on Barra and had toured through it from the south, had engaged a boat on the northern coast of the island which had landed them at the inn at Pollachar two miles south of my schoolhouse; they had tried to get tea at the inn but had been told to go to the hotel—I was surprised at hearing this of my friends at the inn and resolved to try and ascertain the reason of it at my next visit. The two cyclists intended riding north through our island after spending this night at the Lochboisdale hotel. We now had the light of early summer evenings, so that when our visitors after thanking us set out on their six-mile ride to the hotel, we had no misgivings about their safe arrival at the hotel. The next time I visited my friends at Pollachar inn I made a point of referring to the two cyclists. The inn-keeper's wife at once said: 'Oh, yes, they came here and demanded that they be served with tea. I did not like their tone nor their manner, so I told them to go on to the hotel and shut the door on them.' I made no comment on this and changed the subject. The people of the island were naturally courteous themselves, and always very much resented discourtesy in others.

When the letters from Lochboisdale were brought in the evening of the day following that on which we heard of the four missing fish-buyers, I asked the postman if there were any news of them. He answered that they were safe at the hotel, and then explained what had happened. Some fishermen on Eriskay on the Sunday afternoon were crossing the hills when one of them, more keen-sighted than the others, pointed far out to sea and remarked that there was a boat tossing on the waves. They all stood and watched it till they began to think there was something strange about its behaviour. Taking its bearings they hastened down to the shore, and put off in a boat to investigate. Sailing before a good breeze they soon came up with the strange boat seen from the hill-top. Lowering sail and coming alongside they found it contained four exhausted men, two stretched on the floor of the boat, another lying across a thwart, and the fourth hanging half over the side! Making fast the two boats the fishermen clambered across and did their best to revive them. Eventually one of the four recovered sufficiently to be able to tell their rescuers that they were four fish-buyers from Lochboisdale hotel on our island. With the least possible delay their boat was taken safely to the harbour that they had left so light-heartedly some thirty-odd hours before. Well cared for at the hotel they were almost their normal selves again next day, and little the worse for their adventure. They had set out for their sail with a good breeze on the Saturday morning and were far out at sea when the breeze died away and it became a dead calm. They lowered the sail and tried to return by rowing; but the tide and currents were against them. The calm continued and night came on when a light wind arose. Immediately they tried to hoist the sail, when the rope broke; the helpless boat now drifted about all night till morning. The only food they had taken with them, a few sandwiches, had been eaten early in the previous afternoon—they were now in a parlous state and gradually getting weaker as the hours passed. Not being practical seamen who would soon have spliced the broken rope, they were helpless, and had it not been that a keen-sighted sailor had noticed them they would probably have been lost and the sea have claimed four more victims.

In talking the matter over afterwards my sister and I surmised that the solitary boat which we had seen while crossing the hills on Saturday and which seemed to be in sole possession of the seas was that containing the four buyers of fish.

Chapter Twenty-five

SHOULD an aeroplane observer fly over the lands of the Outer Isles he would be surprised at the number of lochs there, the great majority of which are fresh-water lakes. South Uist contained more than three hundred of them; some were very large, very small ones being quite the exception. I believe that it was only a few of them not inhabited by trout, either the brown trout, or the silvery sea trout. They contained no coarse fish such as pike; the only enemy of the trout was the otter, but the game-keeper and his dogs prevented the latter from becoming much of a menace to the fish.

There must have been means of communication between lochs situated at considerable distances from each other. Evidence of this was brought to my notice on one occasion. Anglers from the mainland of Scotland, England and even from abroad used to stay at Lochboisdale hotel during the season. It was the custom for parties of them to be driven in vehicles some eight or ten miles north each morning after breakfast. They took their lunch with them, and after the day's fishing, drove back early in the evening in time for dinner. One Saturday afternoon I happened to be at the pier when I met Duncan, the hotel keeper's son, with his fishing rod. I accompanied him to a neighbouring loch and watched him casting. Nothing happened for a time: then there was a swirl in the water; he struck and hooked a fish which had taken his tail-fly. After a few rushes and runs the fish was netted and landed—a nice five-pound fish. Duncan killed it with a blow on the head. He was then about to remove the hook from where it had caught in the fish's lip, when we saw that a broken cast of three flies was hanging from the side of its mouth. 'Greedy beggar!' was Duncan's comment.

Returning to the hotel we found that parties of anglers had returned and were laying out their respective 'catches' on the grass in front of the hotel, and were comparing them. We told them of the fish we had caught and of the broken cast. Much surprise was shown and one of them said 'One fish broke me and got away with the cast. But it could not be the same fish for it was on Loch K - - -, and that is quite eight miles away?' Then one of the other anglers asked him whether he remembered what flies he had had on the cast at the time. Quite readily he gave them: march brown, teal and green, and zulu. Duncan went indoors, then returned with the cast. This on examination convinced us that it came from the identical fish that had been hooked earlier in the day. It must have travelled for miles through a chain of lochs only to be killed eventually near the sea in the evening of the same day.

Quite often my sister accompanied me on my fishing expeditions to the lochs in the locality of my school, where there were about a dozen of them. She became an adept with the landing-net; but she almost invariably turned her head aside when I killed the fish and said 'Poor thing'!—suffering always much moved her. The diversity of the bird life on the island interested her greatly, and her constant question to me was 'What bird is that?', for we came across a new species on almost every one of our numerous expeditions. The corn-crake, of course, she knew, as also the seagull, though she had never seen the large black-backed gull before; while the myriads of skylarks we saw on our way rising in scores at a time filling the sky with song were a delight to her; of sparrows there were none on the island. The gannet, or solan goose, descending like a thunder-bolt into the sea and rising into the air again, prey in beak, the great northern diver disappearing below water at our approach and reappearing perhaps at a spot some two hundred yards from where it dived, the sandpiper running swiftly along the sands, and the curlew with its melancholy cry were all quite new to her. One day we had just climbed over the brink of a high bank on the shore of a secluded loch and and had sat down under its brow, when we heard a deafening whirring of wings: a large covey of wild duck passed just overhead and alighted in the loch almost at our feet. We two kept perfectly still, and our presence was evidently unsuspected for some time for the birds happily disported themselves in the water immediately before us. Probably some involuntary movement on the part of one of us betrayed our presence and, with shrill cries, they at once rose in a body from the surface of the loch, and rapidly disappeared over the tops of the neighbouring hills.

On another occasion we were all at home in the kitchen. It was a warm day and the doors were wide open. Suddenly there was a noise of beating wings, and a bird flew through two open door-ways into the far corner of the long kitchen shelf. It was a skylark; and there the poor little thing lay, palpitating in terror. Thinking that it had taken refuge there from a cat, I seized a stick, passed out at the kitchen door and through the smaller kitchen into the open air with the intention of scaring off the pursuer of the bird. Not seeing a cat about, and wondering what had frightened the bird, I re-entered at the door of the smaller kitchen when here I saw a large bird on a shelf. It was nearly two feet high and much resembled an eagle, with its large piercing eyes which were fiercely glaring at me; it had a cruel-looking downward-curved beak and large sharp talons. Filled with a momentary resentment towards the creature, and pity for the little skylark, I raised the stick, sprang forward and struck it down. In a few minutes it was dead—it was a very fine specimen of the peregrine falcon! Had I been on the mainland, I should have had it stuffed and mounted. This bird lives on smaller birds, and being of very rapid flight—it has been calculated that it travels at the rate of a hundred and fifty miles an hour—it easily overtakes its prey, slices off its head and devours it while still flying through the air. Among other birds we saw were the skua, or pirate-bird, which being fond of fish, robs gulls and other birds which had recently swallowed fish. The skua is so large and ferocious that its victim, when attacked, disgorges the fish in its terror. The attacker is so rapid in flight that it usually captures the prize ere it reaches the sea beneath. Eider duck we often saw, fine birds, almost as large as geese. Very rarely seen was the fulmar which seldom lands except on an almost inaccessible cliff and whose especial breeding place was the rocky face of St Kilda. It is a bird so powerful in flight that it flies easily against high winds. The hooded crow was much in evidence, and the crofters' wives had to keep a constant eye on their chickens for fear of this marauder. More troublesome still were the ravens which were unusually large and very numerous. Sometimes, when walking along the shore, I mistook a raven at a little distance for a small black sheep. The islanders, in boats, used to visit the islets which were the breeding grounds of these birds; armed with sticks and clubs they destroyed all the eggs and young birds they could find. It must have been nasty work for the men returned bemired and bloody; they told me that this work was necessary as the ravens attacked the sheep by alighting on their heads and pecking out their eyes: from loss of blood the sheep died and their carcases provided the birds with food. Once only I heard the formerly familiar song of my old friend the cuckoo; it was probably passing over our island on its way to the mainland. As far as my knowledge goes there are no snakes, frogs, toads, nor foxes there. An occasional wild deer appeared among the hills; but these probably had swum from North Uist where there was a 'deer-forest'.

Many were my trout-fishing excursions to the local lochs, sometimes alone, and at other times with my sister who liked to join me in such expeditions, and she helped me enthusiastically. On occasion my friend Craig came and had a day's fishing among these lochs. He told me he had heard that one of them was the lair of a monster trout which no one could catch. Though anglers from the hotel and others had tried it was always without success. At first we could gain no information whatever of the whereabouts of any such loch; but, on inquiring from our friend of the inn, we were assured that the report about the monster trout was true. It sometimes had been hooked, so it was alleged, but had got away each time. Moreover it was said to have seized young ducks swimming on the loch waters.

Ascertaining from our host the situation of this loch we proceeded on our quest for it. Crossing over moorland we came to a cluster of crofters' houses, and situated right in the midst of them lay a small loch. It was evidently the one indicated by our friend; but it looked so small and insignificant that we much doubted the story of the fish we had heard. A man came out from a cottage door and Craig called out 'Are there any fish in this loch?' The answer was 'Aye, but they are

verra seldom.' We were soon carefully casting, and we methodi-
cally fished the whole of the water. The loch was so small that
we thrice covered its surface in very short time, and though it
was favourable weather for fishing, no sign of fish did we see.
We left the loch with an impression of our having been 'taken
in' by 'another fishing story'.

On several subsequent occasions, when my friend visited me,
we fished this loch without obtaining any evidence of there
being a fish in it. When on my way to other lochs lying south
of the schoolhouse, I usually made a detour so as to make a
few casts over the waters of this little loch, ever hopeful of
getting a response as a reward for my perseverance. Fish life
there, always seemed to be non-existent, till one Saturday
morning! As usual I had made my detour to the loch, rather
as a matter of habit than with any expectation of a rise as I
sent my flies out over the water. They fell lightly; there was a
movement in the water and something had taken the middle
fly off my cast! I struck, but the line met with a dead resistance
and not a movement! At first I thought that the hook must be
fixed into some inanimate object such as an old boot or a log.
I tugged and pulled without response. Then the object (whatever it was beneath the surface I could not decide) began to
move. There was no rush or plunge of a fish, but there was an
irresistible force taking my steady gliding taut line through the
water. I felt joy and pride for I did not doubt that I had
hooked *the monster trout*! At the west end of the loch there were
some bulrushes, and I began to fear the fish getting among
them; so I gave him the butt of the rod and put on the utmost
weight and pressure I dare. This made no impression whatever
upon him! The fish's steady glide simply continued, up and
down the loch, across it and back again; backwards and forwards it went at just the same steady rate. For all the effect of
my rod's pressure on him he might have been a sack of coal
instead of a fish. I had met my master, and I now began to
have the feeling that he was playing with me, and that he was
amused at my efforts to disturb his imperturbability or to bring
him to the water's surface—I was helpless against him!
Suddenly as though weary with the game he had been playing,
he stopped. Then he swam direct for the rushes at the end of
the loch. Frantically I tugged, jerked and pulled with both

hands; but I might as well have been trying to stop a horse! Without deviating in the least from his course, he headed directly into the bulrushed water. There my line became stationary. After my pulling very hard, it came away, was reeled in but minus the flies! My feelings may be better imagined than expressed as I ruefully gazed at the waters before me. During the whole of the time—(I was going to say 'that I was playing the fish', but, perhaps, 'that the fish was playing with me' would be the more appropriate)—not a glimpse of the fish did I get, not even a fin; nor was there any swirl of water as the fish calmly turned in its course. I, and many others afterwards essayed to catch this 'demon trout'; but, as far as I learned no one ever met with success.

Not many days after my disappointing adventures with the 'monster trout', another fishing excursion provided me with an amusing though unfortunate incident. My sister had accompanied me to a loch less than two miles from home, and we had had fair sport. After casting out from the bank for a while, I was moving along at some distance from my sister when I heard her call me with an alarmed note in her voice. Hastening to her I found her with my spare reel in her hand, and the line running out from it into the loch. She had no rod so amused herself by fastening a hook to the end of the spare fishing line, baiting it with a worm and dangling it in the water. To her consternation a fish had seized the bait. By very careful handling of the rodless reel we managed to land the fish, a pounder; but I had to play it for a considerable time before it could be manœuvred into the landing-net. We started for home by way of the hills. Coming to a small ravine, we stood for a moment searching for the best point from which to descend. Walking along the top edge I stepped on to a large flat rock embedded in the soil and looked for the easiest way down. Without warning, the rock beneath my feet gave way and I felt myself falling with the rock into the ravine below. How quickly one thinks, at times! Even as I plunged I threw myself sideways and I remember visualizing myself lying below crushed beneath the fallen rock. The latter landed well to my left while I lay on the soft ground safe, but unable to move because of the pain my right ankle caused me. My sister speedily descended to me, fortunately without mishap. She bathed and bound the injury and helped me to rise. With the support of her shoulder and the rod I managed to reach the schoolhouse; but it took us more than three hours to cover the distance which was barely a mile. Owing to the pain of my ankle we had to pause on the way almost every few yards. It soon yielded to treatment at home; but some little time elapsed before it was sufficiently healed to enable me to venture out again.

Chapter Twenty-six

ONE of Craig's greatest friends was Alasdair MacLeod, whose father had a very large farm situated near the middle of the island. He was a well-educated young man. Several of the large farmers were very serious about the education of their sons and daughters, sending them to the mainland and even abroad to study and complete their scholastic attainments. Alasdair was a fine handsome fellow, a good horseman, an accurate shot, and a keen angler. I had met him on various occasions and meeting Craig and me returning together from a fishing excursion, he invited us both to join him in a day's fishing on the lochs of his father's farm. The school holidays were pending so we fixed a day early in the holiday. So that we might have a longer time at the sport he promised to bring a horse and trap to pick us up at Craig's house early in the morning of the day decided upon. Of course, we accepted the invitation with alacrity.

The morning of the day appointed broke favourably with a soft west wind, and I was at Craig's house early. Our young friend with his trap soon appeared, and without delay we three happy sanguine young men were shortly on our way north. The trap was a comfortable commodious vehicle and the horse was a good one so that we made good progress and I, for one, much enjoyed the rapid drive and the varied scenery. We had driven, perhaps, six miles when we slackened pace at seeing ahead a large phaeton drawn up on the grass verging the road. As we passed by I judged that the equipage must belong to an important personage: a liveried coachman and footman with cockaded hats stood by the heads of the two well-groomed horses, whose highly polished harness glistened in the sunshine. On the grass near the vehicle several dead grouse lay. At a bend of the road a little further on a lady was approaching, and I noticed, as we passed her, that she was of tall, handsome and commanding appearance, and was carrying a small dog in her arms. She bowed as we raised our caps in passing, and immediately afterwards as we drove on Alasdair said: 'Lady Cathcart! I suppose her husband is up on the moor among the grouse.'

Soon afterwards we reached a point where we left the road and drove on to a stretch of fairly level land clothed in grass and purple heather, with the mountain range ahead of us. Continuing on a short distance we came to the end of a large loch whose waters stretched far away to the east. Here we un-harnessed the horse, removed the bridle and tethered it to the trap with a long rope. Leaving it to graze, each of us gathered his fishing gear and with Alasdair leading the way, we proceeded east along the south shore of the loch. Though much tempted to stop and try my luck in the likely-looking water, I restrained myself till we arrived at a large arm of the loch which lay before us, narrowing on our right till it joined the sea. I was glad now that I had resisted the temptation to lag behind the others for this looked an angler's ideal spot. Here we decided that we should have a competition as to who would have the heaviest 'catch' for the day. My two friends chose to cross the stream much lower down and to fish along the shore on the opposite side to me where the arm of the loch was about fifty yards across; I elected to start from where I was—the wind was favourable for fishing from either shore so that we were all three at equal vantage.

When my fellow competitors arrived on the shore opposite to me, and had taken their chosen positions, so that we all three were ready, Alasdair shouted across to me 'Go!' and three rods were whirled in the air. Three casts of flies, almost simultaneously, fell lightly on the water's surface; there were three splashes and we had each hooked a fish. Both Alasdair's and mine dashed away towards the main waters of the loch. We endeavoured to restrain them, but they were too big and strong so we had, at first, to give them a little head. Craig, at some little distance, had his hands full with his fish, and while he was trying to control it a little, it suddenly darted completely across the track of the two other fish. Snap went my top joint when I put a heavy strain on it in an effort to divert it from its course;

a moment later, three thwarted anglers were looking at their three lines entangled, all minus their three good casts of flies. Fortunately I had with me a spare top to my rod, and before long we all had refitted our tackle and resumed our fishing.

I do not remember which one of us in our competition was the winner but I do remember the onerous task we had, at the end of the day, in carrying the spoil and loading it into the trap. It was well into the evening when, having harnessed the horse, we drove off to MacLeod's farm. We had eaten our lunch long hours before, so we willingly accompanied Alasdair to his father's house on his inviting us there for a meal. It was dark when we arrived and entered the large hall of a well-lighted house. Depositing our impedimenta here we were shown into a long spacious room, evidently the dining-room for at one end of a lengthy table was spread, on a clean white laundered table, a substantial meal for three people—this seemed to be evidence that we had been expected.

While Alasdair was away—for he had asked us to excuse him for a few minutes—I looked round the room. It was comfortably, but substantially furnished with long heavy table, chairs, and large sideboard of polished solid oak, and a few good pictures on the tastefully papered walls. I was interestedly looking at the double casements to the windows and was thinking to myself: 'That is the only way to prevent the Hebridean wind from forcing rain into a room,' when Alasdair returned to us. A tall, grey-bearded fine specimen of a Scottish farmer then entered with a gentle-looking little lady. I recognized them as we had met before at Lochboisdale. They were welcoming us when a maid entered with a tray bearing coffee and tea-pots; at this point they bade us to make a good meal and left the room; wholeheartedly we hastened to obey their injunction—I, for one, was very hungry.

Our welcomed and hearty meal over, we were asked to adjourn to the drawing-room. Here we found quite a company assembled: our host and hostess, their daughters Marion and Jessie, two young cousins from Inverness, Isabella and Ronald Macintosh, and the doctor. Some of these we knew, and we were introduced to the others. Introductions over, polite inquiries about our day's fishing were made, and with the relating of experiences of other members of the company conversation became general. At this juncture our host, Mr MacLeod, approached Craig and me with a request for us to stay at the farm till the morrow. Both of us, knowing that our absence from home for a night would not cause any anxiety there, consented to stay when Mrs MacLeod had joined her persuasions to those of her husband.

Music was now resorted to; one of the young ladies seated herself at the piano and sang one of Scotland's old songs. She sang and played well, and, I remember, she made quite a charming figure in her dark skirt, white blouse, with a shining silver belt enclosing her waist, and her fair hair crowning her head. The doctor knew that I could sing, so he hauled me out to join him in the duet 'Larboard Watch'. Cakes and lemonade were then served by two maids, after which card games were indulged in. Alasdair and his mother and father introduced me to the card game of 'Catch the Ten'. This game was a variety of whist; it was played in exactly the same manner, the only difference being in the scoring. As far as I remember a score of thirty-one points won a game: the ace of trumps scored four points, the king three, the queen two, the knave one, and the ten of trumps ten points in the tricks taken by a pair of partners, while two more points were scored by the partners who took the majority of the tricks in a hand, so that it was possible to score twenty-two points in one hand. I found this an interesting change from the game of ordinary whist as the main interest of the opposing partners seemed to be in winning a trick containing the ten of trumps—hence the title of the game, 'Catch the Ten'. Several games had been won and some lost by my partner, Alasdair, and myself when the ladies began to take their leave and to retire to rest. Soon we six men-folk only were left in the room and our host prescribed 'a night-cap' for us before we retired also. A tray with glasses, spoons, and lump sugar was brought in and a small kettle of hot water was set to boil on a spirit-lamp. When the water boiled our host produced a bottle of whisky and told us to help ourselves. Ronald Macintosh was about to pour some whisky in his tumbler before adding the hot water when Mr MacLeod called out: 'You will spoil it, man! I'll show you boys how to make toddy.' In the glass he placed a spoon and two lumps of sugar, then into this he poured just sufficient boiling water to cover the bowl of the spoon; removing the spoon he held it in a slanting position against the inside of the glass at a distance above the surface of the hot water; into the sloping spoon bowl he poured whisky very gently so that it trickled down the inside of the glass and spread itself on the surface of the water. Telling Macintosh to wait while the whisky heated through, he performed the same process for each of us. When the steam began to rise from the heated whisky he told us that it was ready to be drunk. There was no doubt that his method of toddy-mixing brought out the full flavour of the whisky. Our 'night-caps' finished, Alasdair with lighted candle conducted Craig and me to our bedroom where very soon we were wrapped in slumber.

Breakfast next morning was laid in the dining-room, and a brave show it made. The long table was covered with snowy linen and it almost must have groaned under the weight of the viands laid upon it. Foremost, at the head of the table, was an immense dish bearing a number of the large trout that we three had caught on the previous day; a whole ham, boiled; a big round of beef; plates of cheese, butter, oatcakes and scones, besides jams and jellies presented to me, at least, a formidable sight. Ten of us sat down to table, our host at the head of it, the doctor at the foot, and the hostess about half-way down on the opposite side to Craig and me. There was a pause and Mr MacLeod bent his head and all did likewise— presumably saying silent 'Grace'. Then all of us sat silent and a maid came forward with a tray bearing ten wine glasses and a decanter. Solemnly Mr MacLeod filled a glass, and drank the contents, replacing the glass on the tray afterwards. The maid proceeded to the next person, one of the young ladies, who took a sip only. As the tray neared me, I whispered to Craig, who sat at my side: 'What is it?' He whispered back: 'An appetizer.' By this time the maid was serving us. I took my glass and put my lips to it, taking a sip. It was neat whisky which I had never tasted before, and I replaced the glass on the tray. 'Go on, man!' said Craig. 'It's a grand appetizer!' and he tossed off the contents of his glass. I felt a little foolish, but having a good appetite already, no whetting of it seemed necessary. There was no smile on the face of anyone during the time the maid passed to each one in succession—they all appeared to look upon the matter as quite a serious business, but the ceremonious decorum with which the affair of an 'appetizer' was carried out caused me some secret amusement. Another maid now brought in hot tea and coffee; tongues broke loose at once and all were merry and bright over a substantial breakfast.

As the weather was fine Craig proposed to me that we should walk home along the 'machair', and the proposal met with my immediate acceptance for the summer beauty of the beflowered shore-lands was then at its fullest. After breakfast we announced our intention of walking home. At first there was much opposition to this, and Alasdair showed disappointment at the prospect of losing his drive, but we were firm in our intention, so he told us he would walk some of the way with us. Many regrets at the parting were expressed on both sides as we three set off south, well provided with sandwiches supplied by our kind hostess.

We had the whole day before us; consequently there was no need for us to hasten on our way, so we talked and smoked, as we strolled along; now and then the ground, rising a little, gave us a glimpse of the blue, summer sea; we stopped at times to gather some of the rarer flowers or to listen to the carolling of the skylarks, or to watch the flight of heron, plover, hawk, or of the skua.

Some two miles had been covered when Craig, who was a short way ahead, stopped and stood looking downwards, at the same time giving to us a low call 'Come here'. Quietly hastening to his side we found that he was looking intently into a stream that was running towards the sea, and directly across our path. The stream was about six or seven feet in width and running in a clean-cut channel across the 'machair'. At first I did not see what he was gazing at; then I became aware that hundreds and hundreds of trout were rushing inland up the stream; they were so closely packed that the water seemed scarcely sufficient to contain them. We all three stood silently watching them as they sped past us at our feet: all sizes of fish from a foot to three or four feet in length were hurrying madly upstream: so thick were they in the water that even the big fish seemed to find difficulty in getting past their smaller brethren and, by sheer strength and their weight, they forced their way through the packs of speeding fish.

We stood watching them for nearly an hour, and still then the stream was packed as full of them—there must have been thousands of them—I remember remarking to my companions: 'We could almost walk across the stream on their backs!' Craig, at last, gave a deep breath and said in a voice full of feeling: 'Well, boy and man I have fished the eastern rivers of Scotland, from the Ythan to the Tweed, but I have never seen such a sight as this before.' Alasdair told us that this stream was an effluent of the Howmore River and these waters were strictly watched and preserved for the sport of the proprietor and his friends. He had often seen the trout ascending the stream, but he had never seen them in such numbers before. Here we had to part with our friend; so, giving one last look at the fine fish we so much coveted, we each stepped back a few paces, took a run forward and leapt the stream. Not trusting ourselves to look into it again we waved to Alasdair and resumed our way homeward.

A few days later, meeting the factor, he was interested in my account of the stream packed with rushing fish. He said that we should have got into serious trouble had we attempted to interfere with the fish. I asked him whether anyone had been able to obtain permission to fish the Howmore River. 'Only once,' was the reply. He then told me that one of the anglers at the hotel, a very rich man from London who came every year for the fishing, had often importuned him to try and get him permission from the proprietor to fish the river, but though the landowner was so seldom on the island, permission was always refused by him when approached. The London man told the factor that he would not mind what he paid, and he told the factor to ask the proprietor how much he would take for a permit for a week's fishing on the river. So, on the next occasion that the landlord was leaving the island the factor spoke to him on the matter again. 'Oh! Choke him off and tell him that I should want £200,' was the reply. When the man from London heard of this, he was delighted and paid the money cheerfully. 'And it was well worth it,' was the verdict of this angler after his week's fishing.

NOTE. There was no big farmer called MacLeod in South Uist in Rea's time. He must either have forgotten the right name, or be trying to conceal the person's identity.

Chapter Twenty-seven

THE weather was consistently fine for the holiday, and harvesting was in full swing. All hands, men, women and children, were busy reaping, binding and stacking the corn, which consisted principally of oats, barley and rye; the 'lifting' of the potato crop was not done till last of all. My sister enjoyed going into the fields, for she now seemed of robust health thus much rejoicing our mother and myself.

Among the clergy whom I had met on our island was a Father McColl who was in charge of the mission on Benbecula, across the South Ford. He had been introduced to me while visiting in our locality; his bright smile, happy disposition, and his enthusiasm about his work made us friends at once. Consequently, when I received an invitation from him to spend a week of my holiday at his own place, I, urged by mother and sister to accept, did so. Though Father McColl's hair was perfectly white, he was a comparatively young man, full of vigour, and was very pleasant company, so I anticipated enjoying my stay with him. Having received instructions how to proceed, midnight found me boarding a cargo steamer which was on its way round the islands delivering goods ordered from the mainland, and picking up a cargo *en route*.

We passed several beacons and lighthouses, and morning brought our entry into an inlet of the sea along which we steamed. This was Loch Carnan, the eastern entrance to the South Ford which, at high tide, separates Benbecula from South Uist. About five o'clock in the morning, our vessel slowed up, two anchors were let fall, and we stopped close to the southern shore. A busy scene now ensued; on board, the donkey-engine was at work hoisting sacks of meal, trusses of hay, packing-cases, and furniture from the hold of the ship; long, heavy two-masted boats were brought alongside, men scrambled from them on to the ship's deck and began sorting and collecting the goods. One of these came up to me and said: 'Are you Mr Rae? Well, Father McColl is expecting you and we are to take you in our boat.' Then he added that they would not be starting for another hour, and looking at my fishing-rod hinted that there was a good loch for trout just over the neighbouring hill. This hint was quite sufficient for me, so, leaving my handbag with him, I ascended the hill rod in hand.

Below me lay a small loch glistening in the morning sunlight. Quickly I reached its shore and cast my flies on its waters. The trout were simply mad for them, tumbling over each other to get at them, so that I sometimes had three fish on my line at once: I almost laughed at their eagerness. Time was now very short, so, keeping only the larger fish, I returned to the boat with a creel of good-sized trout. The boats were already loaded and no time was lost in making sail and taking advantage of the flowing tide. The heavily laden boats were low in the water but we made good way. Passing westward along the channel, which was about a mile in width, the shore on either hand seemed to consist of low banks of sand intermingled with boulders of rock. It was a pleasant sail; and, after about three miles, sails were lowered and we ran into a cove where my white-haired friend was waiting to welcome me. Near by was an hotel, and here a horse and trap awaited to convey us to Father McColl's house. A short drive took us there where a hearty breakfast awaited us, to which my freshly caught trout, quickly broiled, formed a welcome supplement. After breakfast my host proposed that we should visit the local school which was in charge of the graduate master whom Craig and I had met earlier in the year at the examinations. On arrival there I was surprised at the fine large buildings which composed the school and the headmaster's house. My colleague seemed very pleased to see me and showed us over his house and school. Compared with those more recently built over which Craig and I had charge his place seemed almost palatial: his dining-room was lofty and from twenty to thirty feet in length with three large windows; there were seven or eight large bedrooms, a study, and several other rooms. The school was quite as generously planned and was well equipped with furniture. A little

later, Father McColl explained to me the reason of this difference from the schools on the island where I was domiciled. It
appeared that, before the advent of school boards and Education Acts, the proprietors of these islands had built, and provided
for, at their own expense, this school to form a centre of education in their Hebridean possessions. Pupils came there, and
some of them, from homes at a distance, had to reside at the
school. Since the Education Act had come in in 1872, however,
schools had been built at convenient places throughout the Isles,
so that all children, even the poorest, were provided with a
school near to their own homes. As my clerical friend took me
around the neighbouring townships, I could but notice the
effect of the influence of this educational centre. The houses
appeared to be better and more substantially built than was
usually the case with crofters' houses, and English was spoken
more generally and fluently than I had yet heard in the Isles.

This small island of Benbecula, three to four miles long, and
seven to eight broad, had a population of two thousand, the
great majority of whom were engaged in farming small farms
or crofts. A sound, or strait, on the north and another on the
south separated it from the North and South Uist. Both these
straits were fordable at a certain state of the tide, but dangerous
for strangers to cross without a guide. There was no port of call
on Benbecula; postmen had to cross these fords with letters
from the seaports in North and South Uist. The cargo boat
which brought me to the entrance to the South Ford was the
only means by which flour, grocery and other goods from the
mainland could be brought to the island. A weekly visit of this
steamer was usual; but, in rough weather, it could not call, and
the people had to wait a week longer for their goods. My host
told me that, sometimes, owing to bad weather, a month ensued
between the visits of the ship. On some of these occasions he
himself had been forced to subsist for a week or so almost
solely on potatoes and fish, as the entire island would be run out
of the supplies of meal and groceries.

At Father McColl's house, in the evening, we talked well on
into the night so interested were we in the various subjects for
conversation. I remember that, among these, he spoke of having
been chaplain at a smallpox hospital previous to his taking
charge of his mission on the island. 'But,' I exclaimed, 'were

you not afraid?' He looked at me, and said: 'Why?' 'Were you not in fear of catching the disease and dying?' I asked. A smile broke over his face as he answered: 'What is a priest's life for, but to give for the sick and suffering!' I am afraid that I had never realized this before.

On the morrow, after breakfast, my host proposed that we should visit a school near the North Ford. The weather had changed, and as we walked along, mile after mile, my impression of the scenery of the island was far from favourable, and I congratulated myself that the school to which I had been appointed was situated on South Uist. The land here was almost level and intersected in all directions by lochs so the island seemed to be composed of as much water as of earth; far away to the east lay a grey line of low hills, so that the whole scene gave an appearance of dullness in the extreme.

Heading due north, we at last came to the north coast of Benbecula and the entrance to the North Ford. Never before had I seen a more forbidding-looking spot; before us lay miles of mud and water, interspersed with islets and black rocks and dark tangles of seaweed clinging to them. My companion pointed north-east and indicated the line of the path across this perilous ford. 'Do you see those two high rocks out there looking like two sentinels?' said he. 'Well, the path lies on a straight line between here and there. It is about two miles in length, and a yard or two on either side of it means that you are in quicksands which immediately swallow any man, horse, cart, or trap that deviates from that path. From those two rocks out there you have to pick up a mark to the north-west and proceed straight for that mark which stands at the other extremity of the ford.' I looked at the entrance to this treacherous ford. From where we stood on the shore a path of shingle sloped sharply down to a passage between two immense, high, rocks; this passage, about seven or eight feet wide, and whose floor seemed to be composed of mud and sand, was the beginning of the four- or five-mile path across the North Ford. Turning to my companion I said: 'Have you ever crossed this ford, Father?' 'Often,' was the reply. 'I was lost in it one night as I was returning from a sick-call on the other side. It was a wild night and I mistook my bearings in the darkness. While trying to correct them, I lost my horse and trap in the quicksands. The tide overtook me and washed me away; but in the end I reached an islet out west there, and so remained till two men in a boat found me the next evening.' Then, removing his hat, he patted his snow-white hair, and smiled whimsically as he said: 'It gave me this;' and abruptly turning he led the way to the school which was quite near. We found it closed for the holidays and the teachers were away. The buildings were very similar to mine in South Uist, but on a smaller scale because accommodation for about seventy pupils only was needed for that district. Again I congratulated myself on my lot when comparing it with that of the schoolmistress in charge of the school by the depressing North Ford.

With the evident purpose of affording me amusement my host, in the evening, announced that he had arranged for us to go heron shooting on the afternoon following. Though personally diffident in regard to this kind of sport, I dissembled and affected an interest, not really felt. Accordingly late in the afternoon of the next day we set out for the west coast and were joined by a party of four men carrying their guns as well as two spare ones for Father McColl and me. The memories of the rest of the expedition are now rather hazy, for I did not really care for the sport and remember that I did not enjoy myself that night. The main recollections of that night are of our tramping for hours over bogs in the growing gloom of the evening; of seeing the bright beam from a beacon or lighthouse as night came on and we splashed our way through reeds; of the cries of birds in the semi-darkness as we came to a halt, then separated. I have visions of seeing the flash from guns on either hand of me, of a great clumsy creature above me which fell on me when I fired; of my falling into a tangle of water reeds, feathers, claws, and huge wings; of the others joining me as I recovered myself and seized the now dead bird. What followed I do not remember distinctly, but I know that, wet, cold, hungry, and tired I was heartily sick of the whole business, and was only too thankful when we reached the house. Sleep came unbidden, surely, to me that night.

During the rest of my stay on the island I fished or accompanied my host on some visits to his parishioners in the daytime, and we spent the evenings in conversation or reading. He was that delightfully tactful companion who knows when to talk and when to be silent and not for a moment did we seem to jar on each other.

My appointed day of departure arrived and I had to start early to catch the South Ford when it 'opened', or the tide had retired sufficiently for walking across the mile of sand not to be dangerous. My host insisted on accompanying me to the other side of it and seeing me into the postman's trap which would take me ten miles on my way home. Reaching the north shore of the ford a mile of wet sand lay before us across which was seen the sandy bank of the north shore of South Uist. Two very tall crofters were waiting for us and we all four descended the bank together on to the sands of the ford. A short distance across, in front of us, was a channel of sea water about three feet deep and twelve to fourteen feet across and evidently connecting the Atlantic and the Minch. Here the two men with us took off their shoes and stockings and rolled up their trouser legs high on their thighs. I was wondering if we should have to do the same when one of them went in front of Father McColl and turned his back to him who at once put his arms round the man's neck, raised his legs and rode pick-a-back while his bearer descended into the water and waded across to the other side of the channel. The other man came to me and I knew he expected me to be carried across. Even now I cannot say exactly why I refused the help: perhaps it was due to an Englishman's prejudice against being made to look ridiculous. At any rate, I was always good at a long jump, so I judged the distance, retired a few paces and cleared the water channel easily. The man waded across to my side, looked at me, but said nothing—his look seemed to betoken a doubt of my sanity. Near the opposite shore was a channel of water similar to the one we had crossed, but as it was not quite as wide nor as deep; I breathed a sigh of relief on reaching the top of the bank which was the north shore of the island of my home.

Though the South Ford did not appear as dangerous as the North Ford it is a fact that it had taken more lives than the other. This was partly due to the two channels we had crossed. A man might cross one, but by the time he reached the other the tide had turned and was running like a mill-race in the channel which, of course, was then much deeper and wider, so that he was caught between the two channels of the tide.

We found the postman, with his horse and trap, waiting for us outside the inn; this stood beside the north end of the main road that stretched for over twenty miles south, and whose extreme south end lay at Pollachar inn near my school. Leave takings with my friend were short as the postman was impatient to be on his way; so, mounting beside him in the trap, we started south, leaving my late host and friend standing with his white head bared and waving his hand. My trap companion was rather taciturn and gave only short answers to any questions of mine. We soon came in sight of an immense loch* directly to our front; it was so large I thought at first it was the sea as it stretched for miles to the east and west. When we had approached nearer I saw that the main road was built right across it at its narrowest part in sight. As we drove along this part of the road, about a mile, with the immense sheet of water on either hand of us, I tried to imagine crossing here in a winter gale; this thought tended to reconcile me with the apparent taciturn humour of my companion. Only once, on the way, did he make a voluntary observation and that was when we had covered some eight miles of the road. We were near the base of the two highest mountains rearing their towering heads two thousand feet above us on our left. Looking towards these, he gazed in their direction for a moment, and then, shaking his whip, exclaimed: 'The peckarrs (beggars)!' In reply to my question as to what was wrong he uttered the word 'Eagles', and again shook his whip. Looking intently I saw, circling high up mountain summits, several very large birds. Turning his head near the towards me my companion remarked: 'After the sheeps and lambs; the peckarrs!', and he drove on south as before.

Two miles further we came to a straggling township, and the trap was pulled up by the door of a thatch-roofed cottage on the wall of which was a board bearing the hand-painted legend 'Post-office'. My driver descended from the trap and began to unharness the horse, so I got out with my bag and fishing-tackle. The postman left his horse for a moment, pointed down the road, looked at me and said: 'Schoolhouse'; then he resumed tending the horse. He shook his head at me and turned away when I tried to recompense him for my drive. I knew the island

* Loch Bee.

204

people: he thought far more of my vigorous shake of the hand and my thanks than of any money I could give him. So, creel on back, bag in one hand and cased rod in the other, a quarter-mile walk took me to the schoolhouse. The schoolmistress here, whom I had previously met at some gathering, was at the house and invited me in for refreshment.

The weather was fine; and, as it was not long past mid-day, I told her that I should enjoy the twelve- or thirteen-mile walk to my house and taking it leisurely expected to reach home in the early evening. 'Call in and see Father John;' she said, 'he would be glad to see you, and you could get a rest there.' When she had given me directions for finding Fr. John Mackintosh's house which would be about half-way to my home, I thanked her and resumed my journey south.

The walk was lonely, for mile after mile was passed without my meeting or seeing anyone; but I enjoyed the sweet air, the scenery, and the thoughts that occurred to me on the way. About an hour, perhaps, after leaving the schoolhouse, a thudding sound reached my ear as I walked along; gradually it grew louder and louder. Standing still and listening to locate and to ascertain the meaning of this sound which was rapidly drawing near, I was just in time to see that a stampede of cattle was coming from the north before they were upon me. Without a moment's hesitation I threw myself into the deep ditch beside the road only barely escaping the leaders as they thundered past. There were hundreds and hundreds of them, long shaggy black or brown haired, and with wide-spreading horns; the road was crowded with them jostling and goring each other in their wild impetuous rush south. The large startled eyes of the huge creatures nearest the ditch, when they saw me, made me fearful of their being pushed off the road on top of me by the surge of beasts behind them. The ground in the ditch trembled beneath me while they were rushing by; then came the hindermost who passed by me in almost a flash and disappeared southwards in a cloud of dust. Next I heard shouting and half a dozen well-mounted men carrying stock-whips appeared and were accompanied by numerous dogs. These were all in full career in pursuit of the cattle. When they had disappeared and all was quiet again, I ventured to climb from the ditch, and, though my clothes and shoes were somewhat soiled, continued my journey, but I cast more than one nervous glance behind me ere I reached the gate of Father John's house.

It would be about four o'clock in the afternoon when on opening the gate a private road of two or three hundred yards in length lay before me and the house and chapel of Bornish were visible at the end of it. In a paddock beside the road a mettlesome black horse raised his head, galloped round, then came to the fencing and gazed at me with ears erect. Passing on I approached the porch of the house; the door was wide open, but no one was in sight. Making sure that no person was about outside, I returned to the porch and knocked loudly on the open door, but all was silent but for the humming of the bees, busy with the flowers of plants in pots that adorned the interior of the porch. Standing in the open doorway, I noticed the sporting guns and fishing rods standing in its corners which corroborated what I had heard: that Father John was a keen sportsman.

All continued silent and no sound broke the quiet of the still summer's afternoon except the droning of the bees; so I knocked again, more loudly than before. After waiting quietly for a few moments and listening, there was a sound like the slow padding of soft slippers on the floor of the hall which apparently led off at right-angles to the porch. Then something emerged from the hall and stood facing me, waiting at the wide-open door. At first I was too startled to think what it was: a donkey, a lion, or what; immediately after I recognized it as a dog. It was the largest I have ever seen. In memory I can see it now, distinctly; the eyes almost level with mine looking me calmly in the face, a huge head with heavy black drooping lips, long dark-tawny powerful body, and great paws. I stood perfectly still like a statue; the dog did the same; if I moved it might attack me as an interloper, so all I could think of doing was to wait and hope that someone would soon come and call off the dog. Standing there tense and motionless it seemed ages to me before I heard firm heavy steps in the hall; a stalwart black-bearded man in clerical dress appeared in the porch. 'Back, Hamlet,' he said to the dog which immediately retired into the house. He smiled, and came forward with outstretched hand on my announcing myself, and asked me in to tea. Stowing my baggage in a vacant corner of the porch I followed him into a large room, library and sitting-room combined, judging by its furniture. The huge dog was stretched at full length at one end of the room where the wall was completely occupied with shelves of books. The table was laid for tea, and after an old lady had brought in extra plates and cup in saucer, we sat down at table. Over the meal I learned that the dog was a large specimen of Danish boarhound and was quite inoffensive unless roused; also that Father John wore a beard to protect his rather sensitive throat. When I told him of the cattle stampede, he explained that they belonged to a local farmer and had been running wild on the mountain-side for a year; the farmer's men had been collecting them for market purposes.

Afterwards we sat in armchairs, smoking and talking while the table was cleared. I do not remember exactly how the subject of chess entered into the conversation unless it cropped up when we were discussing games of skill and I happened to mention that I sometimes played chess with my mother at her bedside. My host sprang to his feet and exclaimed: 'Chess! Do you play chess?' He hastened across the room to an old sideboard and returned to the table where he set out a chess-board and placed the men. Placing two chairs in position he said: 'Oh! I am so glad. I have not had a game of chess since I came to the Isles.' We were well matched and he was delighted as our success varied, some games he won and some fell to me. We were so lost in the game that time seemed not to exist for us till, suddenly, he looked at the clock and 'Two o'clock! We must go to bed after this game and I will drive you south tomorrow.'

After breakfast next morning, he put the board and men on the table and looking at me said eagerly: 'Shall we?' Down we sat and again lost all sense of time. I became almost as keenly interested as he was, and the interest increased as we began to realize each other's game and make more subtle moves. We played on and on, game after game throughout the day, only snatching a hasty dinner and tea so as to return the more quickly to our game. Sometimes I wonder what the old housekeeper must have thought of us—possessed! I expect. It was long past midnight when we relinquished play and retired to bed. We were just as enthusiastic for a game the next morning and we played throughout that day and on into the night. We had had about three days of chess and agreed that I must return home the next day. I felt really happy that I had been able to help my host to indulge in the intellectual game of playing chess.

Father John had business at the pier next day, so drove me in his trap as far as the house of my friend Craig at Daliburgh. Here I took leave of him; then finding that Craig was out, I wended my way home.

NOTE. Rea's recollection of the identity of the parish priest of Benbecula seems to have been confused. It was the Rev. Alexander MacDougall who held this position from 1891 to 1903. Fr Donald McColl had been parish priest of Iochdar from 1877 to 1887. Fr John Mackintosh left Bornish in 1900.

The school referred to on p. 199 was at Torlum, Benbecula. According to the statement of Angus MacLennan, sub-factor of South Uist in 1883, 'this school was built about fifteen years ago, at an expense of £600. An addition was made in 1876, which cost about £180. During the past five years about £145 has been expended on improvements and repairs in connection with the school, and over and above this its management, including payment of teacher and assistant, costs over £150 annually' (*Minutes of Evidence of the Crofters Commission*, p. 2871).

Epilogue

SOON after I had returned from my visit to the north my mother's health failed, which caused me and my sister some alarm. Our doctor visited and treated her, but she became weaker. Often she asked if the windows and doors were wide open, for she said that she could not breathe. I asked the doctor to get further advice on her case if possible. Fortunately a celebrated Edinburgh doctor was staying at the hotel at this time on holiday for fishing and shooting. He was called in for consultation with our doctor. After examination of my mother and conferring together, they gave me their verdict: she was to leave the Isles as soon as possible. They had come to the conclusion that the strong air was too much for her weakened vitality; though most beneficial to the normal person, it was deleterious to her delicate state of health and she should be removed to her native climate.

Naturally, the responsibility weighed upon me rather heavily, and I considered as to what was to be my wisest course. My sister was now thoroughly restored to health so I decided to obtain a post in Birmingham, our native place and establish a new home there. Quite soon a good post in my native city was offered me, and I accepted it.

I feel it best to draw a veil over the farewells, the mutual regret expressed on all sides at the necessity for our leaving. Father Allan, who came over several times to see us, was the greatest comfort and support to me in my endeavour to act as my duty should lead.

As the steamer that bore us, mother, sister and brother, steamed eastwards across the Minch and I stood at the taffrail taking my last look at the Outer Isles now faint on the western horizon, my thoughts were of the people I had left behind;

simple folk, brave, enduring, generous and warm hearted, true and faithful friends. Then my thoughts flew to the man on his small island ministering to the poor fisherfolk—how truly he personified that picture in the *Clergy Review* of the ideal parochial pastor:

A man of real learning, sane and skilled in judgment; kindly and companionable; devoted to his work; unobtrusive, tactful and sympathetic; energetic and manly, a leader to his people and fellow-priests; pious without show, having in the strength, simplicity and sincerity of his devotion the secret of his ascendancy with souls.

Index

Spotter's Guide to
FISHES

Alwyne Wheele~

Illustrated by
Annabel Milne & Peter Stebbing
with additional illustrations by
Christine Howes and Joyce Bee

Contents

Edited by
Jessica Datta
and Rosamund Kidman-Cox

The illustrators would like to thank Charles Wiard of Billingsgate Fish Market for his assistance and advice. Also many thanks to Roy Bruce and Robert Thompson for their help.

Printed in Great Britain

First published in 1978 by Usborne Publishing Limited, 20 Garrick Street, London WC2

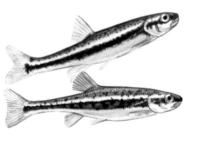

Text and Artwork © 1978 by
Usborne Publishing Limited

All rights reserved. No part of this publication may be reproduced, stored in a retrieval system, or transmitted by any means, electronic, mechanical, photocopying, recording, or otherwise, without the prior permission of the publisher.

The name Usborne and the device are Trade Marks of Usborne Publishing Ltd.

How to use this book

This book is an identification guide to some of the freshwater and sea fishes of Britain and Europe. The book is arranged with freshwater fishes first, followed by sea fishes. The fishes are also grouped by the places where they live.

The description next to each illustration tells you about the fish – where it lives, what it eats, where it lays its eggs. It also tells you the normal maximum length of an adult fish measured from head to tail. Given good conditions, fishes can continue growing throughout their lives. The ones you will see or find may therefore be any size up to this maximum, depending on the age of the fish, and its food supply.

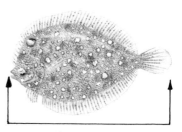

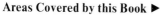

Length in metres or centimetres

Areas Covered by this Book ▶

This book covers the countries (and their coastlines) coloured red on the map and all the seas (shown blue). Not all the fishes that live in these areas are included in the book. Some of the fishes shown are very rare in British waters, or do not live here at all, but are common in other countries of Europe. Look for them if you go on holiday abroad.

Tick off each fish when you have seen it ✓

Scorecard ▶

The scorecard at the end of the book gives you a score for each fish that you spot. A common fish scores 5 points and a very rare one is worth 25 points. Some of the fishes in the book, the ocean fishes for example, are very difficult to spot. Tick them off if you see them in an aquarium, a museum, on television or in a film.

Page	Fish	Score	Date May1	Date Jun7	Date
6	Grayling	15		15	
6	Trout	5	5		

The pictures on this page name and show you the different parts of a fish. You may find the names useful when you use the book. Other special words are explained in the glossary on page 59.

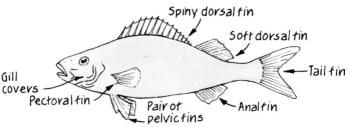

The pointed, torpedo-like shape of most fishes is good for moving through water. A fish swims by moving its tail fin and the back part of its body. The other fins help it to keep its balance. Most fishes have a swim bladder inside them. This is a bag full of gas which helps stop the fish from sinking in the water.

Fishes are **vertebrates,** which means that they have a backbone made up of many small bones called **vertebrae.** (You can see the backbone easily when you eat a fish.) Unlike mammals, most fishes are not warm blooded. Their body temperature changes with the temperature of the water. Most of them lay eggs and do not give birth to live young.

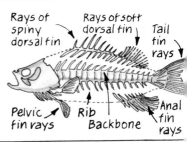

Breathing In   **Breathing Out**

Fishes take oxygen from the water by passing the water over their **gills.** They gulp water in through their mouths with the **gill covers** closed. Then the gill covers open and the water flows out through the gills. Some fishes feed on plankton (microscopic plants and animals) which is sieved from the water by gill rakers.

There are over 20,000 **species** (or kinds) of fishes and most of them live in the sea. Although many of them live in the same kind of habitat (places where animals live), they can all survive together because they eat different foods. This balance can be upset when people pollute or over-fish the seas or rivers where fishes live.

4

What to Take

When you go spotting, take this book and a notebook and pencil with you to record what you see. Draw the fishes that you see and note where and when you spotted them. Take a tape measure if you are going to watch people fishing or to visit the fishmonger's.

Try attracting fishes by dropping small pieces of bread and maggots into the water. A fine net and jam jars will be useful for catching and studying small fishes, but always put them back when you have finished looking at them.

If you are looking in rock pools, in a freshwater pond, or in the sea off a sandy beach, take a face mask for looking under water. If you are a good swimmer, you could use a snorkel for longer periods of fish-watching. A clear plastic box, placed on the water surface, is also useful for underwater viewing.

Notebook and pencils

Pieces of bread

Tape measure

Snorkel

Face mask

Shrimping net

Jam jars for collecting fishes

Plastic box

Where to Look

You can see freshwater fishes in ▶ rivers, ponds, canals and lakes. Stand on the bank or on a low bridge and watch carefully. Don't make a noise or let your shadow fall on the water as this can disturb the fishes.

◀ You can see many kinds of sea fishes at a fishmonger's or at a fish market. If you live near the sea or go on holiday to the sea, you may be able to watch fishing boats docking and the catch being unloaded.

You can spot small sea fishes in rock ▶ pools and in the shallow water of sandy beaches.

There are many aquariums in Britain where you can see unusual fishes, and most museums have a natural history section where you can find out more about fishes.

Hill streams and highland lakes

The water is usually clear, cold and fast-flowing. The fishes shelter behind or under rocks. In lakes, many of the fishes spend the winter in deep water and eat very little.

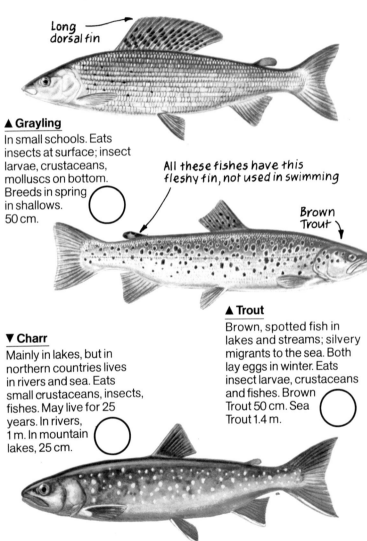

Long dorsal fin

▲ Grayling

In small schools. Eats insects at surface; insect larvae, crustaceans, molluscs on bottom. Breeds in spring in shallows. 50 cm.

All these fishes have this fleshy fin, not used in swimming

Brown Trout

▼ Charr

Mainly in lakes, but in northern countries lives in rivers and sea. Eats small crustaceans, insects, fishes. May live for 25 years. In rivers, 1 m. In mountain lakes, 25 cm.

▲ Trout

Brown, spotted fish in lakes and streams; silvery migrants to the sea. Both lay eggs in winter. Eats insect larvae, crustaceans and fishes. Brown Trout 50 cm. Sea Trout 1.4 m.

Hill streams and highland lakes

Fleshy fin

▲ Powan
Mostly in mountain lakes, but found in rivers around the Baltic Sea. Feeds on small crustaceans. In rivers, 70 cm. In mountain lakes, 20 cm.

▼ Minnow
Large schools near surface often in shallow water. Eats insects, their larvae, crustaceans. 8 cm.

Male in breeding colours

▲ Bullhead
Hides under rocks and in dense plant growth by day. Active at dusk and dawn. Lays its eggs in a cavity under a large stone. 10 cm.

▼ Streber
Bottom-living, mainly solitary fish. Found in eastern Europe. Lives in fast-flowing streams. Eats insect larvae and crustaceans, mainly at night. 15 cm.

Middle reaches of rivers

The water current is moderate with fast-flowing stretches and also slower deep pools. The water is fairly clear and there are lots of water plants.

Sucker

Seven gill openings

▲ Lampern

Spawns in gravelly shallows. Young live in small streams, buried in mud. Migrates to sea to feed on other fishes by sucking their blood. 50 cm.

▼ Salmon

Migrates to Greenland to feed on shrimps and fishes, then returns to fresh water to lay its eggs in gravel streams in winter. Young stay in the river for up to three years. 1.5 m.

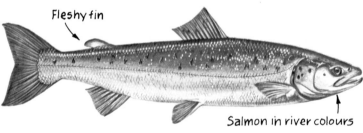

Fleshy fin

Salmon in river colours

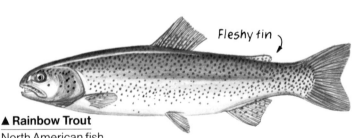

Fleshy fin

▲ Rainbow Trout

North American fish introduced into Europe. Young eat insects, their larvae and crustaceans. Adults eat other fishes. 1 m.

Middle reaches of rivers

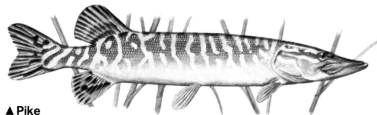

▲ Pike
Hides among water plants waiting to attack prey. Eats all but biggest fishes, and sometimes ducklings and water mammals. Lives up to 20 years. 1.3 m.

▼ Dace
Likes moderate current and clean shallow water. Usually in schools. Eats insects at the surface. Spawns in gravelly shallows. 30 cm.

▼ Chub
Forms schools when young, but large fish live alone in deep pools under trees and river banks. Eats fishes, insects and crayfish. 50 cm.

The shape of the anal fin will help you tell the difference between Dace and Chub

Bleak ▶
Lives at the surface of the water in schools. Eats water fleas and other crustaceans, and insects on the surface. 15 cm.

Anal fin

9

Middle reaches of rivers

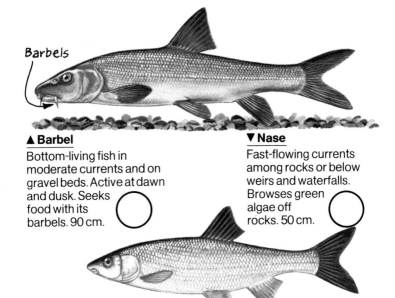

Barbels

▲ Barbel
Bottom-living fish in moderate currents and on gravel beds. Active at dawn and dusk. Seeks food with its barbels. 90 cm.

▼ Nase
Fast-flowing currents among rocks or below weirs and waterfalls. Browses green algae off rocks. 50 cm.

Sides are rounded

▼ Spined Loach
Lives in soft mud and green algae. Comes out to feed on tiny crustaceans at night. Spine under each eye. 11.5 cm.

Sides are flattened

▲ Stone Loach
Hides under stones or in weed-beds by day. Hunts for bottom-living insect larvae, crustaceans and worms by night. 10 cm.

Middle reaches of rivers

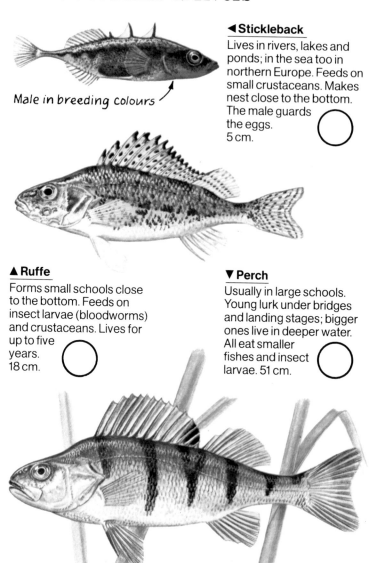

◀ Stickleback

Lives in rivers, lakes and ponds; in the sea too in northern Europe. Feeds on small crustaceans. Makes nest close to the bottom. The male guards the eggs. 5 cm.

Male in breeding colours

▲ Ruffe

Forms small schools close to the bottom. Feeds on insect larvae (bloodworms) and crustaceans. Lives for up to five years. 18 cm.

▼ Perch

Usually in large schools. Young lurk under bridges and landing stages; bigger ones live in deeper water. All eat smaller fishes and insect larvae. 51 cm.

Lowland lakes and ponds

Mostly reservoirs, gravel-workings and farm ponds. Depending on size and age, the water varies from clear and well-oxygenated to coloured and stagnant. Usually full of plant and animal life. Fishes grow fast and large.

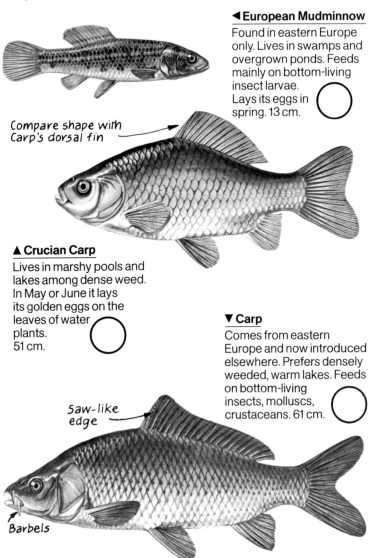

◀ European Mudminnow

Found in eastern Europe only. Lives in swamps and overgrown ponds. Feeds mainly on bottom-living insect larvae. Lays its eggs in spring. 13 cm.

Compare shape with Carp's dorsal fin

▲ Crucian Carp

Lives in marshy pools and lakes among dense weed. In May or June it lays its golden eggs on the leaves of water plants. 51 cm.

▼ Carp

Comes from eastern Europe and now introduced elsewhere. Prefers densely weeded, warm lakes. Feeds on bottom-living insects, molluscs, crustaceans. 61 cm.

Saw-like edge

Barbels

Lowland lakes and ponds

Angle of mouth is steep

▲ Rudd

Lives in overgrown ponds as well as lakes. Forms schools. Feeds on surface-living insects, as well as larvae and plants. 40 cm.

▼ Tench

Lives in dense weed-beds. Burrows in mud in winter. Eats insect larvae, snails, crustaceans, and occasionally plants. 50 cm.

▲ Weatherfish

Often lives in overgrown stagnant ponds. Gulps for air at the surface. Becomes restless in thundery weather. Northern and eastern Europe only. 15 cm.

▼ Nine-spined Stickleback

In dense weed-beds, and can live even in ditches. Male makes a nest just off the bottom. He guards the eggs. 7 cm.

There can be 7 to 12 spines on the back

Male in breeding colours

Lowland rivers

Usually slow-flowing with a gentle slope, winding through flat land.
Fishes prefer clouded water, little current and muddy bottoms.
Dense weed beds at edges provide food, shelter and places to spawn.
Often slightly polluted.

Lower jaw
sticks out

▲ Whitefish

In mountain lakes in
Britain and the Alps; in
rivers in northern Europe;
and in Baltic Sea. Eats
mainly fishes and
crustaceans.
Lakes, 25 cm.
Rivers, 35 cm.

▼ Goldfish

Comes from China and
Japan and now widespread
in Europe where pet fish
have escaped. In dense
weed where it
spawns in June
and July. 30 cm.

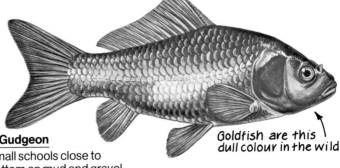

▼ Gudgeon

Small schools close to
bottom on mud and gravel
Uses long barbels to find
snails, crustaceans
and insect
larvae.
15 cm.

Goldfish are this
dull colour in the wild

Lowland rivers

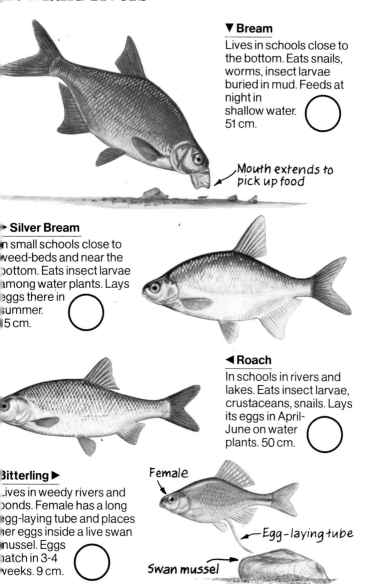

▼ Bream
Lives in schools close to the bottom. Eats snails, worms, insect larvae buried in mud. Feeds at night in shallow water. 51 cm.

Mouth extends to pick up food

► Silver Bream
In small schools close to weed-beds and near the bottom. Eats insect larvae among water plants. Lays eggs there in summer. 15 cm.

◄ Roach
In schools in rivers and lakes. Eats insect larvae, crustaceans, snails. Lays its eggs in April-June on water plants. 50 cm.

Bitterling ►
Lives in weedy rivers and ponds. Female has a long egg-laying tube and places her eggs inside a live swan mussel. Eggs hatch in 3-4 weeks. 9 cm.

Female

Egg-laying tube

Swan mussel

Lowland rivers

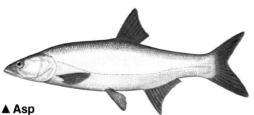

▲ Asp
Prefers moderate currents
but will live in lakes.
Young form schools; adults
mainly solitary. Sweden
and Germany
eastwards.
60 cm.

▼ Wels
The only native European
catfish. In deep, still
water. Hunts mainly at
night. Eats mostly
fishes, ducklings,
frogs. Rare. 3 m.

Barbels

Raised
nostrils

▼ Zander
Comes from central
Europe but now spread
throughout northern
Europe. Found in schools
in cloudy water. Eats
smaller fish
mainly at dawn
and dusk. 70 cm.

▲ Burbot
Only member of the cod
family living in fresh water.
Under tree roots and
holes in banks. Active
mainly at night.
Extinct in
Britain. 51 cm.

River mouths and estuaries

Water is fresh upstream and salty at the mouth. Fresh water often runs downstream above the sea water, which comes and goes with the tide. Usually muddy-bottomed with sand banks and few plants.

▲ Sea Lamprey

Eats larger fishes by sucking their blood. Migrates into fresh water to spawn, then adults die. Larvae spend three years buried in river mud. 91 cm.

▼ Sturgeon

Breeds in large rivers over gravel bottom. Migrates to sea to feed on bottom-living fishes, crustaceans, worms and molluscs. Now very rare and may die out completely. 3.5 m.

Yellow Eel
(see page 54)

▲ Eel

Breeds in mid-Atlantic. Eel larva takes three years to float to Europe. Changes to an elver and swims upriver even into the tiniest streams. May live for 20 years in fresh water. 1 m.

▼ Twaite Shad

Large relative of the herring. Lives in the sea, but migrates up rivers to spawn on gravelly shallows. Eats crustaceans and small fishes. 55 cm.

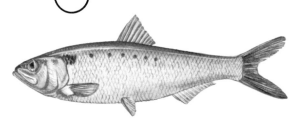

17

River mouths and estuaries

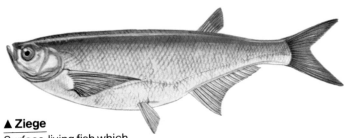

▲ Ziege
Surface-living fish which migrates in schools from the sea up rivers. Feeds mainly on fishes. Found in Baltic and Black Sea countries. 51 cm.

▼ European Toothcarp
In shallow pools at the sea's edge and in marshy estuaries. Eats small crustaceans and insect larvae. Mediterranean only. 5 cm.

Male colouring

▼ Meagre
Uncommon in northern European seas, but elsewhere young are common in estuaries. Eats small fishes, and makes a loud rumbling sound as it hunts for food. 2 m.

River mouths and estuaries

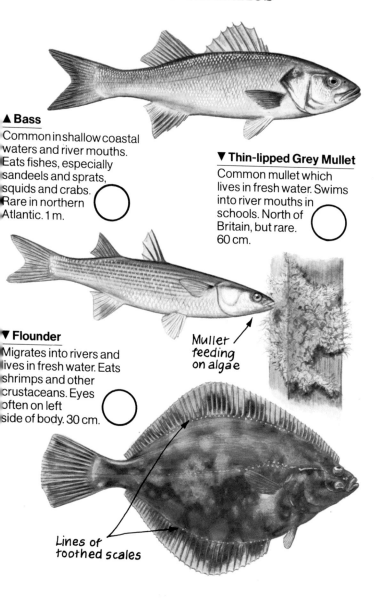

▲ Bass
Common in shallow coastal waters and river mouths. Eats fishes, especially sandeels and sprats, squids and crabs. Rare in northern Atlantic. 1 m.

▼ Thin-lipped Grey Mullet
Common mullet which lives in fresh water. Swims into river mouths in schools. North of Britain, but rare. 60 cm.

▼ Flounder
Migrates into rivers and lives in fresh water. Eats shrimps and other crustaceans. Eyes often on left side of body. 30 cm.

Mullet feeding on algae

Lines of toothed scales

Sandy beaches and shallow water

Many fishes burrow into the sand in shallow water and come out at high tide to look for food on the water-covered shore. Others live in schools, which gives them some protection, as there is no seaweed to hide in.

Greater Pipefish ▶

Common on muddy or sandy bottoms. Eats young fishes and tiny crustaceans. Male has a skin fold under his tail in which the eggs develop. 45 cm.

Barbels

▲ Five-bearded Rockling

Common in shallow water and on rocky shores. Young are silvery and live at the surface of the sea. Not in the Mediterranean. 25 cm.

Jellyfish

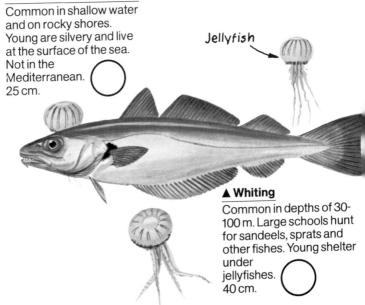

▲ Whiting

Common in depths of 30-100 m. Large schools hunt for sandeels, sprats and other fishes. Young shelter under jellyfishes. 40 cm.

20

Sandy beaches and shallow water

▲ Eelpout

Common fish on sandy and
rocky shores in pools,
under stones and algae.
Gives birth to young about
4 cm long.
North Atlantic
only. 19 cm.

▲ Sand Smelt

Usually in huge schools.
Breeds in shore pools in
summer. Eggs have long
threads which get
tangled with
seaweeds. 9 cm.

▼ Thick-lipped Grey Mullet

In coastal waters in large
schools, migrating north
in summer. Eats fine algae
on rocks and on soft mud
surface, which
contains small
animals. 75 cm.

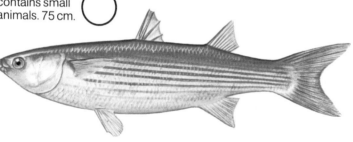

Hook

◀ Hooknose

Lives in shallow water
2-40 m deep. Often caught
in shrimp nets. Feeds on
small crustaceans,
worms and
molluscs. 20 cm.

21

Sandy beaches and shallow water

Lesser Weaver ▶
Lies buried in sand in shallow water with its venomous spines sticking up. Feeds mostly on small shrimps and other crustaceans. DO NOT TOUCH. 14 cm.

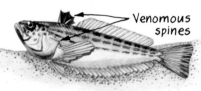

Venomous spines

▼ Sand Goby
Lives on sandy shores to 10 m deep. Eats small crustaceans and is often eaten by birds and fishes. Lays its eggs in a hollow shell. 9 cm.

▲ Sandeel
In huge schools close to the bottom. Burrows head-first in the sand. Eaten by other fishes and birds, like terns and puffins. Not in Mediterranean. 20 cm.

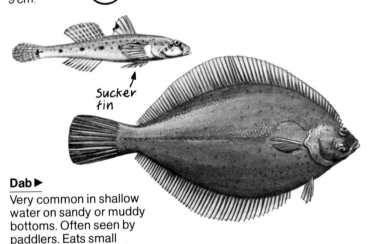

Sucker fin

Dab ▶
Very common in shallow water on sandy or muddy bottoms. Often seen by paddlers. Eats small crustaceans. Not in Mediterranean. 25 cm.

Rocky shores and shallow water

Rich in animal and plant life. Fishes live in pools, under stones or among seaweed. Many spend most of their lives on the same shore.

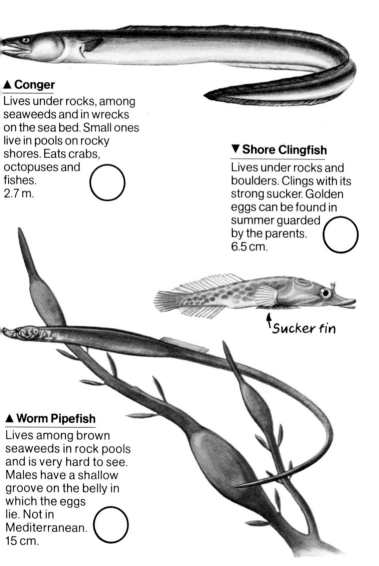

▲ Conger

Lives under rocks, among seaweeds and in wrecks on the sea bed. Small ones live in pools on rocky shores. Eats crabs, octopuses and fishes.
2.7 m.

▼ Shore Clingfish

Lives under rocks and boulders. Clings with its strong sucker. Golden eggs can be found in summer guarded by the parents.
6.5 cm.

Sucker fin

▲ Worm Pipefish

Lives among brown seaweeds in rock pools and is very hard to see. Males have a shallow groove on the belly in which the eggs lie. Not in Mediterranean.
15 cm.

Rocky shores and shallow water

Lower jaw sticks out

▲ Pollack

In schools in midwater, close to rocks when adult. Eats fishes, especially sandeels and herrings. Not in eastern Mediterranean. 1.3 m.

▼ Shore Rockling

Most common on rocky shores in pools and under seaweed. Its three barbels help it to locate shrimps, small crabs and worms, which it eats. 35 cm.

Barbels

Sea Scorpion ▶

Common fish in shore pools and among seaweeds. Eats shrimps, small crabs and fishes. Not in Mediterranean. 17 cm.

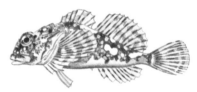

Flaps of skin help camouflage fish

◀ Scorpionfish

Lies motionless among rocks and under seaweeds in shallow water. Hunts for crustaceans and fish at night. Not in north Atlantic. 25 cm.

Rocky shores and shallow water

14 to 16 spines

▲ Sea Stickleback

Lives entirely in the sea among seaweeds and eel-grass. Male builds a cup-sized nest in the seaweed. Not found in Mediterranean. 15 cm.

▼ Cardinalfish

In small groups in caves or crevices in rocky outcrops. Hunts actively at night. Male holds the eggs in his mouth until they hatch. Mediterranean only. 15 cm.

▼ Damselfish

Very common in Mediterranean. Forms large schools close to rocks. Lays its eggs on flat patches of rock. Male guards the eggs. 15 cm.

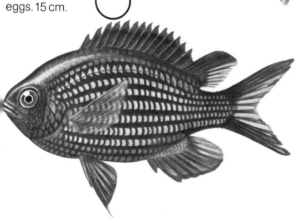

25

Rocky shores and shallow water

◄ Saddled Bream

In small schools close to rocks often 2-3 m below the surface. Eats small bottom-living animals and seaweeds. Not in north Atlantic. 30 cm.

"Saddle"

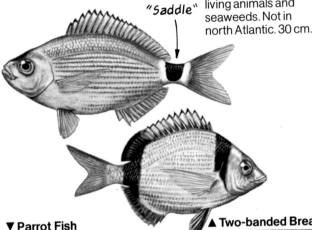

▼ Parrot Fish

Small groups swim around rocks. They scrape algae off rock with their strong teeth. Mediterranean only. 50 cm.

▲ Two-banded Bream

Common in small groups close to seaweed-covered rocks. Eats crustaceans and worms. Not in north Atlantic. 25 cm.

Broad teeth make mouth look like a parrot's beak

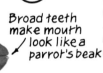

Goldsinny ►

Lives close to seaweed-covered rocks and in eel-grass beds, occasionally in shore pools. 15 cm.

Rocky shores and shallow water

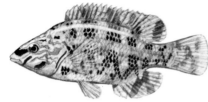

▲ Five-spotted Wrasse
In shallow water among rocks and seaweeds. Male makes large seaweed nest for female's eggs. He guards the eggs. Mediterranean only. 15 cm.

▼ Ocellated Wrasse
In Mediterranean at moderate depths near rocks and sand. Builds seaweed nest for its eggs. Eats parasites which live on the bodies of other fishes. 13 cm.

Colour varies

▲ Ballan Wrasse
Large wrasse. Common except in Mediterranean. Lives in loose schools around rocks. Feeds mainly on mussels. 60 cm.

▼ Cuckoo Wrasse
Rather uncommon wrasse. Lives near rocks. Male displays his bright colours to female before she will lay her eggs. 35 cm.

Male in breeding colours

27

Rocky shores and shallow water

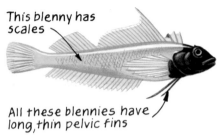

This blenny has scales

All these blennies have long, thin pelvic fins

◀ Black-faced Blenny

Found on rocky shores in shallow water where it basks in the sun. Male has a territory about 1 m wide which he defends. Only in Mediterranean. 8 cm.

Montagu's Blenny ▶

In rock pools almost bare of seaweeds. Eats acorn barnacles fastened to rocks, biting their limbs off when they come out from their shells. 8.5 cm.

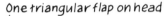

One triangular flap on head

Other blennies have no scales

▲ Shanny

Very common shore fish in pools and among seaweeds on sandy and rocky shores. Eats small crustaceans. 16 cm.

▼ Peacock Blenny

Very shallow water on mud and sand near rocks. Lays eggs under empty shells or in hollows in rocks. Mediterranean only. 10 cm.

Rocky shores and shallow water

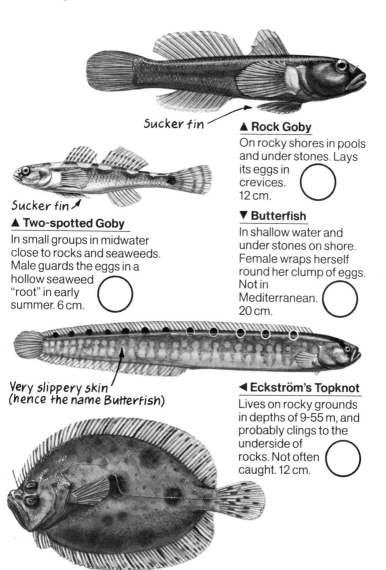

Sucker fin

▲ Rock Goby
On rocky shores in pools and under stones. Lays its eggs in crevices. 12 cm.

Sucker fin

▲ Two-spotted Goby
In small groups in midwater close to rocks and seaweeds. Male guards the eggs in a hollow seaweed "root" in early summer. 6 cm.

▼ Butterfish
In shallow water and under stones on shore. Female wraps herself round her clump of eggs. Not in Mediterranean. 20 cm.

Very slippery skin
(hence the name Butterfish)

◀ Eckström's Topknot
Lives on rocky grounds in depths of 9-55 m, and probably clings to the underside of rocks. Not often caught. 12 cm.

Inshore bottom-living fishes

Many of these fishes burrow or match their colouring to the sand on sandy bottoms. Others find food and shelter in rocky areas and wrecked ships.

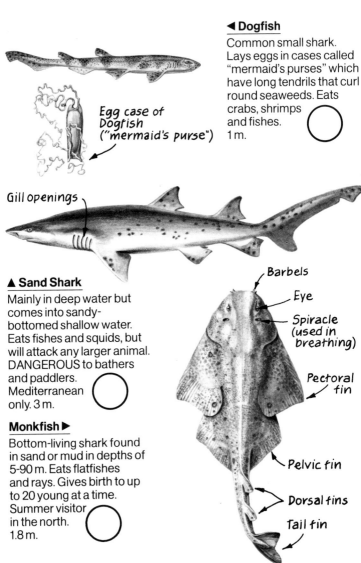

◀ Dogfish

Common small shark. Lays eggs in cases called "mermaid's purses" which have long tendrils that curl round seaweeds. Eats crabs, shrimps and fishes. 1 m.

Egg case of Dogfish ("mermaid's purse")

Gill openings

▲ Sand Shark

Mainly in deep water but comes into sandy-bottomed shallow water. Eats fishes and squids, but will attack any larger animal. DANGEROUS to bathers and paddlers. Mediterranean only. 3 m.

Monkfish ▶

Bottom-living shark found in sand or mud in depths of 5-90 m. Eats flatfishes and rays. Gives birth to up to 20 young at a time. Summer visitor in the north. 1.8 m.

Barbels

Eye

Spiracle (used in breathing)

Pectoral fin

Pelvic fin

Dorsal fins

Tail fin

Inshore bottom-living fishes

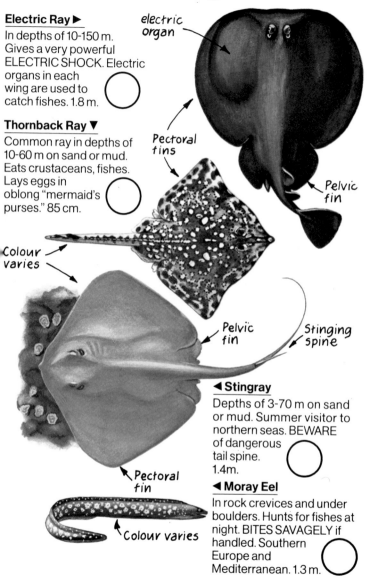

Electric Ray ▶
In depths of 10-150 m. Gives a very powerful ELECTRIC SHOCK. Electric organs in each wing are used to catch fishes. 1.8 m.

Thornback Ray ▼
Common ray in depths of 10-60 m on sand or mud. Eats crustaceans, fishes. Lays eggs in oblong "mermaid's purses." 85 cm.

electric organ

Pectoral fins

Pelvic fin

Colour varies

Pelvic fin

Stinging spine

Pectoral fin

Colour varies

◀ Stingray
Depths of 3-70 m on sand or mud. Summer visitor to northern seas. BEWARE of dangerous tail spine. 1.4m.

◀ Moray Eel
In rock crevices and under boulders. Hunts for fishes at night. BITES SAVAGELY if handled. Southern Europe and Mediterranean. 1.3 m.

31

Inshore bottom-living fishes

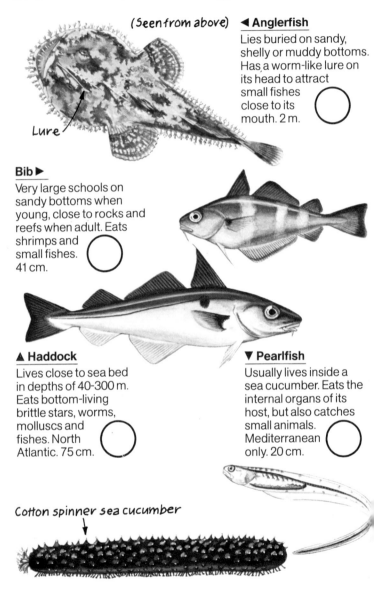

(Seen from above)

Lure

◄ Anglerfish
Lies buried on sandy, shelly or muddy bottoms. Has a worm-like lure on its head to attract small fishes close to its mouth. 2 m.

Bib ►
Very large schools on sandy bottoms when young, close to rocks and reefs when adult. Eats shrimps and small fishes. 41 cm.

▲ Haddock
Lives close to sea bed in depths of 40-300 m. Eats bottom-living brittle stars, worms, molluscs and fishes. North Atlantic. 75 cm.

▼ Pearlfish
Usually lives inside a sea cucumber. Eats the internal organs of its host, but also catches small animals. Mediterranean only. 20 cm.

Cotton spinner sea cucumber

Inshore bottom-living fishes

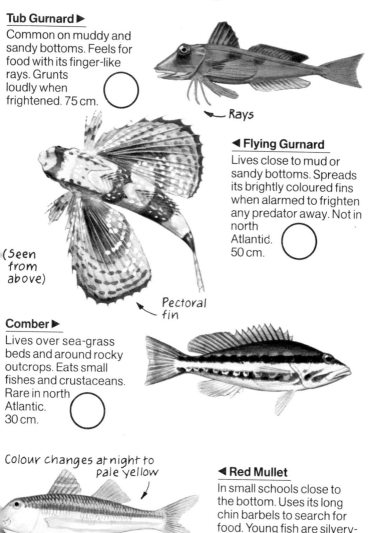

Tub Gurnard ▶

Common on muddy and sandy bottoms. Feels for food with its finger-like rays. Grunts loudly when frightened. 75 cm.

Rays

◀ Flying Gurnard

Lives close to mud or sandy bottoms. Spreads its brightly coloured fins when alarmed to frighten any predator away. Not in north Atlantic. 50 cm.

(Seen from above)

Pectoral fin

Comber ▶

Lives over sea-grass beds and around rocky outcrops. Eats small fishes and crustaceans. Rare in north Atlantic. 30 cm.

Colour changes at night to pale yellow

◀ Red Mullet

In small schools close to the bottom. Uses its long chin barbels to search for food. Young fish are silvery-blue and live at the surface of the sea. 35 cm.

Barbels

33

Inshore bottom-living fishes

Red Band-fish ▶

Burrows in stiff mud in depths of 6-20 m. Comes out of its hole to snap up passing small crustaceans, and is occasionally eaten by other fishes. 50 cm.

Male

▼ Rainbow Wrasse

Common in the Mediterranean close to rocks and in sea-grass beds. Lives in small schools led by the biggest male fish. Females change to males with age. 25 cm.

▲ Peacock Wrasse

Very common in the Mediterranean among weed-covered rocks at about 20 m. Females often change into males as they grow older. 20 cm.

Eyes

Adult male

Small electric organs

▲ Stargazer

Lies buried in sand with only its eyes showing. Lures small fishes by vibrating its tongue. Detects them with weak electric currents. Mediterranean only. 25 cm.

Inshore bottom-living fishes

Butterfly Blenny ▶

Lives on shelly or rocky bottoms in depths of 10-100 m. Often "owns" a broken pot or hollow in which it lays its eggs in spring. 20 cm.

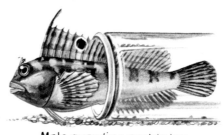

Male guarding nest in jar

▲ Wolf-fish

On rocky bottoms 20-300 m deep. Eats crabs, sea urchins and whelks. Crushes shells with its large teeth. North Atlantic only. 1.2 m.

▼ Dragonet

Near the bottom, 20-100 m deep. Often buries itself. Eats molluscs, crustaceans and worms. Male displays his long fins at spawning time. 20 cm.

Male

◀ Turbot

On gravel, shell and sandy bottoms in quite deep water. Eats bottom-living fishes like sandeels, dragonets and gobies. 80 cm.

35

Inshore bottom-living fishes

Wide-eyed Flounder ▶
Shallow sandy areas. Feeds on small fishes and crustaceans. Male's eyes spaced wide apart. Mediterranean only. 20 cm.

Eyes

Male

◀ Plaice
Common fish on sea bed on sandy, muddy and gravel bottoms. Feeds mainly on shellfish, worms and crustaceans. 50 cm.

Halibut ▶
Largest known flatfish. Depth of 100-1500 m on mud, sand and gravel. Hunts for fishes in mid-water. North Atlantic only. 2 m.

All these fishes can camouflage themselves by changing colour

Sole ▶
Common flatfish. Burrows in sandy bottom but hunts worms and crustaceans at night. Young in sandy pools on the beach. 40 cm.

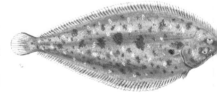

Inshore midwater fishes

Most midwater fishes in inshore waters (up to 100 m deep) are schooling fishes. Only the largest fishes can live without the protection of a school

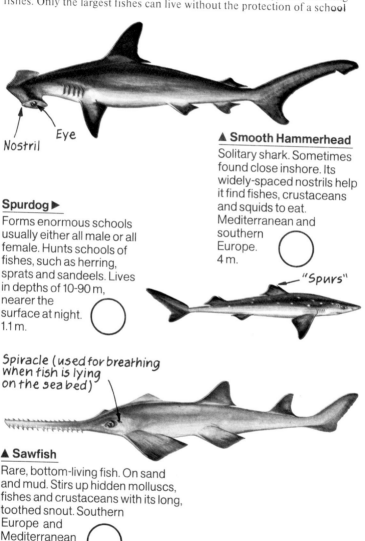

Nostril

Eye

▲ Smooth Hammerhead

Solitary shark. Sometimes found close inshore. Its widely-spaced nostrils help it find fishes, crustaceans and squids to eat. Mediterranean and southern Europe. 4 m.

Spurdog ▶

Forms enormous schools usually either all male or all female. Hunts schools of fishes, such as herring, sprats and sandeels. Lives in depths of 10-90 m, nearer the surface at night. 1.1 m.

"Spurs"

Spiracle (used for breathing when fish is lying on the sea bed)

▲ Sawfish

Rare, bottom-living fish. On sand and mud. Stirs up hidden molluscs, fishes and crustaceans with its long, toothed snout. Southern Europe and Mediterranean only. 4.5 m.

Inshore midwater fishes

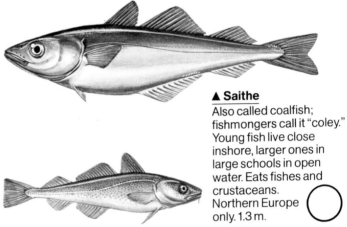

▲ Saithe
Also called coalfish; fishmongers call it "coley." Young fish live close inshore, larger ones in large schools in open water. Eats fishes and crustaceans. Northern Europe only. 1.3 m.

▲ Cod
Very common in midwater and near sea bed. Large schools. Eats many kinds of fishes and crustaceans. Northern Europe only. 1.2 m.

▼ Ling
Common fish around rocks and wrecks as deep as 400 m. Eats mainly fishes and crustaceans. Not in the Mediterranean. 2 m.

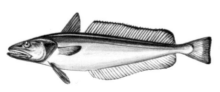

◄ Hake
Lives in quite deep water, just above bottom, coming nearer the surface at night. Eats fishes and squids, and, when young, crustaceans. 1.8 m.

Inshore midwater fishes

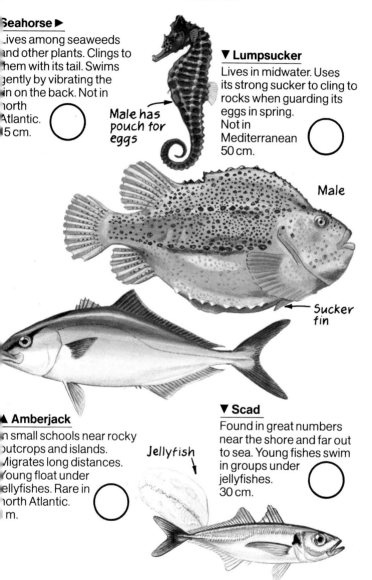

Seahorse ▶
Lives among seaweeds and other plants. Clings to them with its tail. Swims gently by vibrating the fin on the back. Not in north Atlantic.
15 cm.

Male has pouch for eggs

▼ Lumpsucker
Lives in midwater. Uses its strong sucker to cling to rocks when guarding its eggs in spring.
Not in Mediterranean
50 cm.

Male

Sucker fin

▲ Amberjack
In small schools near rocky outcrops and islands. Migrates long distances. Young float under jellyfishes. Rare in north Atlantic.
1 m.

Jellyfish

▼ Scad
Found in great numbers near the shore and far out to sea. Young fishes swim in groups under jellyfishes.
30 cm.

39

Inshore midwater fishes

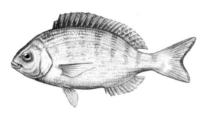

▼ Red Sea-bream
In schools when young, but adults form only small groups and live in deeper water (to 100 m). Eats fishes, crustaceans and squids. 50 cm.

▲ Black Sea-bream
Lives around wrecks and rocky outcrops close to sand. Hollows a nest in the sand for the eggs. The male guards them until they hatch. 35 cm.

▲ Saupe
Swims in close-packed schools in shallow water. Feeds by grazing fine algae off rocks and other seaweeds. Not in northern Europe. 30 cm.

◄ John Dory
Swims slowly. Lives alone. Lies in wait in the shadows for small fishes and snaps them up with its huge jaws. 40 cm.

Inshore surface fishes

Surface-living fishes are mostly plankton eaters (like the Mackerel) or fishes that hunt plankton eaters (like the Porbeagle Shark). Smaller fishes live in schools and most are silvery or white underneath and blue-green above.

Large gill openings

▲ Basking Shark

Largest fish in European seas but feeds on tiny plankton (larvae of crabs, molluscs and fishes). Hibernates in deep water in winter, probably on the sea bed. 11 m.

▼ Porbeagle

Active hunter of schools of fishes, such as herring, mackerel and pilchards, as well as squids. Gives birth to one or two well-developed young in summer. 3 m.

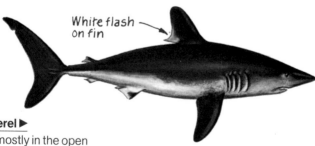

White flash on fin

Mackerel ▶

Lives mostly in the open sea often close to the surface. Eats surface-living crustaceans and young fishes, but in winter hibernates close to the sea bed. 40 cm.

This is a good example of "counter shading" (see page 53)

Inshore surface fishes

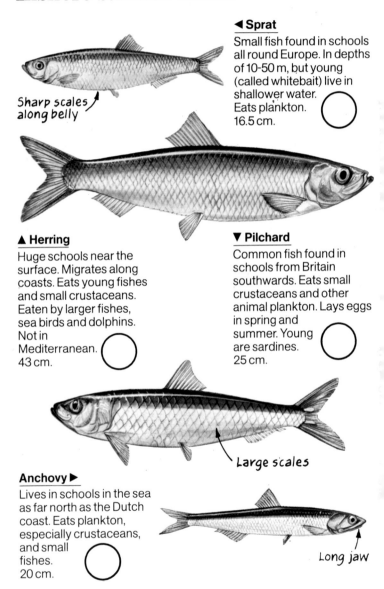

◀ Sprat
Small fish found in schools all round Europe. In depths of 10-50 m, but young (called whitebait) live in shallower water. Eats plankton. 16.5 cm.

Sharp scales along belly

▲ Herring
Huge schools near the surface. Migrates along coasts. Eats young fishes and small crustaceans. Eaten by larger fishes, sea birds and dolphins. Not in Mediterranean. 43 cm.

▼ Pilchard
Common fish found in schools from Britain southwards. Eats small crustaceans and other animal plankton. Lays eggs in spring and summer. Young are sardines. 25 cm.

Large scales

Anchovy ▶
Lives in schools in the sea as far north as the Dutch coast. Eats plankton, especially crustaceans, and small fishes. 20 cm.

Long jaw

Inshore surface fishes

▲ Garfish

Common at the sea's surface where it eats young fishes, like herrings and sandeels. Its eggs have long threads on their surface which tangle with floating seaweeds. 94 cm.

▼ Barracuda

Common in Mediterranean. Lives in large schools usually close to the surface. Hunts small fishes. 50 cm.

(Tropical Barracudas are very dangerous)

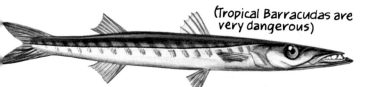

Spines can be locked in an upright position, so that the Triggerfish cannot be dragged out of rock crevices

▼ Triggerfish

In open sea and drifting with floating wreckage from the tropical Atlantic in summer. Eats crustaceans. 35 cm.

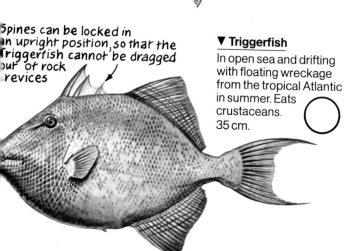

Ocean surface fishes

Most surface-living ocean fishes are blue-green above, white or silvery below. Many eat smaller, plankton-eating fishes which usually live in schools. Most migrate, moving into warmer water in winter.

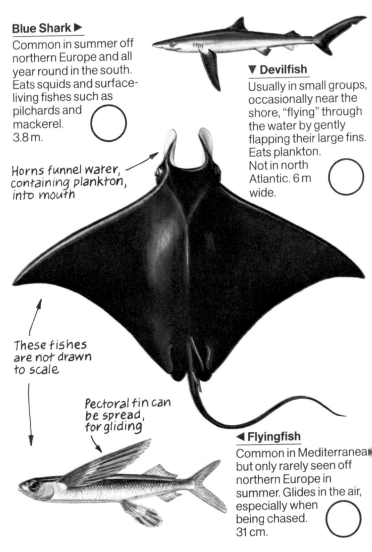

Blue Shark ▶

Common in summer off northern Europe and all year round in the south. Eats squids and surface-living fishes such as pilchards and mackerel. 3.8 m.

Horns funnel water, containing plankton, into mouth

▼ Devilfish

Usually in small groups, occasionally near the shore, "flying" through the water by gently flapping their large fins. Eats plankton. Not in north Atlantic. 6 m wide.

These fishes are not drawn to scale

Pectoral fin can be spread, for gliding

◀ Flyingfish

Common in Mediterranean but only rarely seen off northern Europe in summer. Glides in the air, especially when being chased. 31 cm.

Ocean surface fishes

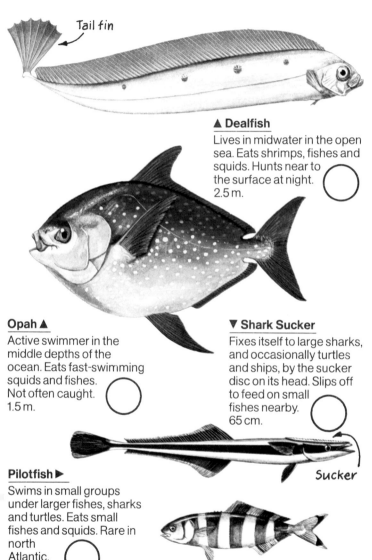

Tail fin

▲ Dealfish
Lives in midwater in the open
sea. Eats shrimps, fishes and
squids. Hunts near to
the surface at night.
2.5 m.

Opah ▲
Active swimmer in the
middle depths of the
ocean. Eats fast-swimming
squids and fishes.
Not often caught.
1.5 m.

▼ Shark Sucker
Fixes itself to large sharks,
and occasionally turtles
and ships, by the sucker
disc on its head. Slips off
to feed on small
fishes nearby.
65 cm.

Sucker

Pilotfish ▶
Swims in small groups
under larger fishes, sharks
and turtles. Eats small
fishes and squids. Rare in
north
Atlantic.
40 cm.

Ocean surface fishes

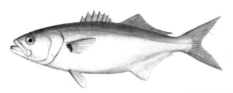

▲ Bluefish
Very active predator.
Forms schools and attacks
smaller fishes. Occasionally
found in coastal water.
Only in Mediterranean
and south
Atlantic.
70 cm.

▼ Dolphinfish
Fast-swimming migratory
fish which hunts at the
surface. Forehead
becomes steeper with age.
Not in north
Atlantic.
1.9 m.

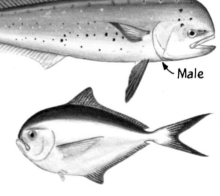

← Male

Ray's Bream ▶
In deep water to south,
but migrates northwards
and is often stranded on
northern coasts. Feeds on
crustaceans
and fishes.
55 cm.

◀ Scabbardfish
Found in water 100-400 m
deep over sandy bottoms.
Eats mainly fishes.
Caught on deep lines and
in trawls. Not
in north
Atlantic. 2 m.

Ocean surface fishes

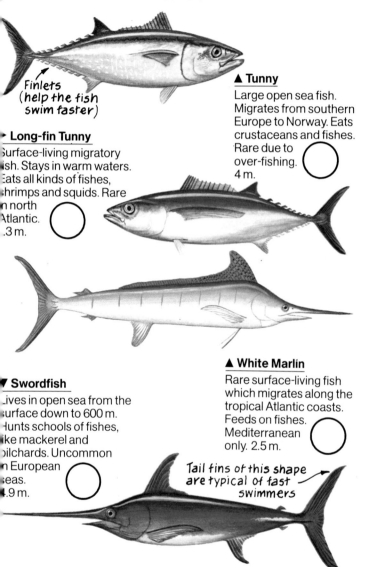

Finlets
(help the fish
swim faster)

► Long-fin Tunny
Surface-living migratory
fish. Stays in warm waters.
Eats all kinds of fishes,
shrimps and squids. Rare
in north
Atlantic.
.3 m.

▲ Tunny
Large open sea fish.
Migrates from southern
Europe to Norway. Eats
crustaceans and fishes.
Rare due to
over-fishing.
4 m.

▼ Swordfish
Lives in open sea from the
surface down to 600 m.
Hunts schools of fishes,
like mackerel and
pilchards. Uncommon
in European
seas.
4.9 m.

▲ White Marlin
Rare surface-living fish
which migrates along the
tropical Atlantic coasts.
Feeds on fishes.
Mediterranean
only. 2.5 m.

Tail fins of this shape
are typical of fast
swimmers

47

Ocean surface fishes

Sunfish ▼

Open sea fish which feeds
on jellyfishes. Lives near
the surface of the sea.
Its skeleton is
light and paper-
thin. 4 m.

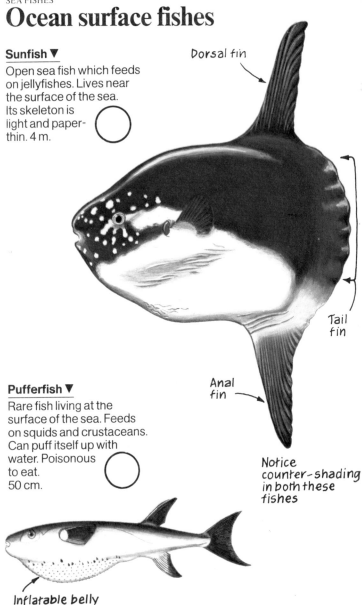

Dorsal fin

Tail
fin

Anal
fin

Notice
counter-shading
in both these
fishes

Pufferfish ▼

Rare fish living at the
surface of the sea. Feeds
on squids and crustaceans.
Can puff itself up with
water. Poisonous
to eat.
50 cm.

Inflatable belly

Shape and movement

The fastest swimming fishes have the most streamlined shapes.

Garfish
Streamlined: fast movement.

Anglerfish
Not streamlined: slow movement.

Most fishes swim by moving the back part of their bodies from side to side, but some fishes have a non-streamlined shape that may prevent them from moving in this way. Below are some fishes which, because of their feeding habits or for camouflage or defence, have strange body shapes.

PLAICE — Body moving

Fins moving   RAY

Rays and Flatfishes
These fishes swim by bending their bodies up and down. For more gentle movement, their fins curve in a wave motion.

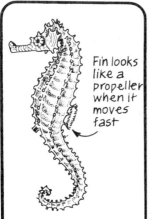

Fin looks like a propeller when it moves fast

Seahorse
Swims upright using its back fin as a propeller. Wave-like ripples pass along it.

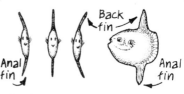

Back fin

Anal fin

Anal fin

Sunfish
Has large back and anal fins. It moves them from side to side at the same time.

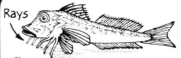

Rays

Gurnard
Several rays are separated from the pectoral fins and are used to feel for food on the bottom.

Mouths and feeding

A fish's mouth and teeth can tell you what sort of food it eats and if the fish feeds at the surface of the water, or on the bottom.

Surface feeders have upturned mouths. Bottom feeders have downturned mouths, or mouths set lower down on the head. Fishes that eat other fishes have wide mouths and sharp teeth.

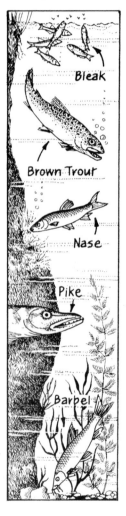

Bleak
Feeds near the surface on plankton and insects. Its mouth turns up.

Brown Trout
Feeds at all levels on crustaceans, fishes and insects. Large, toothed jaws for catching large prey.

Nase
Eats green algae off rocks. It has a rough-lipped, slit-like mouth for scraping.

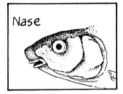

Pike
Hunts at all levels for fishes. Also eats small mammals and ducklings. Huge mouth with straight lower teeth for seizing large prey, and small, backward-pointing upper teeth that prevent prey from escaping.

Barbel
Feeds at the bottom on insect larvae and worms. Fleshy mouth in lower position. Barbels are used to feel for prey.

Some fishes, the shad for example, have long bony strips on their gill arches which are used as filters to strain plankton food out of the water.

Other fishes have developed special food-catching devices. The swordfish uses its sword to knock small fishes unconscious. The electric ray (page 31) gives off an electric shock, which stuns its prey, and the anglerfish (page 32) has a false bait to lure small fishes close to its mouth.

Mackerel
Feeds mostly near the surface on small fishes and crustaceans. Quite large mouth for catching prey.

Swordfish
Feeds on fishes near the surface. Stuns them by hitting them with its sword. Large mouth.

Hake
Feeds in midwater on fishes and squids. Large wide mouth and many sharp teeth.

Conger
In holes and under rocks. A constant hunter of large fish, crabs and octopuses. Huge mouth and rows of sharp, cutting teeth.

Strong sharp teeth

Sole
Lives on the sea bed feeding on crustaceans and worms. Its small, semi-circular mouth extends underneath.

Mouth continues round to underside

Sole

Defence

Large fishes, such as some sharks, escape their enemies by swimming fast. Small fishes, unless they are also fast swimmers, usually protect themselves by grouping together in large numbers or by camouflaging themselves. A group of fishes of the same species swimming together is called a school.

Fishes that live by themselves and slow-swimming fishes need special defences. Most commonly they have spines. If a predator managed to grasp a spiny fish in its jaws, it would have great difficulty in swallowing it since the spines would stick in its throat. Other fishes have protective armour and some, like the pufferfish, can make themselves too big to swallow by puffing themselves up with water.

Fins form two "wings"

Flyingfish
Escapes predators by jumping out of the water and gliding for short distances above the surface.

Leathery skin

Sunfish
Slow swimmer, but protected by tough, leathery, almost bullet-proof skin.

Armoured head   Bony plates

Sturgeon
Protected by five rows of hard, bony plates and an armoured head.

Skin of belly and sides covered with spines

Pufferfish
Spiny skin. If threatened, can blow itself up to twice its normal size.

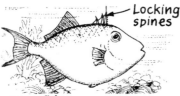

Locking spines

Triggerfish
If threatened, strong spines on its back lock into a raised position. It jams itself into a crevice.

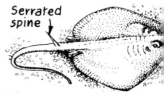

Serrated spine

Stingray
If disturbed, lashes out with its tail which has a large, venomous, sword-like spike.

Camouflage

A fish with a good camouflage is hard to see against its background and is therefore difficult for an enemy to find.

The most common disguise for surface and midwater fishes is "counter shading". This means a dark back and a light or silvery belly and sides. Seen from above, by other fishes and by sea birds, the fish blends with the darkness of the water. Seen from below or from the side, the silver reflects the colour of the water and the fish becomes almost invisible.

Some fishes have stripes, spots or a strange shape which break up the normal outline of the body and confuse enemies. The dark colour or pattern of bottom-living fishes blends in with the mud, sand or stones of their background.

Mackerel
Counter shading. Ripple marking breaks up the outline of the back.

Anchovy
Swims in schools. When schools move the flashing sides of the fishes confuse enemies.

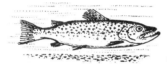

Sea Trout
Spots break up its outline, so it is hard to see against a stony bottom.

Pearlfish   Backbone visible
Its body is transparent and so is very difficult to see.

Worm Pipefish
Hides among seaweeds and pretends to be one of the stems.

Butterfish
A row of spots along its back look like eyes and confuse enemies.

Flounder
Can change its pattern and colour to match any surface it is lying on.

Shanny
Colour and pattern match colour and pattern of rocks and seaweeds.

Breeding: eels and elvers

The eggs from female fishes and the sperms from male fishes are called spawn. Nearly all fishes have a spawning time. This is the time of year when a particular species is ready to breed.

At spawning time, fishes of the same species collect together in a large group or school. The fishes release their sperms and eggs into the water at the same time. Cod, herring and eels all do this. Some species make a long journey to a special spawning ground hundreds of miles from their normal feeding area.

Eels and Elvers

Until the beginning of this century, biologists had no idea where the spawning ground of the common eel was or what a newly-hatched eel looked like, although they knew that elvers came from the sea. Biologists began the long search for younger eels by fishing west of Europe and found that the further west they went the smaller were the baby eels they found. The smallest ones came from the Sargasso Sea. Today the whole life cycle of the common eel is known.

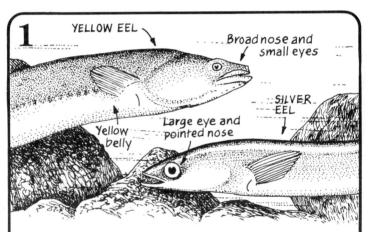

1 YELLOW EEL — Broad nose and small eyes — SILVER EEL — Large eye and pointed nose — Yellow belly

The adult eel has a yellow belly and is called a yellow eel. It lives in streams, rivers and estuaries.

When the male yellow eels are 8 to 10 years old and the female eels 10 to 18 years old, they begin to change their shape and colour. They stop feeding and their breeding organs start to develop. Their eyes get larger, their heads more pointed and the colour of their bellies changes from yellow to silver. They are now called silver eels.

2

In autumn, the silver eels leave the streams and rivers in Europe and swim across the Atlantic Ocean to the Sargasso Sea. Here they release their eggs and sperms. Then they die.

Routes from Europe

SARGASSO SEA

Breeding ground

3

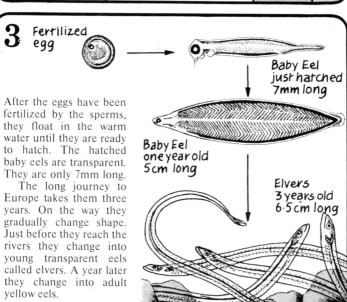

Fertilized egg

Baby Eel just hatched 7mm long

Baby Eel one year old 5cm long

Elvers 3 years old 6·5cm long

After the eggs have been fertilized by the sperms, they float in the warm water until they are ready to hatch. The hatched baby eels are transparent. They are only 7mm long.

The long journey to Europe takes them three years. On the way they gradually change shape. Just before they reach the rivers they change into young transparent eels called elvers. A year later they change into adult yellow eels.

Making a stickleback aquarium

You can study sticklebacks at home if you keep them in an aquarium. Catch them in April so that you can watch their nest-building and mating display.

Catch sticklebacks in a pond or ditch with a fine net. You will find them hiding among the grasses and plants at the water's edge. Try to catch one male and two or three females. You can tell the difference because the males have red bellies and blue eyes.

Net

Jam jars

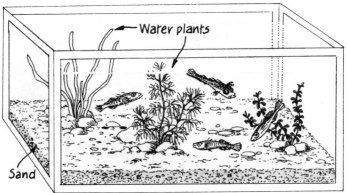

Water plants

Sand

To set up an aquarium, you will need a large tank made of glass or strong plastic. Line the bottom with clean sand about 5cm deep. Collect water plants from the pond or buy them from a pet shop. Secure them in the sand with small stones. Put some large stones in too.

Use pond or rain water to fill your aquarium. (If you use tap water, mix it with some pond water first.) To avoid disturbing the plants and sand, begin by pouring water into a saucer on the bottom. Then take the saucer out of the tank. Put the aquarium near a window, not in direct sunlight.

Feed your sticklebacks with small earthworms and daphnia (water fleas and tiny crustaceans you can catch in the pond with your net). If the aquarium begins to smell nasty, change the water and clean the bottom after taking the sticklebacks out.

Put the sticklebacks carefully into the water. The male builds a nest out of plant material. Watch him dance to attract the females to the nest. You can tell when they have laid the eggs because the male guards the nest and attacks any females that swim too close. Take the females out and return them to the pond where you found them.

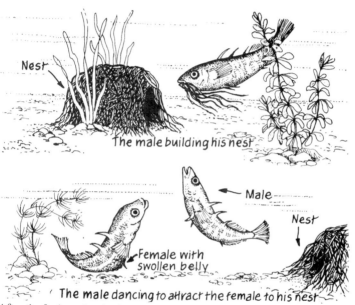

The male building his nest

Female with swollen belly

Male

Nest

The male dancing to attract the female to his nest

After the fry have hatched out, they hover over the nest in a school. The male guards them fiercely. Put a small stick into the water and see how he attacks it. When the fry grow larger and break away from the school, put them and the male back in the pond.

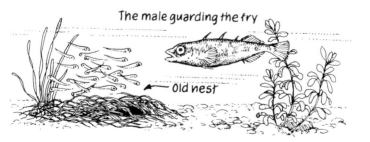

The male guarding the fry

Old nest

Making fish prints

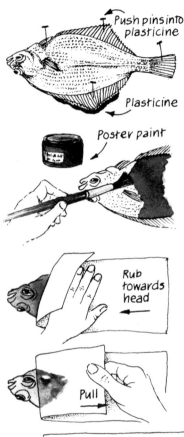

Push pins into plasticine

Plasticine

Poster paint

Rub towards head

Pull

You can use a fish to make prints. You will need: a small fish from the fishmonger (a dab works well), poster paints, drawing paper, a paint-brush, plasticine and some pins.

Cover a table with layers of newspaper. Lay the fish on them. If the fish is not flat, put some plasticine under the fins and tail to hold them up and pin them in place.

Add water to the paint until it is very thin. Paint the upper side of the fish. Start at the tail end and paint towards the head, making sure you spread the paint evenly. Leave the tail and fins until last as they dry quickly. Do not paint the eye.

Lay the drawing paper on top of the fish. Rub your hand over the paper, pressing down gently on the fish's scales. Be careful not to smudge the paint or wrinkle the paper.

Carefully lift off the paper, starting at the head end. Lay your print down flat. When it is completely dry, paint the eye in. You can paint a background too.

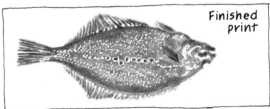

Finished print

You can make more than one print from your fish. Try using different coloured paints and paper for unusual effects.

Glossary

Algae – simple plants that range from minute plankton in the sea and in fresh water to large sea-weeds.

Barbels – sensitive feelers. Fishes use their barbels to find their food on the bottom.

Camouflage – when the colour of a fish matches its background and makes it difficult to see.

Crustaceans – animals, such as crabs, prawns and shrimps, that have a hard shell.

Display – when a male fish attracts a mate. Some fishes dance to attract the female's attention. Some are brightly coloured.

Fry – Young fish after the larval stage.

Hibernation – the sleepy state in which some fishes spend the winter.

Host – an animal on which animals called parasites live and feed.

Larva – (plural: **larvae**) – of fishes – the stage immediately after a fish hatches out its egg – of insects – the stage in an insect's life after it has hatched (e.g. maggot).

Mermaid's purse – Egg case of a ray or dogfish.

Middle reaches – the portion of a river between the fast-flowing mountainous and the slow-flowing lowland portions.

Midwater – the water between the surface and the bottom of the sea.

Migration – the regular movement of fishes from one place to another; usually between spawning and feeding grounds. Migrating fishes are called migrants.

Molluscs – animals, such as mussels and squids, that have a soft body, often protected by an outer shell.

Over-fishing – when the fishing industry endangers the numbers of certain species of fishes.

Plankton – microscopic plants and animals that drift in water.

Pollution – occurs when chemicals, litter or waste matter damage the natural habitats of plants and animals.

Predator – any animal that eats other animals.

Prey – an animal that is hunted by another animal.

Rays – bony parts of a fish's fin.

School – a group of fishes of the same species that swim together.

Spawn – to breed.

Spawning ground – breeding place.

Species – fishes that all look alike, behave in the same way and breed together.

Territory – the area "belonging" to one fish or group of fishes. Males often defend their territory in the spawning season.

Venomous – capable of injecting a venom by means of a bite or sting.

Index

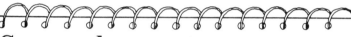

Scorecard

The fishes on this scorecard are arranged in the same order as they appear in the book. When you go spotting, fill in the date at the top of one of the blank columns, and then write in that column your score, next to each fish that you see. At the end of the day, add up your score and put the total at the bottom of the columns. Then add up your grand total.

Page	Fish	Score	Date	Date	Date	Page	Fish	Score	Date	Date	Date
6	Grayling	15				8	Salmon	10			
6	Trout	5				8	Rainbow Trout	5			
6	Charr	15				9	Pike	5			
7	Powan	20				9	Dace	5			
7	Minnow	5				9	Chub	5			
7	Streber	20				9	Bleak	5			
8	Lampern	5				10	Barbel	10			
	Total						Total				

Page	Fish	Score				Page	Fish	Score			
10	Nase	25				17	Sea Lamprey	10			
10	Stone Loach	5				17	Sturgeon	25			
10	Spined Loach	15				17	Eel	5			
11	Stickleback	5				17	Twaite Shad	10			
11	Ruffe	15				18	Ziege	25			
11	Perch	5				18	European Toothcarp	20			
12	European Mudminnow	25				18	Meagre	20			
12	Crucian Carp	5				19	Bass	5			
12	Carp	5				19	Thin-lipped Grey Mullet	10			
13	Rudd	10				19	Flounder	5			
13	Tench	10				20	Greater Pipefish	10			
13	Weatherfish	20				20	Five-bearded Rockling	5			
13	Nine-spined Stickleback	10				20	Whiting	5			
14	Whitefish	20				21	Eelpout	10			
14	Goldfish	5				21	Sand Smelt	10			
14	Gudgeon	5				21	Thick-lipped Grey Mullet	5			
15	Bream	5				21	Hooknose	10			
15	Silver Bream	10				22	Lesser Weever	10			
15	Roach	5				22	Sandeel	5			
15	Bitterling	20				22	Sand Goby	5			
16	Asp	25				22	Dab	5			
16	Wels	20				23	Conger	5			
16	Burbot	25				23	Shore Clingfish	10			
16	Zander	5				23	Worm	10			
	Total						Total				